AMERICAN
INDIVIDUALISM

AMERICAN INDIVIDUALISM

How a New Generation of
Conservatives Can Save the
REPUBLICAN PARTY

Margaret Hoover

CROWN
FORUM
NEW YORK

Copyright © 2011 by Margaret Hoover

Published in the United States by Crown Forum, an imprint of the
Crown Publishing Group, a division of Random House, Inc., New York.

www.crownpublishing.com

CROWN FORUM with colophon is a registered trademark of Random House, Inc.

Library of Congress Cataloging-in-Publication Data

Hoover, Margaret.
American individualism : how a new generation of conservatives can save the Republican Party /
Margaret Hoover.
p.   cm.
Includes bibliographical references.
1. Republican Party (U.S.: 1854–)   2. Conservatism—United States.
3. Generation Y—United States.   I. Title.
JK2356.H66 2011
324.2734—dc22   2011008362

ISBN 978-0-307-71815-0
eISBN 978-0-307-71817-4

Printed in the United States of America

Book design by Leonard W. Henderson
Jacket design by Jean Traina
Jacket photograph by Deborah Feingold

10 9 8 7 6 5 4 3 2 1

First Edition

For my husband, John Avlon,
the love of my life

CONTENTS

INTRODUCTION

This book has its origins in a lightning-strike moment I experienced during the presidential campaign of 2004. At the time I was just another bubbly young junior staffer, still savoring my good fortune at having secured a position with the Bush-Cheney 2004 reelection campaign. I bounded through the halls of the redbrick office building in Arlington, Virginia, that housed President George W. Bush's campaign headquarters. After a morning staff meeting, I decided to swing by my office-mate's desk, tucked in a corner facing south toward the Potomac River, with a clear view of Georgetown and the rest of Washington, D.C. She was a coordinator in the political department, and that morning she seemed troubled.

"Look," she said, pointing to supporting documents that spelled out what became known as the anti-same-sex-marriage strategy.

The regional political directors of President Bush's campaign had been tasked with ensuring that battleground states sponsored ballot initiatives defining marriage exclusively as a union of one man and one woman, thus prohibiting same-sex marriage. As an additional measure to boost political enthusiasm, President Bush would ask Congress to pass an amendment to the Constitution that would federally define all marriages as being between a man and a woman. President Bush's plan was to campaign in these battleground states in support of the Federal Marriage Amendment, in a joint effort with statewide candidates to energize social conservatives, who, it was feared, might otherwise not come out to vote. While they were in the voting booth casting a ballot against same-sex marriage, the thinking went, they would also pull the lever for candidate George W. Bush, the man for whom I worked.

That moment remains vivid in my memory. After an instant of confusion, I felt a wave of disappointment crash over me. A series of questions raced through my mind: Why on earth did the campaign care about defining marriage as being between a man and a woman? Did President Bush really believe it was important to make laws that discriminate against gays and lesbians? Was this strategy necessary to ensure the president's reelection? Did President Bush think that mobilizing people against gay rights was a good thing? I looked up from the papers on my office-mate's desk and stared out through the window over the treetops toward the nation's capital, feeling sick to my stomach.

That was my Ms.-Hoover-Goes-to-Washington moment. I suddenly realized as never before that the Republican Party—my party—was falling seriously out of step with a rising generation of Americans. These up-and-coming young voters value the ideal of individual freedom when it comes to gay rights, as they value some degree of reproductive freedom. And they do not support conservative activists' hard-line positions on immigration and environmentalism. It was on these questions, I felt, that the Republican Party was turning young voters away. In the years since 2004, the problem has only worsened. Unless the party can connect with a younger generation and, at the same time, offer solutions to meet the challenges of modern America, it is destined to remain at best a minority party— or worse, to fade into irrelevance. That would be tragic, because a modern brand of American conservatism is more urgently needed now than ever before.

Today, the United States faces a daunting array of challenges that threaten to imperil the American dream. Skyrocketing deficits and debt that amount to generational theft are staking a claim to the future prosperity of the youngest Americans. Our economy has lost its vibrancy, a quality that is increasingly associated with our less democratic trading partners in foreign markets. America's status as a world leader has diminished at a time when the world's most volatile region, the Middle East, is in a state of upheaval and the threat of Islamic supremacy looms. A failure to reconcile our twin needs for secure borders and new immigrants has led us into a protracted and divisive immigration crisis. Our schools, rather than facilitating equality of opportunity, increasingly constrict the upward mobility of young people. America's challenges all have one thing in common: They will likely be with us for a long time, and the next generation of Americans will have to solve them, or face American decline.

I believe that the next generation of Americans—the first to come of age in the new millennium—understands our situation well. The "millennials," born roughly between the years 1980 and 1999, perceive our political system at an impasse. They fear that as a nation we are incapable of addressing our problems. From every corner, they hear exhausted ideological rhetoric and see political gamesmanship at the expense of practical solutions.

Millennials thought they had found a candidate to break through the rhetorical divisions and excuses for inaction when they voted overwhelmingly for Barack Obama in 2008. They believed they were electing a man who, as he had promised, would bring change to Washington. His rhetoric spoke to their desire to move beyond the partisan divide of red states and blue states, to unify the country in order to solve problems. They have been disappointed.

As a result, millennials have yet to solidly commit to a political party. As a group, they are confident, open to change, globally oriented, techno-savvy, hyperconnected, and 50 million strong. By political orientation, the largest bloc are Independents, followed by Democrats, with Republicans a distant third. Though likely to call themselves liberal, millennials are not proponents of the big-government orthodoxy of modern liberalism. And yet, they are *socially liberal,* adhering to the least traditional views of family, homosexuality, and gender roles. In this sense, they are passionate about expanding individual freedom. They also have idealistic expectations about what government can and should do, and are optimistic about the competence of their elected leaders.

Yet the millennials also demonstrate decidedly conservative tendencies, even though relatively few call themselves Republicans. They show signs of fiscal conservatism and cherish individual freedom, self-expression, and the ability to choose their own way in life. They have favorable attitudes toward business and individual entrepreneurship and are less likely than their parents to say that the government should take on more debt in order to help those in need.

Some might call them "fiscally conservative but socially liberal." They are ripe for a political party to come along and make the case for maximum freedom, fiscal responsibility, equality of opportunity, social mobility, individual responsibility, and service to community and country. They are likely to frustrate the ambitions of old-line political purists, because they do not fit neatly into the traditional partisan or ideological boxes.

Neither party, in my view, has secured a connection with millennial sensibilities. While Barack Obama succeeded in appealing to them in the 2008 election campaign, his party failed to do so during the 2010 midterms. Republicans, meanwhile, have never managed to connect. Nor have they seriously tried. That's the purpose of this book: to make the case to millennials that they should give the Republican Party a fair hearing and to make the case to my fellow Republicans that millennials are not a lost cause.

Republicans have generated some of the best ideas for tackling the most pressing problems facing millennials—the debt and the deficit, education reform, immigration reform, market-based healthcare reform, and practical approaches to environmental conservation.

And when it comes to protecting individual freedom, the Republican Party has always prided itself on taking the lead.

But let's face facts: The Republican Party's brand is damaged. The perception that the Religious Right and *social* conservatives dominate the party apparatus is part of what has caused millennials to tune us out. Increasingly disconcerted by this widening gap between the perception of the Republican Party and the expectations of millennials, I undertook a journey in search of a fresh way for my party to appeal to the millennial generation.

I arrived at my destination with the help of an unexpected source: the writings of my great-grandfather, President Herbert Hoover, the thirty-first president of the United States. Growing up a Hoover, I had plenty of insults thrown my way simply on account of my family name. When you're related to one of the great mythical villains of American political history, you grow up constantly on the defensive. My friends' parents, my teachers in grade school and high school, my professors in college—they all pilloried my great-grandfather's presidency, indeed his entire career, as a failure of the highest order.

I won't say that this didn't cost a few tears or leave me without emotional scars, but being a direct descendant of Herbert Hoover has given me a special connection to an extraordinary individual. I never met my great-grandfather, but through family stories and my own exploration of the historical record, I learned about his orphan childhood, his success as a mining engineer, his globe-trotting years in business as a self-made millionaire before the age of forty, and his unprecedented achievement in building up nongovernmental organizations. Herbert Hoover was responsible for saving more lives from hunger and disease than anyone who has ever lived. His career as the most effective secretary of commerce in our nation's history and his efforts to build a public-private coalition to provide power to the nation's western states led to one of the most successful infrastructure projects in history: the Hoover Dam.

Herbert Hoover was millennial in spirit long before the term came into existence. He was like the Bill Gates or Mark Zuckerberg of his day—an innovator who believed in practical solutions, who dedicated his material and intellectual wealth to the service of the world, who believed in a philosophy encapsulated in the title of a little book he published, "American Individualism."★

I discovered this modest work, published in 1922, and was struck by its immediacy. It seemed it could have been written just yesterday, so contemporary were its themes. Largely overlooked by historians who hold forth on my great-grandfather's presidency, it is a powerful document: a broad and forceful statement of political philosophy and an extended essay on the relationship between the individual and the state. What I found most extraordinary was the relevance of its message and how it made the case for modern conservative thinking in an original way. Its author never refers to himself as a "conservative," yet he offers a compelling explanation for the vital importance of limited but *energetic* government in America's democratic system. His book celebrates America's diversity of religious traditions and heritages. It emphasizes the individual's responsibility to serve his or her community. It presents what modern-day conservatives would appreciate as a fundamentally individual-centered view of society, and it defends that view in a refreshing and convincing manner. The influential American historian Frederick Jackson Turner said it "contains the New and Old Testament of the American gospel."

That earlier booklet inspired me to write this book. This is a moment when modern conservatism needs to be fresh and convincing. It has lately become deeply nostalgic for the Reagan years, which makes sense, as Reagan was the last conservative leader to enjoy broad political support. He was also the last leader to unite the various tribes of the conservative nation—the neocons, paleocons,

★For those of you interested in reading Herbert Hoover's "American Individualism" in its entirety, I've posted it on my website, margarethoover.com.

social conservatives, fiscal conservatives, and libertarians. Conservatism has always been tribal, but in the absence of a charismatic leader, it has become a contentious and self-cannibalizing movement. And within the conservative nation are plenty of tribal warlords who devote their energies to eliminating rivals who they think aren't conservative enough. It's hardly the description of a political movement ready to lead America forward.

American individualism is not only a philosophy that can appeal to the millennial generation, but a prescription for how the conservative movement and the Republican Party can rise above their internecine feuding. By invoking the principles of American individualism, we have a template for addressing the challenges of the twenty-first century in a way that can make modern conservatism relevant for the rising generation.

I recognize that in writing this book, I am taking some risks. Anytime someone writes anything about an entire generation, they risk overgeneralization—and usually commit it. At the outset, let me say that millennials are like every other generation in certain respects. They are for one thing a diverse group. Just as baby boomers were not all wild-eyed, drugged-out attendees at Woodstock, neither are all millennials the hyper-texting Obamaites they are often made out to be. That said, those who study generational shifts in America can describe demographic groups by their shared experiences, by the historical context of their formative childhood years, and perhaps more important, by their outlook, as measured by opinion polls. In these ways, millennials are indeed different from those who came before them, and they do have certain features in common, by and large.

Experts will tell you that generational dividing lines are never carved in stone, that there is an arbitrariness to any generational divide. As someone born on the cusp of Gen X and the millennial generation, I share sensibilities of both but don't entirely identify with either. This makes my position advantageous, as an observer who can translate from one group to another and help bridge the divide between an older generation of Republicans and what I hope will become a new one.

This book is the culmination of that quest I undertook in search of a Republican-rooted philosophy that can appeal to a broad section of Americans, especially millennials. That a major source of my inspiration proved to be a work written nearly a century ago might be surprising. But millennials might also be surprised to discover fresh thinking and new ideas within the Republican Party, and in these sources find the hope and change they are looking for.

AMERICAN
INDIVIDUALISM

CHAPTER 1

GROWING UP HOOVER

"You have to do your own growing,
no matter how tall your grandfather was."
—IRISH PROVERB

THIS PAST CHRISTMAS I read a letter from my great-grandmother to my grandfather written on White House stationery. It was September 1931 and the envelope was addressed simply: "Allan Hoover, Stanford University." The nation's capital had awoken to a morning thunderstorm, she reported. In Europe, the banks and financial markets were in disarray. Here in America, investors were panicking, borrowers were in default or imminent danger of default, increasing numbers of loans once considered solid were becoming worthless, and American companies could not find the capital to stay in business. America's economy—the global economy, in fact—was grinding to a halt due to factors and forces that no economist had ever before witnessed. And my great-grandfather, the president of the United States, was trying to manage it all. This letter, from mother to son, cast the historic moment in personal terms: "He certainly has had his hand on the tiller in a hard storm and one still wonders what is going to happen next."

In most American families, the personal and the political rarely overlap so completely. Notes from mothers to sons are not typically

1

written on White House stationery. After all, there have been only forty-four presidents. And as a direct descendant of one of them, I have been extraordinarily privileged to hear stories about how history was made from those who were in the room. I have read, and held in my hands, many letters like the one above detailing the inner thoughts of the people who were confronted with the greatest challenge in our nation's economic history.

And yet this privilege has come with a great cost. To be a direct descendant of Herbert Hoover is to inherit the full weight of history's disapproval. My eighth-grade textbook blamed my great-grandfather for everything from Black Tuesday's stock market crash in October 1929 to the 25 percent unemployment rates and breadlines that followed in the Great Depression. Countless history books have detailed "Hoovervilles," the cardboard shelters of the homeless; "Hoover hogs," edible armadillos; "Hoover flags," penniless pockets turned inside out; and "Hoover blankets," newspapers repurposed for outdoor sleeping. Hoover's name was so synonymous with hard times that the midwestern drought that led to the dust storms and failed harvests of the Dust Bowl somehow seemed to have been his fault.

We Hoovers have been in a defensive crouch for eight decades. Today, people say that our political culture has become coarse, uncivil, and even violent. But after Franklin Roosevelt defeated my great-grandfather for the presidency in 1932, my family bore the psychological scars for decades. I remember talking to my grandmother about what it was like in the 1930s when Hoover was in the political wilderness and Roosevelt had captured the nation's heart. She reminisced next to a photo of her father-in-law, "the Chief," smiling and smoking a favorite pipe at the Bohemian Grove. She spoke of his kindness and intelligence—and of the million dollars that the Democratic National Committee spent to destroy his reputation. The worst part about the attacks was that they worked. Roosevelt did not just win an election: he won the approval of history.

Now my great American ancestor gets invoked every time a politician wants to score easy points by calling an opponent the "worst president since Herbert Hoover."

When my father was growing up in the 1950s, the Depression was still fresh in Americans' minds. My dad's experience was searing, as he was forced to defend himself in fistfights on school playgrounds. "Your granddad caused the Depression!"—*whack!* Compared with that, I had it easy. By the early 1990s, when I was in school, I found that just the mention of my family name could still evoke negative feelings among some of my friends' parents, especially the committed Democrats. They didn't even try to hide their disapproval when it came to my political heritage.

I suppose some children might have tried to distance themselves from the family name. Some presidential descendants do exactly that in an attempt to wriggle out from under the shadow of history. But I knew about another Herbert Hoover. I knew from my grandparents about the private man, about his indomitable will, his surprising wit, and his capacity to put ideas into action. I knew that he was from modest means and had been orphaned at a young age, and that despite this background, he grew up to become one of the wealthiest self-made men in the world. I knew that before he was president, he was regarded as one of the leading lights of his generation. I knew he had risked his fortune in order to save Belgium from starvation during the First World War. I knew he had helped organize a massive effort to feed the people of Central and Eastern Europe after the war. I knew he was called "the master of emergencies," was considered a pioneer of international nongovernmental organizations, and was a man known to his contemporaries as the Great Engineer and the Great Humanitarian. And he achieved all that before the age of forty-five!

As a teenager, I could see that the world perceived Herbert Hoover as a cartoon villain. And like any teenager aroused to defend the defenseless, I thought it profoundly unjust. Sure, I had a distinct interest in seeing his name redeemed, but I also felt something deeper: the determination to help set history's record straight.

But to defend him, I had to learn far more about Herbert Hoover's life and times. I would have to peel back the layers of conventional wisdom that often obscure complex events. I would have to question those who offered a simplified explanation for a decade of economic upheaval. I also would have to rein in my instinct for defending the family name at all costs. I knew that I would have to forget at times that my last name was Hoover, and just see where the facts led me.

As it turns out, this quest ended up changing me profoundly. I learned not to blindly trust what others proclaimed to be historically true, because even the best scholars make errors and all "intellectuals" have their own biases. I learned not only that history is often written to serve the interests of the winners, but also to explain everything that follows in a coherent narrative—even when the facts are as elusive, ambiguous, and difficult to interpret as they were for the people living through them and looking for clarity at the time.

The advantage I had is that I started my work from a position of absolute skepticism about the conventional wisdom. I began to think independently. I discovered early on that anyone could be wrong in her or his assumptions. I learned to distrust groupthink and ideological orthodoxy. I saw how even self-described critics of our society—feminists at the women's college I attended, avowed Marxists in the Latin American Studies programs where I was enrolled—were often incurable go-along-to-get-along types who would never dare challenge their own ideological conventions. These were conformists parading around as nonconformists; they all dressed in the same clothes, read the same books, knew the same people, and voted for the same politicians.

And I learned something else: The more I pressed and the more I questioned, the more I liked uncovering the fuller, forgotten truth. It became infectious—a habit of mind that I began to turn to other parts of my life. I didn't just go along to get along. I was my own person. And that turned out to be the greatest gift my great-grandfather bestowed upon me across the generations: the courage to think independently.

I began my quest by reading the works of others: historians such as George H. Nash, Eugene Lyons, Richard Norton Smith, and great writers like William F. Buckley Jr. They had looked more seriously at Hoover's life and presidency, and they had discovered a picture far different from the one often presented by the traditional historical narrative. The picture of Hoover that emerged was of an organizational wunderkind, an extraordinary American whose life story had contemporary resonance. There is an abundance of objective information that can be used to vindicate his legacy. Enough time has passed that it is now possible to view Herbert Hoover through a nonpartisan lens as an American original.

Hoover's path was hardly easy. Unlike his contemporaries among the Eastern elite, he was born with no material advantages. He was the second son of an Iowa frontier blacksmith who died of a heart attack when young "Bertie" was six years old. Three years later typhoid fever took his mother, an outspoken Quaker minister, and the orphaned boy was separated from his siblings and sent to live with an eccentric uncle in Newberg, Oregon. In 1891, at age seventeen, he demonstrated sufficient character and promise to be admitted to the first class of Stanford University, which became his spiritual home. The rest of his life was shaped by his years at Stanford. He graduated with a degree in geology, a field valuable to some of the fastest-growing global industries of that day. It was there that he met his future wife, Lou Henry, who became Stanford's first woman to graduate with a degree in geology.

After Stanford, Hoover got his start on the lowest rung of the mining industry, pushing an ore cart in California mines, earning two dollars a week working ten-hour night shifts. He graduated to an office job as an assistant to a prominent mining engineer who then recommended him to an English firm that hired him to explore undeveloped mines in western Australia for possible investment. Good fortune shone upon him: Hoover recommended a site for a mine that turned into one of the largest gold veins in western Australia, and it remained active for more than six decades.

At age twenty-four, at the close of the nineteenth century, Hoover was a true global citizen. After Bert cabled a marriage proposal to Lou Henry from Australia, the couple wed in Monterey, California, and the next day set sail for China, where Hoover established new coal mines for his firm. There the newlyweds had front-row seats at one of the watershed events that ushered in the twentieth century: the Boxer Rebellion. My great-grandmother swept bullets from her porch each morning and passed the days avoiding artillery fire and studying Mandarin Chinese, adopting the character "Hu" as her name, which became my Chinese name when I studied Mandarin in Beijing one hundred years later. Trapped in the final encampment of foreigners in China, protected from thousands of Boxers by just two thousand Russian and British soldiers, Bert organized food supplies and Lou tended to the wounded. Tianjin was relieved by an international force in July of 1900, and the Hoovers escaped to England in a German mail boat. My great-grandmother kept amazing notes detailing her time in China in a journal her father had given her as a wedding present. She had a pioneering spirit to match her husband's.

Herbert Hoover referred fondly to his life prior to America's entrance into the First World War as his "years of adventure." This was no exaggeration. By the time he was in his late twenties, he had circumnavigated the globe five times by steamship, overseen mining operations on virtually every continent, and barely escaped the political upheaval that marked the end of colonial empires in China.

Hoover was put in charge of building and managing mines on every continent except Antarctica. He was like one of the tech tycoons of our age—by the time he was twenty-eight, he was the highest paid person in the world under the age of thirty, according to the *San Francisco Chronicle,* which reported his annual salary as $33,000 (equivalent to more than $850,000 in 2010). Later, at the height of his career as an international businessman, he employed more than 100,000 people on four continents.

But Hoover's run of business success was halted by the outbreak of world war, after Germany invaded Belgium and France in 1914. With as many as nine million French and Belgian citizens in imminent danger of starvation, Hoover was asked by the American ambassador in London to organize what would become the first-ever international republic of relief, the Commission for Relief in Belgium (CRB). Hoover oversaw an effort to deliver food relief to these millions, and thanks to his success he became an international hero. Operating under its own flag, and with a monthly budget of $12 million supplied by voluntary donations and government grants, the CRB enjoyed a support system that included navy ships, factories, mills, and railroads. The CRB was managed so efficiently that after the war, Hoover was able to draw on its surplus operating funds and transform them into a scholarship fund to enable Belgian and American exchange students and scholars to pursue advanced degrees in the partner country. Since that time, the Belgian American Educational Foundation (BAEF) has provided more than three thousand Belgians and nine hundred Americans with the opportunity to spend a period of advanced study in the United States and Belgium. The ninety-year-old BAEF both commemorates and perpetuates the special Belgian-American friendship launched by Herbert Hoover.

After the United States entered the war, President Woodrow Wilson appointed him food administrator, in charge of managing the country's, and the army's, food supply. After the war he became, in essence, the food administrator for the world, as he oversaw the distribution of food relief to more than twenty countries throughout Europe and the Near East. In 1921 he led a successful campaign to combat a catastrophic famine in Soviet Russia. Hoover despised the system of Soviet Communism but insisted, "Twenty million are starving. Whatever their politics, they shall be fed!" and managed to secure a $20 million grant from the U.S. Congress for Russian food relief. PBS recently documented this heroic undertaking in the American Experience film *The Great Famine*, which tells the story of how Hoover-led relief saved the lives of many millions, and how the Soviet regime later thoroughly erased the episode from Russia's history books. It was the first case of massive humanitarian aid being delivered to the population of an ideologically hostile government.

Seventy years later, I had the privilege of meeting one of those men whose lives he helped save. He was an eighty-year-old Russian man, who had seven decades earlier walked ten miles daily to a food distribution point for condensed milk and "Hoover rolls." He wept as he grasped my young hand. My brother and I stammered, and tried to tell him how grateful we were for his thanks. But the truth is, we felt so unworthy of his thanks and were humbled to be related to a man whose compassion and resourcefulness had saved this man's life, and the lives of millions of others like him. Through this old man's still-thick Russian accent, he told us how his entire outlook on life had been transformed by the example of Herbert Hoover's generosity. He decided to come to America, believing that a country that fed its enemies must be great. He went on to become an inventor and developed a substance that was used to remove static from the Space Shuttle's surfaces. With a wink, he informed me that if we rubbed a golf ball with it before teeing off, it would fly fifty yards farther than normal. I was thirteen at the time, and since then I have often contemplated how radically different this man's life would have turned out without the intervention of Herbert Hoover.

This man was hardly alone. According to Hoover's biographer, George Nash, Hoover was directly responsible for saving the lives of as many as one-third of Europe's population during and immediately after World War I.

Here was someone who could have devoted himself completely to making money. Instead, he spent years trying to rescue millions from hunger and starvation, making an emphatic decision to "let the fortune go to hell." That impulse—to use one's skills for as elevated a purpose as possible—reminds me of the values cherished by many of my friends in their twenties and thirties today, millennials with a commitment to public service. Like Bill Gates, who stepped down as the head of Microsoft in order to pursue worldwide philanthropy, Hoover decided to become an international activist in order to advance the greater well-being of mankind. He was an enormously successful businessman who believed that the best way to build on his success was to serve society as a whole.

As a Quaker with pacifist instincts, Hoover found himself profoundly impacted by his experience as a witness to the human suffering and "rivers of blood" caused by Europe's wartime carnage and revolutionary aftermath. He was also influenced, during the First World War, by the autobiography of Andrew White. White, the first president of Cornell University, was also a historian and diplomat whose personal collection of artifacts and documents relating to the French Revolution greatly contributed to posterity's understanding of that watershed event. Reading White's autobiography, Hoover realized that he himself was in a position to collect artifacts and documents relating to the tumultuous military, political, and economic events unfolding all around him. While overseeing postwar food relief efforts throughout Europe, he began to organize the collection of such materials, and in 1919 he made a gift of $50,000 to Stanford University to house what began as the Hoover War History Collection and would become the world's largest private repository of documents relating to twentieth-century political history. The Hoover Institution on War, Revolution and Peace, as it is known today, is my great-grandfather's proudest legacy. It remains dedicated to its original purpose. The Hoover Institution's mission, as Hoover stated it in 1959, is, "from its records, to recall the voice of experience against the making of war, and by the study of these records and their publication, to recall man's endeavors to make and preserve peace, and to sustain for America the safeguards of the American way of life."

Hoover returned home a hero after the war, one of the best-known men in America. After serving in Woodrow Wilson's Democratic administration, he was encouraged to run for president by people in both parties, including one young assistant secretary of the Navy named Franklin Roosevelt, who wanted him to run as a Democrat. Instead, after the 1920 election, Republican president Warren Harding made him commerce secretary. Harding's successor, Calvin Coolidge, called him "Wonder Boy." A newspaper cartoonist joked that his title was "Secretary of Commerce and Under-Secretary of Everything Else."

Hoover was not a man brought up in politics and patronage. As secretary of commerce, he took no interest or pleasure in settling scores or carving out special deals for political allies. Instead, he set out to solve some of the basic problems of a modern industrial economy. We take for granted that businesses will compete on a level playing field. We assume that every electrical appliance will use the same AC/DC current and that most products will be sized using the same standard. But in Hoover's day, that wasn't the case. So he aimed to bring order out of chaos.

In his role as commerce secretary, he sought to turn the federal government into a kind of referee for the free market. Ever wonder why you purchase eggs by the dozen? Or why bricks are all $3\frac{5}{8}$ × $2\frac{1}{4}$ × 8 inches? Or why milk is pasteurized and sold in quarts and gallons, why tires for automobiles are of standard sizes, or why traffic lights and highway safety standards don't vary from state to state? All these standardizations occurred because Hoover believed the government could make industry more efficient. He didn't believe in forcing industries into compliance through legislative action, but instead initiated hundreds of conferences and meetings to build consensus about the best path forward. He focused on how voluntary cooperation between industry and government, driven by common goals, could improve industry's performance.

Hoover recognized that government has an important role to play. He championed efforts to significantly reduce the incidence of child labor. He pushed to eliminate the seven-day workweek in the steel industry. Both efforts succeeded not because Hoover jammed the legislation down the throats of businesses, but because he used conferences, studies, and public exposure to show industries how they could benefit from improving efficiency through standardization. For example, he encouraged the home construction industry to standardize their key building materials. The result was a significant decrease in the cost of building a home, making home ownership more affordable for Americans of modest means, and thus increasing the overall size of the home construction market.

In his work, Hoover drew on a diversity of thinking and ideas. He wanted the government to be a *catalyst* for solutions, not a designer of them. He delighted in the search for fresh approaches that emerge from genuine collaboration. Eight decades later, this approach to problem solving is the same one preferred by members of the millennial generation.

Hoover was also a believer in the power of technology. He recognized the capacity of radio to transform communications, and was the first person ever to appear via television transmission (in 1927!). He anticipated the future of air travel, and the first airfield in the Washington, D.C., area was called Hoover Field in recognition of his role in establishing aviation standards.

When his governing philosophy emerged, it was different from what had prevailed in the Harding and Coolidge administrations: laissez-faire policies that he scornfully regarded as "every man for himself and the devil take the hindmost." He saw a vigorous—but limited—role for government to play, establishing the rules of the road: helping to ensure a fair-framework of equal opportunity within which people would be free to live their lives to the best of their abilities.

In 1922, he articulated his philosophy in a commencement address that he never delivered but which was published as a small book called "American Individualism." It was a statement of his beliefs and a defense of the American system at a time when ideologies like communism and fascism had begun to challenge old-world assumptions. At the time of its publication, the *New York Times Book Review* wrote that it was "among the few great formulations of American political theory" and Fredrick Jackson Turner wrote that "it contains the New and the Old Testament of the American gospel." "American Individualism" not only offered a sketch of Hoover's political philosophy. It suggested a path forward for America, one that remains relevant enough today to have animated my own thinking on the subject—and to have inspired the title of this book.

In the spring of 1927, Hoover was again called on to oversee humanitarian relief, this time in the American heartland, when the

Mississippi River flooded well beyond its banks. The Great Mississippi River Flood of 1927 was the Hurricane Katrina of the 1920s:
it displaced more than one and a half million Americans, destroyed
two million acres of crops, and killed thousands of cattle and other
livestock. Hoover left Washington and went to the Midwest to co-
ordinate with local governments to build tent cities complete with
beds, electricity, running water, hospitals, and kitchens. He managed to have these facilities in place by the time the floodwaters had
crested.

Hoover did all this without federal dollars, choosing instead to
raise private funds for the relief efforts. The fund-raising drive succeeded, bringing in $25 million in donations and low-interest loans,
all of which were repaid. Later, in his memoirs, he remarked about
the rescue efforts that "those were the days when citizens expected
to take care of one another in time of disaster and it had not occurred to them that the Federal Government should do it."

Hoover's heroic coordination of the Mississippi River flood relief
catapulted him to new heights in American politics. The chorus at
the 1928 Republican National Convention was "Who but Hoover?"

Toward the end of his triumphant 1928 campaign for president,
Hoover gave a speech that summed up his Republican Party's philosophy. He called it "Rugged Individualism." It is a speech that is still
cited today—and it was in many ways a campaign-style distillation
of the ideas expressed in "American Individualism" six years earlier.

"The American system," Hoover said, "is founded upon the
conception that only through ordered liberty, freedom, and equal
opportunity to the individual will his initiative and enterprise spur
on the march of progress. And in our insistence upon equality of opportunity has our system advanced beyond all the world."

Hoover saw the 1928 presidential election, and the differences
between the Republican and Democratic parties, as a "choice between the American system of rugged individualism and a European

philosophy of diametrically opposed doctrines—doctrines of paternalism and state socialism. . . . Every step of bureaucratizing of the business of our country poisons the very roots of liberalism—[namely] political equality, free speech, free assembly, free press, and equality of opportunity. It is not the road to more liberty, but to less liberty."

The "Rugged Individualism" speech endures, as do the underlying differences between the Republican and Democratic parties. On the one hand, a focus on the individual and the free market, and on the other hand an emphasis on government intervention into private industry by means of regulation and bureaucratization—a contrast highlighted in our current political debates and at Tea Party rallies. The choice remains between an American model and a European model of governance, and the long-term stakes remain the same: the road to liberty or the road to serfdom.

Hoover won the presidency by the largest landslide in American history, capturing almost 60 percent of the popular vote, the only civilian to have ascended to the presidency without previously holding elective office.

But his run of good fortune and success soon ended. Seven months after he assumed office in 1929, the stock market crashed, triggering a series of events that led to the Great Depression. Hoover hardly sat on his hands in the wake of the sudden decline in the economy—instead he set to work launching or accelerating public works efforts. He proposed to Congress a $160 million tax cut along with a doubling of outlays for public buildings and dams, highways and harbors. By the spring of 1930, Hoover's response to the crisis had received widespread acclaim, as the New York Times editorialized: "No one in his place could have done more. . . . Very few of his predecessors could have done as much."

But it was not enough. The collapse of foreign banks and international trade along with persistent drought conditions in the

Midwest drove unemployment up from five million to more than eleven million by 1931. The economy would not recover for more than another decade.

Circumstances beyond Hoover's control greatly complicated his efforts to revive the economy, and there was one area where my great-grandfather was truly at a disadvantage. He was trying to cope with a global depression in a modern industrial economy without the benefit of some of the core theories of modern economics. Most major theories of macroeconomics were developed, in fact, by studying what happened during the Great Depression. John Maynard Keynes, Friedrich von Hayek, Milton Friedman, and other prominent economists emerged from that period with critical theories about monetary and fiscal policy, trade, and the interrelationship of taxes and the economy as well as the value of countercyclical policies. But none of this expertise was available to Hoover in 1930.

Not surprisingly, he made some mistakes. He signed the Smoot-Hawley legislation that increased U.S. tariffs on imported goods, contributing to a global decline in trade (although this affected only 4.2 percent of the U.S. economy, so its impact, it has been argued, has been overstated by later economists). He pressed employers to maintain wages, which made it harder for employers to hire workers. And he cooperated with Congress to balance the budget with the expiration of Coolidge-era tax cuts in 1932, which resulted in the largest tax increase in history. The fact is, a modern-day conservative would find none of these mistakes easy to explain, let alone defend. But in each of these cases, he was responding to political pressures without the ability to gauge how his actions might affect the economy, and his actions were certainly less radical than those he was urged to adopt by his political rivals or those later pursued by his successor. In our current debates, the *context* for Hoover's decision making has been entirely lost.

I believe that the most effective defense of Hoover is not just that he did better that anyone could have, but that his successor did no better. Roosevelt's administration enacted dozens of laws, in the process creating an alphabet soup of agencies to attend to almost every aspect of American life and transforming the relationship between government and the individual. But Roosevelt's economic record was no better than Hoover's. The little-known truth is that the American economy actually *worsened* during Roosevelt's second term, and did not begin to recover until the Second World War jump-started industry. Yet, somehow, Hoover still gets all the blame.

Roosevelt did succeed in one important respect: he *appeared* to care more than his predecessor. Politics is perception, and this image of FDR was a direct outgrowth of his well-oiled political machine. During the 1932 campaign, Charles Michelson and the Democratic National Committee were armed with a million-dollar budget to organize a smear operation to destroy Hoover's reputation. Michelson was the hyperpartisan hack who coined the term "Hoovervilles" and continually attacked Hoover as an uncaring, do-nothing, apathetic leader who ignored the hardships suffered by "the little man." Historian Thomas Fleming characterizes Michelson's attacks as a series of "atrocious assaults on President Hoover, portraying him as a vicious egotist who had self-promoted his greatest living American title out of raw ambition for power." Nothing could have been further from the truth, and the smear campaign drove my great-grandmother to write long letters to her children for posterity detailing how deeply her husband did indeed care for "the little man."

During the Bonus Marches of 1932, when World War I veterans marched on Washington demanding their war bonuses early (which Congress categorically denied), twenty thousand men were camping out at the Anacostia Flats in Washington, D.C. Hoover secretly arranged for tents, food, and water; yet unlike today's politicians, he took no credit for this effort. Brought up in the Quaker tradition, he did not believe that glory should follow those who did good works. In this case, he didn't have to worry.

After his defeat in the 1932 election, Hoover retreated to his Palo Alto home (now occupied by the president of Stanford University). Unlike most ex-presidents up to that point, he remained active in public policy. Yet the bitter partisanship of the 1932 campaign did not let up. Immediately following his swearing-in ceremony, FDR personally rescinded Herbert Hoover's Secret Service detail. As William F. Buckley Jr. wrote, "Mr. Hoover went away unguarded, discredited, unloved." Harold Ickes, secretary of the interior, changed the name of one of Hoover's greatest achievements, the Colorado River Project, from Hoover Dam to Boulder Dam when it was dedicated in 1936, an injustice so petty and grotesque that Harry Truman corrected it upon assuming the presidency after Roosevelt's death.

Within one month of entering the Oval Office, Harry Truman summoned Herbert Hoover from the shadows and into the White House, rekindling his career in public service. Truman dispatched Hoover to Europe on a thirty-eight-nation tour to oversee food relief in the wake of the Second World War, thereby empowering him to reprise the role he had played so effectively three decades earlier. In 1947, Truman established the first of two "Hoover Commissions," each helmed by my great-grandfather and dedicated to streamlining the postwar executive branch and improving government efficiency. The two presidents' bipartisan friendship inaugurated an extended period of energetic activity during which Hoover wrote a dozen books and became a much sought-after counsel for political leaders of both parties, a performance that shaped the modern postpresidency.

And so Hoover turned the page to a new chapter in his life. No longer the mining engineer, the relief organizer, the cabinet officer, or even the president, Hoover became, in the words of historian

Richard Norton Smith, "a philosopher of modern conservative thought." He had begun to play this role with the publication of "American Individualism" in 1922.

Hoover had seen firsthand Europe's experiments with socialism and Bolshevism and the rise of fascism, and he felt he ought to affirm why America must resist the temptation to follow those paths. He believed fundamentally that America's greatness lay in the individual, using God-given talents and working with others, as the essential building block of society. He believed in America's inherent dynamism—that the absence of old-world social castes in the United States, which allowed an individual to rise from extreme poverty to fabulous wealth within a lifetime, was a unique gift to Americans. He believed that the nation's diversity of faiths was a strength, endowing it with a richness of spiritual traditions, heritages, and beliefs from which it could continue to draw inspiration and new energy. He believed that America's record of welcoming new cultures and initiating new traditions set it apart. He believed that our civic tradition of volunteerism was the backbone of every community and could not be matched by centralized government action. At the core of his philosophy was the profound belief that the individual was the engine driving it all. And ten years later, he had a a stark philosophical counterpoint in Roosevelt's policies.

In 1934, spurred by his alarm at where Roosevelt was taking the country, Hoover wrote a direct rebuke of the New Deal in a book called *The Challenge to Liberty*. He saw in the New Deal a dramatic expansion of the federal government's role in the life of the individual. He saw this as a dangerous encroachment that would "cripple or abandon the heritage of liberty for some new philosophy which must mark the passing of freedom."

Hoover understood that promises extended by the government come with a cost. With every promise to ease the pain of loss comes the price to be paid by ordinary citizens. Once the government takes upon itself by force the role normally performed by the individual, he wrote, it becomes "the master of the man." And indeed, Hoover cited several areas where government had become the master: it devalued the currency and devalued existing debt; it forced collective bargaining on employers; it concentrated corporate power in oligopolies and trusts; it fixed prices; it levied taxes on food and clothing and other essentials; it began to engage in business activity that had always been reserved for the private sector, such as power generation; it told farmers what to grow and how much to grow; and it restricted expansion of business in specific industries. And it did all this with the power to prosecute and jail individuals found in violation of the new rules.

This concentration of power alarmed Hoover. Unfortunately, his words did not persuade Americans to turn away from the New Deal. Far from it: during the eight years before the start of World War II, the federal government grew enormously. And once in place, the new bureaucracy began to generate its own reason for being. Inertia would set in; no argument, even one rooted deeply in constitutional principles of limited government, could defeat it. The legacy of Roosevelt is not the individual programs introduced under the New Deal, but the idea that the federal government should remain a permanent fixture in the life of the individual, from birth until death. It is the legacy that every Democratic president and even some Republican presidents have sought to enlarge upon.

In contrast to the top-down vision of the New Deal bureaucrats, my great-grandfather understood that the proper role of the government was to support the individual's pursuit of opportunity, not to guarantee a particular outcome. He saw the danger in allowing a powerful government to replace many of the essential institutions of civic life—churches, community organizations, families—thus depriving America of the diversity of solutions and ideas that had made it great. He helped lay the foundation for what has become one of

the central tenets of modern conservative thinking: "The government that is powerful enough to give you everything you need is
powerful enough to take it all away."

Vindicating Herbert Hoover's legacy is an uphill battle, because
today Democrats are *still* running against my great-grandfather.
Senator Joe Biden offered this remark during the 2008 presidential
campaign: "I'm proud to say that we Democrats aren't experts at
Herbert Hoover depression economics like John McCain and his
pals. From Franklin Roosevelt to Bill Clinton, we just get elected
to clean up the economic mess these Republicans leave behind."
Senator Harry Reid had this to say about my great-grandfather:
"For Herbert Hoover, I guess ignorance was bliss. It wasn't until the
American people replaced this out-of-touch Republican president
with a Democrat, Franklin Delano Roosevelt, that our nation's economic recovery began."

More disturbing, conservatives and Republicans have joined
this chorus. In 2008, John McCain made history by becoming the
first *Republican* nominee to run against Hoover, when he said, "My
friends, the last president to raise taxes during tough economic times
was Herbert Hoover, and he practiced protectionism as well . . ."
Mitt Romney piled on as recently as the 2011 Conservative Political Action Conference with "Obama's Hoovervilles," and even
Rush Limbaugh has shamefully called our current president "Barack
'Hoover' Obama."

I happen to have an ongoing argument with pundit Glenn Beck,
whom I have gotten to know a bit from our shared perch at Fox
News over the past few years.

If you've watched Glenn Beck's television show during the past
year, or listened to his radio program, you've been exposed to his

crusade against progressivism. Beck has launched a movement to identify and expel progressives from government, and has framed it in a historical narrative that begins with Teddy Roosevelt's Bull Moose candidacy for president in 1912 and extends straight through to Barack Obama's White House. Beck has plopped Herbert Hoover into the middle of this narrative, mischaracterizing him as just another progressive.

I don't fault Beck for making this mistake once, or even twice. After all, Hoover did call himself an "independent progressive in the Republican tradition." He believed, for example, that children shouldn't work in factories, and that government had a responsibility to prevent child labor and unsafe working conditions. But does that make him a socialist? Not at all. Hoover was no progressive in the continuum from Woodrow Wilson to Franklin Delano Roosevelt. He was instead FDR's most prominent and consistent philosophical opponent. He detailed his opposition to socialism, big government, and, later, the New Deal in successive essays and books. Glenn Beck completely overlooks this evidence, and although I have brought it to his attention, he continues to repeat his mistake. I suppose it's easier to hammer away at Herbert Hoover. But on this, Glenn Beck is worse than Joe Biden: he gets it wrong even when he knows better. Certainly the liberal image of Hoover as an uncaring and out-of-touch, do-nothing president was always wrong. But conservatives who dismiss Hoover out of embarrassment, ignorance, or a misplaced sense of principle are just as misguided.

There are signs, however, that the tide is finally beginning to turn. The financial crisis of 2008 and the unprecedented experiments in federal takeovers of banks and auto companies, as well as the creation of penalties and taxes regulating the private health insurance market and now the federal effort to regulate carbon—all these measures have given conservatives, as well as independents, a reason to reconsider their vilification of Hoover. They are taking a fresh look at the history and the economics of the Great Depression and the New Deal.

The columnist and political thinker Thomas Sowell writes that "what was widely believed then and later was that the stock market crash of 1929 was a failure of the free market and the cause of the massive unemployment that persisted for years during the 1930s. Given the two most striking features of that era—the stock market crash and a widespread government intervention in the economy—it is not immediately obvious which was more responsible for the dire economic conditions. But remarkably little effort has been made by most of the intelligentsia to try to sort out the cause or causes. It has been largely a foregone conclusion that the market was the cause and the government intervention was the saving grace."

Amity Shlaes's 2006 bestseller, *The Forgotten Man: A New History of the Great Depression,* inspired a wave of scholarship that has begun chipping away at the perception of FDR as the country's economic savior during the Great Depression. Other books, such as historian Burton Folsom Jr.'s 2008 *New Deal or Raw Deal: How FDR's Economic Legacy Has Damaged America* and the 2009 work by Robert Murphy, *The Politically Incorrect Guide to the Great Depression and the New Deal,* have challenged the predominant narrative that FDR's New Deal saved America from Herbert Hoover's Great Depression. In a *Wall Street Journal* article titled "Did FDR End the Depression?" Folsom answered in the negative: "It's a myth. FDR did not get us out of the Great Depression—not during the 1930s, and only in a limited sense during World War II."

In the reevaluation of Herbert Hoover, Americans are becoming acquainted with his life and career prior to and after leaving the White House, when he made some of his most lasting achievements. Hoover's legacies are as diverse as the electrification of the neon skyline of the Las Vegas Strip, the vast agricultural economy of California, the Hoover Institution's contributions to public policy, and the descendants of the millions of Europeans he saved from starvation. Those who fixate only on making money or winning elections will find it an unhappy existence much of the time. My great-grandfather understood this, and that's why he chose to dedicate his life to serving others.

He was always oriented toward the future. He was, after all, the first president born and raised west of the Mississippi River, which was still considered America's great frontier. It is there where he was laid to rest, on the sunrise side of a hill in the humble hamlet of West Branch, Iowa, overlooking the cottage in which he was born and his presidential library.

Hoover was a globalist and a technologist, and he understood America's rising position in the world. He believed that America could extend its power not just with arms, but also with assistance. Surely no nation in the history of the world had ever done so much to help civilians in other nations as America did under Hoover's guidance. And that is a tradition that continues to this day.

These are all values that I see as familiar, because they are the values of my generation. In some ways, Herbert Hoover can be considered a millennial in spirit: young at the turn of the century, aware of America's past but deeply committed to building its future. His greatest passion and highest calling was service to others, and he measured his life's successes not in dollars and votes but in results achieved. He lived a life that millennials today would embrace, and I believe he gave voice to their interests, and those of every generation committed to the ideals of American individualism.

CHAPTER 2

CONSERVATIVE TRIBALISM

*"The term conservatism has come to cover so wide a range of views,
and views so incompatible with one another, that we shall no doubt see
the growth of hyphenated designations, such as libertarian-conservative
and aristocratic-conservative."*
—MILTON FRIEDMAN, 1962

Which Tribe Do You Belong To?

Paleocons, neocons, lib-cons, enviro-cons, Crunchy Cons, so-cons, Religious-Right conservatives, traditionalist conservatives, southern conservatives, western conservatives, Goldwater conservatives, Tea Party conservatives—if you are somewhere right of center, which tribe do you belong to?

Growing up in Colorado, I was reared in the spirit of what my father described at my wedding as "western conservatism": individualism tempered by responsibility for the community; a predilection for limited federal government, lower taxes, the entrepreneurial spirit, and individual initiative; and an appreciation for the idea of American exceptionalism. Or put more crassly, western conservatives are the ranchers who pump their shotguns before yelling, "Keep your government off my land and out of my bedroom." That's the tribe in which I was raised, and yes, my dad gave me my first shotgun when I was twelve.

But in my journey across the conservative universe—through America's West Coast and East Coast conservative think tanks and its activist groups inside the Beltway and beyond, and as a result of my employment as a staffer on Capitol Hill, in political campaigns, and in the White House—I have discovered that Milton Friedman's description of conservatism is especially apt: Conservatism is a nation of tribes, governed by warlords, spouting often incompatible and irreconcilable philosophies and principles.

Thirty years ago, Ronald Reagan was able to bring harmony to the cacophony of conservative interests, and for a brief time they all sang from the same song sheet. But since then, for most of the time, tribalism has ruled, with one tribe ascending in national influence as another descends. Without a unifying leadership or a pragmatic campaign to rally around, conservatives have spent a lot of time over the past two decades in a proverbial circular firing squad, engaged in a deadly squabble over who is and who isn't conservative enough.

But millennials don't see all that. The truth is, most millennials think conservatism means "social conservatism," and to put it mildly, they are not impressed.

Millennials are the most ethnically diverse, nonwhite generation in American history. They are the most socially liberal. A sound majority of them believes that homosexuality should be accepted by society. They are highly urban and suburban, not small-town or rural. They are worldly, and not necessarily besotted with the idea of American exceptionalism. As a generation, they have the lowest level of affiliation with organized religion, despite being very "spiritual." So what they see, however mistakenly—a Republican Party run by a bunch of old white guys and a few gals from nonurban, mostly southern and midwestern America bent on restricting gay rights and abortion and populated by flag-waving America-firsters—doesn't leave them with a warm and fuzzy feeling.

Of course, the millennials aren't getting the full picture. There is far more to conservatism than the social conservative activists—or so-cons, as I like to call them. Conservatism is actually a pretty vibrant nation, with all our different tribes. So for the benefit of my millennial readers, and anyone else who thinks conservatism is just a one-note movement, in the pages that follow I offer a panoramic view of today's conservative movement. Call it a field guide to modern American conservatism.

A disclaimer first: Serious studies of the American conservative movement, its history and its many facets, have been written by giants such as George H. Nash, William F. Buckley Jr., and Lee Edwards, among others. I encourage anyone interested in the movement to read their works. This chapter isn't meant as a substitute for those works, merely an overview.

The biggest thing to remember is that *conservatism* is a deceptive word. First, conservatism isn't necessarily trying to conserve anything. Second, conservatism isn't an *ism*. It isn't a single political ideology but a movement made up of several mini-movements, each with its own governing philosophy. The movement's most esteemed historian, George Nash, says this: "Perhaps the most important thing to understand about modern American conservatism is that it is not, and has never been, univocal. It is a *coalition,* with many points of origin and diverse tendencies that are not always easy to reconcile with one another. Historically, it has been a river of thought and activism fed by many tributaries: a wide and sometimes muddy river, but one with great power, so long as the tributaries flowed into the common stream."

So where did modern American conservatism begin? The fact is, many elements of America's modern conservative movement have been around forever. You will find strains of modern conservative thinking in the ancient classics of Greece and Rome, the Hebrew scriptures, the Christian Gospel, classical liberalism spun from the French Revolution, the writings of Edmund Burke, and of course among the writings of America's Founding Fathers.

But the event that marked the emergence of an organized modern conservative coalition in America was the publication of the first issue of William F. Buckley Jr.'s *National Review* on November 19, 1955. In his mission statement for *National Review,* Buckley spelled out the priorities for which "conservatism" should stand: resisting government expansion to protect individual freedom; championing "the competitive price system," or classical economic liberalism; confronting concentrations of power in corporations and syndicates; defeating communism; supporting a two-party political system that practices transparent and honest debate; understanding the reality of the human condition; challenging intellectual conformity in the arts, culture, and education; opposing internationalism when it undermines the United States and its autonomy.

What is striking is that Buckley was not trying to promote some kind of preservation of an old-world order, as the word *conservative* misleadingly implies. In the mid-1950s, the dominant political philosophy was the liberalism that had established itself during the twelve years of Franklin Delano Roosevelt's presidency and that had retained prominence afterward, despite the election of Republican president Dwight D. Eisenhower. When Buckley famously declared that conservatives were standing athwart history, yelling "Stop!" he was referring to the seeming inevitability of the growth of government, and what he felt was the transformation of the American character by the fundamental altering of the relationship between the individual and the state. From the very start, the modern conservative movement was defined by its unwillingness to go along with the status quo. It was, at its heart, a rebellious movement identified by opposition to the accepted political establishment of the time. Not exactly conservative—in fact, somewhat revolutionary.

Buckley's mission statement touched on all facets of public and private life: international policy, domestic policy, philosophy, religion, and economics. Buckley's ambition was to bring diverse groups resistant to liberal dogma together under a single banner. The three primary components of this coalition—economic libertarians, traditionalists, and anticommunists—were later joined by new groups, including neoconservatives and the Protestant evangelical Religious Right. And that diversity persists today.

Here are the principal groups that have joined this loose confederation of modern conservatism from its founding down to the present day:

Economic Libertarians and Fiscal Conservatives

The New Deal had its opponents, even during the depths of the Great Depression. People besides my great-grandfather saw Roosevelt's experiments with the economy as unlikely to end the Great Depression. Instead, they saw in them the roots of a radical realignment of the relationship between the individual and the federal government. Economic libertarians, or "classical liberals," were one of the first three coalition partners in the budding conservative movement. They believed that the ever-expanding federal government would be the root of economic stagnation and a permanent impediment to individual initiative and individual liberty. They longed for an unfettered free market, where those with ambition could benefit fully from their talents and wits. To economic libertarians, modern liberalism was merely a softer version of socialism and communism. Indeed, they believed that many aspects of the New Deal were leading to central planning and warmed-over socialism and that the state, through taxation and regulation, would gradually sap society of its productive and creative energies. At the core of this philosophy was a concern for the protection of private property—things owned by individuals should not be appropriated by the state for any reason.

The leading lights of this branch of the movement were think-
ers, not populists. They were not even self-described conservatives.
Friedrich von Hayek's *The Road to Serfdom,* Milton Friedman's *Capitalism and Freedom,* and Ayn Rand's fiction and nonfiction (which
deeply influenced economists like Alan Greenspan) became and remain to this day among the most important works of this tribe, and
are by far the most influential economic contributions of the conservative movement as a whole.

At the same time, a cadre of economists in the last fifty years has
reevaluated the state-driven, Keynesian theories that underpinned
the New Deal and subsequent liberal experiments in economics.
Most notably, Milton Friedman, Ludwig von Mises, and, later, Ar-
thur Laffer have shown that historically the greater the government's
involvement in the economy, the smaller the resulting economy turns
out to be. They have also shown that if you raise taxes, the economy
shrinks somewhat as people react to the disincentives of higher tax
rates, while tax revenue doesn't rise as expected. On the other hand,
these conservative economists have shown if you *cut* tax rates, people see more reason to work and to invest, and the economy grows
faster as a result. In the long run, this course of action produces
greater tax revenues. The underlying assumption is that the economy
is not some static machine. Rather, it is a somewhat temperamental
beast and must be approached cautiously. This simple idea—that the
economy can't be managed very well, and that the more you try
to "fine-tune" it, the less it is apt to grow—is at the core of economic conservatism and the approach most Republicans take when
it comes to taxes, regulations, and economic theory.

Today, Libertarians cluster at the CATO Institute and *Reason*
magazine, which proclaims support for "free minds and free markets . . . by making a principled case for liberty and individual choice
in all areas of human activity." Populated by economic libertarians,

this tribe today is also known for its less stringent approach to social issues like gay marriage, abortion, and drug legalization, advocating limited government intervention.

So-Cons, Traditionalists, and the Religious Right

We all know that the Republican Party has a strong contingent of social and religious conservatives, but not everyone knows how this came to be, or that this element is actually far weaker today than it has been in the past.

At the founding of America's modern conservative movement, the second major partner of Buckley's three-part coalition were the traditionalist conservatives. Historian George Nash calls them the most authentically "conservative" partners because they joined the coalition out of alarm at liberalism's moral relativism. They were mostly Roman Catholic, and some were converts to Catholicism. They were religious and academic elites, such as Russell Kirk and Richard Weaver, and opinion elites, such as Robert Novak (though he came later). They believed that the state was in perpetual competition with God's authority, and that liberalism would naturally try to help the state win that battle. Thus traditionalists focused in particular on battling secular culture. They advocated "a revival of Christian orthodoxy, classical natural law, pre-modern political philosophy, and mediating institutions between the citizen and the state." Traditionalists believed liberalism was "eating away not only at our liberties but also at the ethical and institutional foundations of traditional society, thereby creating a vast spiritual vacuum into which totalitarianism could enter."

By the late 1970s, traditionalists had made common cause with the rising tide of Protestant evangelicals who later came to be known as the Religious Right. These voters had been either apolitical or Democratic-leaning since the New Deal, as were most rural voters in the South. They voted for a Democrat, Jimmy Carter, in 1976.

Carter himself was a born-again Christian and drew upon the language of the Southern Baptist Church. But during the Cold War, Democrats were divided between those who remained determined to defeat communism and those who sought to negotiate with it—an issue that did not divide evangelicals, who viewed godless communism as a special threat to Christianity.

Until the Cold War years, the religiosity of these Americans had not informed their politics. But with the schism over communism, and then after the Supreme Court decision *Roe v. Wade* legalized abortion in the United States, religious Christians felt that it was no longer acceptable for them to remain silent on political matters. They took on not only the abortion issue, but also other social issues, including, in Nash's words, "school prayer, pornography, drug use, sexual deviancy, [and] the vulgarization of mass entertainment." By 1980, leaders such as Jerry Falwell, Pat Robertson, and James Dobson were urging their congregations to participate in the political process and exercise their voting rights against what these leaders saw as America's moral decline. These evangelicals came out in droves to support Ronald Reagan, a moment that marked what scholars now call the "great awakening" of the Religious Right, when they joined the conservative coalition.

Social conservatives also took a strong stance against the feminism of the 1960s and 1970s, which encouraged women to throw off the traditional restrictions of the domestic sphere and to pursue professional careers and sexual independence. Social conservative female leaders such as Phyllis Schlafly affirmed that women were different from men, and that women should not compete with men economically and should cherish traditional gender role divides. To this day, they believe that they are the true feminists, fighting for women to be respected and honored precisely because they have a special gift for domesticity and family building.

In recent years, however, the Religious Right has diversified its political portfolio. For example, the evangelical ministry of Rick Warren's Saddleback Church has focused less on the traditional social issues of the Religious Right and more on a broad ministry of social action that includes fighting HIV/AIDS, caring for orphans, and helping addicts recover.

Today's social conservatives comprise a mix of multiple faiths, not just the evangelicals and traditional Catholics but also Orthodox Jews and religious immigrant groups from South Asia. This variegated group, which could never come to an agreement on theological issues but manages to find common cause in the political arena, has brought moral populism into the broader conservative movement and has helped deliver election victories to Republicans. They turned out in large numbers for the 1994 Gingrich revolution, and were heavily courted in 2004 by George W. Bush after it became clear that its members hadn't supported him with enthusiasm in 2000.

Having worked on the Bush reelection campaign, I can testify to the intensity of the campaign's effort to woo the Religious Right. While these efforts—specifically President Bush's support for the Federal Marriage Amendment and various state ballot initiatives banning same-sex marriage—were intended to drive social conservatives to the polls, further analysis has shown that this election strategy failed. The central myth about the "conservagenzia," a term introduced by Bush campaign chief strategist Matthew Dowd to describe the self-anointed political leaders of the Religious Right, is that social conservative voters care solely about social issues. Dowd's numbers tell a different story: today's so-cons, just like other tribes in the movement, make economic and national security issues, not social issues, their top priority. More on this in chapter five.

Anticommunists and Paleocons

The third tribe of William F. Buckley's new conservative movement in the 1950s were the anticommunists. Largely irrelevant today,

thanks to the collapse of communism and socialism as serious economic and political alternatives to capitalism, this was actually in
some ways the most important tribe of the early conservative movement because it supplied the glue that bound the various ideological
groupings together. Led by a group of former Trotskyites and con-
fessed former communists—people such as Whittaker Chambers,
John Chamberlain, James Burnham, and Frank Meyer—this tribe
denounced communism as a corrupt moral system, and recognized
in free-market economics the core of freedom. Both of the other
conservative factions—economic libertarians and traditionalists—
were alarmed by the ascendance of communism around the globe
because it threatened what was most important to them, be it the
fire of individual initiative and productivity or the primacy of man's
relationship with God.

Anticommunism proved to be the common thread of this loose
coalition: It made dealing with the existential communist threat to
America and the West the overriding priority. And that gave the
sometimes competing, sometimes incoherent conservative factions a
common purpose. This strategy, outlined by Frank Meyer, was called
"fusionism," and it had the effect of curbing the incessant infighting
that characterized the early conservative movement. For roughly four
decades, the fusionism strategy proved to be remarkably effective. But
since the fall of the Berlin Wall in 1989, a moment when conservative anticommunists reached the apex of their influence within the
movement, that glue has dissolved and unity has eluded the movement. Without a commonly perceived existential threat to America's
values, conservatism has been as factionalized as it was at its founding.

Within the anticommunist wing, and largely left behind in the
postcommunist era, are paleoconservatives such as Pat Buchanan,
who are crossbreeds of social conservatives and foreign policy iso-
lationists. They oppose concepts like world government and internationalism, resist the authority of the United Nations, and are

"defiantly nationalist, [and] skeptical of global democracy." In a way, this group predates the modern conservative movement because they had earlier dominated the Republican Party. In the era after World War I, Republicans were deeply distrustful of further international entanglements, and until the Japanese attack on Pearl Harbor they opposed entry into World War II. Today paleoconservatives are ardent nationalists who have increasingly found common cause with the neoisolationist left.

Neocons and National Security Conservatives

At the opposite end of the foreign policy spectrum is the neoconservative tribe. As an intellectual group, they began as mainly Jewish liberals who migrated rightward in the 1960s and 1970s, disenchanted by the excesses of the Great Society and unhappy about the American Left's defense of European socialism and softness on Soviet Communism. Their definition was most famously summarized by Irving Kristol's quip: a neoconservative is "a liberal who has been mugged by reality."

Irving Kristol, Norman Podhoretz, Midge Decter, and Jeane Kirkpatrick were all part of the intellectual migration from Left to Right, and through their perches at *Commentary* magazine and *The Public Interest,* they added intellectual, urban, and even counterrevolutionary heft to the conservative movement. While they certainly recognized the evils of communist totalitarianism, they were often at odds with the social conservative and paleoconservative factions in the movement when it came to specific issues, such as the value of church-state separation and the vital role of American power and alliances around the world. But thanks to their staunch anticommunism and anti-liberalism, they became de facto conservatives.

Because neocons came to the movement after embracing liberalism, they have less patience for some of the more unsavory aspects of conservatism's early history, particularly on the issue of civil

rights. The leaders of the conservative movement—Barry Goldwater, in particular—voted against the 1964 Civil Rights Act and related laws, even though he was clearly not racist (his had been among
the first businesses in Arizona to desegregate). But the neocons were
impatient with such resistance and helped traditionalist conservatives to rethink their opposition to the civil rights movement. While
conservatives remained opposed to affirmative action, mainstream
conservatives have come to recognize that the civil rights movement
deserved their support. Conservatives such as Jack Kemp and George
W. Bush made some inroads within the African-American community, helping to diminish this obvious blot on the conservative movement's reputation.

Today, the label "neoconservative" has come to designate someone who supports a strong national security policy. Although pilloried
for advocating the 2003 Iraq War, they have been steadfast in com-
bating Islamist terrorism and promoting democracy abroad. And at a
time when popular revolutions are erupting in the Middle East, Bush's
"Freedom Agenda," which was derided by Democrats and the Left,
appears to be bearing fruit as of the Arab Spring uprisings of 2011.

Conservative Populists: Tea Partiers, Dittoheads, and Mama Grizzlies

Rush Limbaugh's fans and Sarah Palin's followers are not one and
the same, but they have a lot in common. They have a similar outlook on the world; they are more rural than urban and are more
likely to be blue-collar than white-collar. They resent the elitism of
liberalism to the point where they associate its key elements with
moral degeneration. They deeply distrust government, and resent
paying taxes when they see so much of it wasted on what they think
are useless government programs. They tend to be pro-defense, and
when America is at war they are among the most vocal in supporting
our troops.

While Limbaugh's Dittoheads came into political consciousness in the Clinton era, and Palin's Mama Grizzlies in the 2010 campaign season, these groups have been united by two political twists: the first was the bailouts initiated by George W. Bush and accelerated by Barack Obama; the second was the vast spending programs launched by President Obama and the Democratic House and Senate immediately after President Obama took office. With these two events, Dittoheads and Mama Grizzlies joined forces with the Tea Party. This grassroots movement was a conservative populist revolt against the irresponsible fiscal policies of the late Bush and early Obama administrations. It grew out of Ron Paul's Tea Party protests during the 2008 presidential campaign.

While a return to fiscal conservatism is the animating idea behind these Tea Party protests, they have focused on other major policy areas, and some activists are running for local county councils and school boards. These groups can easily steer Republican nominations to favored candidates, and in certain cases, can help them win elections. But not always: the one clear lesson of the 2010 campaign is that a Tea Party–backed candidate like Sharon Angle or Christine O'Donnell, no matter how loyal her supporters, will lose unless she can appeal beyond the base of the Republican Party. The power of the Tea Party movement will be tested again in the 2012 presidential election campaign.

Crunchy Cons and Enviro-cons

The rise of the green movement has largely been a phenomenon of the Left. And no wonder—there is almost nothing that resonates more strongly with the liberal worldview than the need for government regulation to meet the threat of private industrial pollution. Much of what the Left has produced follows that pattern: punish private enterprise to accomplish goals, without regard to what individual taxpayers may want and be willing to pay for. So, in classic conservative fashion, there have sprung up, in response, environmentally conscious conservatives who look for free-enterprise solutions to environmental problems—like cap-and-trade credits for fighting the pollutants that cause acid rain. And then there is a group known as Crunchy Cons, "political right-wingers with countercultural sensibilities." They tend to be pro-green, anti–urban sprawl, and anti–strip mall. They base their opposition on what they see as the moral corrosion and the environmental ugliness imposed on America by the consumer culture. The countercultural elements of this movement strike me as fundamentally conservative—for example, they don't trust large institutions such as schools, so they homeschool. They are deeply distrustful of authority, so they resent nanny-state ideas, such as anti-smoking laws. In fundamental ways, Crunchy Cons are a wonderful part of the movement.

Reagan, Rush, RINOs, and Me

All this tribalism leads to the question, is there any common theme among conservatives today? How can we reconcile the social conservative impulses to highly regulate sexuality with the libertarian instincts to keep government out of the bedroom? How can the neocons and paleocons agree on a path forward in Afghanistan? Can free-market pro-business types coexist with off-the-grid Crunchy Cons?

Sure, some say, but we need a Ronald Reagan to be our uniter. Always Reagan—he looms large whenever conservatives wax nostalgic for that period of American conservatism's halcyon days. It's as if Reagan were not just a great president, but a conservative saint, someone who performed the miracle of achieving ideological and political unity.

I don't blame people for thinking this way. When Reagan left office, the movement and the Republican Party were in great shape.

And since then, conservatives have either lost politically or lost phil-osophically—often both.

But this nostalgia has left conservatives in a state of inertia, bogged down in a fruitless effort to discover something called "Rea-gan conservatism," as though there is a pure version of conservatism. But there isn't. The movement is too rife with factions and tribes for there to be one true version of conservatism.

And the truth is that there never was. What the Reagan yearn-ers and Reagan revisionists forget is that Reagan wasn't a purist. Reagan, for example, followed conservative economic orthodoxy by cutting taxes, but he later raised them. Reagan didn't like terror-ists and launched air strikes against them, but he also did side deals with the mullahs in Iran. He could be accused of cutting and run-ning from Beirut after our Marines were attacked there in 1983. He signed a massive amnesty bill giving citizenship to illegal immigrants. I point out these facts not to denigrate Reagan. He was the most successful conservative president the United States has ever had. But he wasn't a purist. His politics were pragmatic, in a way that would appeal to today's millennials.

There actually is no such thing as "pure" conservatism. Success-ful conservative leadership is about balancing the competing factions of an inherently diverse and at times factional and self-cannibalizing movement. The modern American conservative movement does not hold together the way many political movements often do. It is not based on one coherent set of principles, but several groups, each with its own set of principles, are united in opposition to various aspects of modern liberalism. As a sometimes knee-jerk response, it can trip over itself: Fiscal conservatives favor smaller government above all and are especially hostile to foreign aid and international organizations. Neocons, meanwhile, support U.S. government aid to key allies as a means of advancing America's interests overseas. These two elements within the movement struggle to coexist, and they often collide—as they do today when some Tea Partiers would like to cut foreign aid as a whole, while neocons would preserve military and economic aid to America's stalwart friends, such as Israel and our NATO allies.

Another example is immigration policy. Most economic conservatives have no interest in restricting the flow of labor into the United States, believing, usually, that immigration adds significantly to the vitality of the American economy. But Tea Party paleoconservatives and even some national security conservatives are alarmed at our porous borders, which they believe imperil our national character and our safety, security, and economy.

These issues divide America, but they also create deep schisms within the conservative movement. They can also turn contentious. Just this past year, some social conservatives opposed even the presence of a gay conservative organization called GOProud at the annual Conservative Political Action Conference (CPAC) convention, one of the most important movement events of the year. For some social conservatives, the mere presence of gays within the conservative movement is problematic. They want to see the gay conservatives banned from participating in the movement, believing that it's impossible to be both gay and conservative. In the interest of full disclosure, I am honored to serve on GOProud's advisory council and to support their work advocating limited government, individual liberty, free markets, and confident foreign policy.

Such battles condemn the movement to weakness. We are best served by being lively and argumentative but always keeping our eye on the fact that we are a coalition. I think that these debates, rather than becoming destructive, can help make room for new ideas and opinions within the Republican Party.

The genius of Ronald Reagan's leadership was best demonstrated by his view that if someone is conservative on eight of ten major conservative principles, that's sufficient. Reagan believed in building a "big tent," capable of accommodating people who broadly agreed on most major issues, although they might occasionally differ on a few. And he drew on the formula of Frank Meyer's fusionism to link the various tribes together—something that few conservative leaders have been able to do since. For example, for the first time he was able to link the neoconservatives, anticommunists, and national security conservatives with social conservatives. He knew that social conservatives opposed communism because of its moral evils; he knew as well that national security conservatives opposed communism because of its security threat to America and the West. So he gave his famous Evil Empire speech to the National Association of Evangelicals. This helped several tribes of conservatism see that their efforts were complementary, and that they needed one another in order to achieve a practical governing coalition. This was Reagan's practical realization of Meyer's fusionism. People on the Right remember only that they agreed with Reagan. They fail to recall how remarkable it was that they *all* agreed with Reagan. Successful conservative leaders have drawn on fusionism, and have found a way to unify conservatism's tribes—not by attempting to define "the true conservatism" but by dexterously managing the people, personalities, and competing interests of conservatism's various strands within a governing coalition tied together by a common purpose.

Which brings me to millennials. If the Republican Party, backed by the conservative movement, is ever going to connect with this generation, it will need a leader who can inspire a new kind of fusionism.

Such a leader has yet to emerge. Many conservatives say that the leader already exists in Rush Limbaugh, but I'm afraid I can't agree. And yet, it's true that among millennials, the people most associated with the conservative movement are entertainers like Rush and Glenn Beck. This is not a good thing for the viability of conservatism with the next generation.

It pains me to say this because I grew up with Rush. I came to political awareness mostly during the Clinton administration, in a Republican household during an age when AM radio appeared to be in its dying days. Then an AM radio host in Sacramento appeared on the scene, and instead of playing golden oldies, he talked. And talked and talked and talked. Rush Limbaugh devoted his entire show to talking about politics mostly, and occasionally American football. He had plenty of material. President Bill Clinton was then stumbling through the first two years of his presidency, and so between noon and three p.m. every day, Rush teed off on Clinton.

Every radio and cable news talking head—conservative, liberal, and in between—owes a debt of gratitude to Rush Limbaugh. He made it possible for politics to be fun, irreverent, and interesting. Before Rush, politics was the province of PBS and mainstream networks, who were deferential to politicians. And cozy with them, too.

Rush broke all those rules. Nobody in Washington knew this guy, and yet he had the attention of millions of people who took his political commentary and analysis quite seriously. He didn't kowtow to politicians of any stripe—he hit Democrats hard, but he would go after liberal Republicans, too. He also was Clinton's biggest and most listened to critic. To the extent that the conservative movement seemed to have died when Reagan left office and the Berlin Wall crumbled, its tribes revived in opposition to Clinton in 1992, thanks largely to the rallying of Rush.

Rush's listeners, for the most part, came to the show with some center-right leanings, but he turned them into a pretty well-informed army of conservatives. They became known as Dittoheads, people who simply said "ditto" to indicate that they agreed with everything he said. Rush would not tolerate dissent or deviation from his orthodoxy, often verbally attacking callers who said they agreed with 99 percent of what he said. "What," he demanded to know, "was the one percent they did not agree with?" And then he would badger them into total agreement. This is what it meant to be a Dittohead.

In the process, Rush transformed conservatism. No longer were conservative ideas batted about only by highbrow intellectual readers of *National Review* and *Commentary*. Rush was a populist who appealed broadly to regular folks and the conservative elites alike. And for the first time, conservatism had a daily megaphone to millions. Rush's success proved that there was an enormous audience hungry for conservative ideas.

I grew up a Dittohead. I appreciated the stark contrast Rush presented to the steady drumbeat of conventional liberalism that dominated the major networks, newspapers, and magazines and my schooling. I actually used the word *Dittohead* proudly on my first political résumé. Listening to Rush was a big part of my political education. While most kids in the liberal midsize American city I grew up in loved Bill Clinton, Rush offered a clever and entertaining philosophical antidote. He didn't make politics taste like medicine but made it fun and appealing. Aside from my parents' rightward political leanings and Herbert Hoover's "American Individualism," Rush's show was the most important influence in my political coming-of-age.

Rush's personality was large, his voice sonorous, his optimism contagious, and his outrage punctuated with humor, creativity, and the notion of the persecuted white male under attack. I found his parodies of Bill Clinton's reckless and decidedly unpresidential behavior to be brilliant.

More important, Rush stood for the important themes of the conservative movement: limited government, lower taxes, the importance of the entrepreneurial spirit, American exceptionalism, liberalism's degradation of individual initiative and dignity through the creation and maintenance of the welfare state, and liberalism's hypocrisy. He argued for a strong national defense prudently deployed. Most of all, he delighted in goosing the mainstream media—he would later coin the phrase "drive-by media"—for their perpetual inability to understand conservative ideas because they were so blind to conservative thinking (because there were few if any conservatives in their midst).

Rush was hardly an evangelical, but he stood with social conservatives. He could be antagonistic toward groups he found distasteful. I was a new student at Bryn Mawr, a women's liberal arts college with more than a few lesbian students, when I first heard his "dykes on bikes" parody, and it seemed cruel, to say the least. I could find no humor in this parody, which seemed to reinforce the notion that gay people should just stay quiet about their sexuality. (He was many years away from the day when, for his third wedding, he invited Sir Elton John, a famously gay activist and artist, to perform.)

But despite his vast influence, to most in the millennial generation Rush Limbaugh is a loud, bombastic white guy with annoying opinions. He is no longer a fresh face. He has been around, as a leading figure in political entertainment and commentary, for more than two decades. Everyone I knew growing up watched David Letterman, not Johnny Carson. Today's young adults watch Jon Stewart; they don't listen to Rush.

Furthermore, while Rush is a force in the conservative movement, he ultimately must build and nurture his audience. He has to be entertaining—that's his primary goal. That means he has to be provocative. If Jon Stewart weren't funny, nobody would watch him. If Rush didn't stir the pot, nobody would tune in. And so just as liberals would be foolish to look to Jon Stewart as some kind of political leader, conservatives need to find someone to build the movement as a way to shape a better America, not just to maintain a loyal radio audience.

The conservative movement owes Rush Limbaugh an enormous

debt of gratitude for reinvigorating conservatism in the 1990s, and for pioneering the market for center-right news analysis in the heartland. While I admire what Rush Limbaugh has achieved as an entertainer, the Maha Rushie (as he calls himself somewhat mockingly) is wrong when he says he represents "true conservatism." In this, he is no more than another conservative warlord who wants his version of conservatism to become "the accepted version" in its purest sense. He has used his radio platform to define for others who is conservative and who isn't. His influence has served to consolidate and perpetuate the schisms within the movement. As a result, on issues such as immigration or gay marriage or even the proper role of government, everyone needs to be holier than the pope—or be drummed out of the movement. But if we are going to call out those among us who we think are insufficiently loyal to the movement, we might as well hang it up right now, because ultimately we'll become an ideology of one.

Which leads me to RINOs and other so-called squishes. Nobody identifies himself as a RINO (Republican in Name Only) on purpose. It's an insult hurled at various members of the broader conservative coalition or Republican Party as a bullying tactic when they aren't adhering to whatever conservative orthodoxy the more vocal members of the coalition demand. Astute members of the conservative movement have been called RINOs in recent years, including some of the smartest and most thoughtful members of the various tribes. The modern political etymology of the word *squish* dates to Nixon's vice president Spiro Agnew, who used it to refer to radical liberals in the 1960s and '70s. Later, in the Reagan administration, members of the broader conservative movement co-opted the word *squish* to refer to James Baker, Reagan's chief of staff, and to George H. W. Bush, the vice president.

This instinct is exactly the opposite of Reagan's 80 percent/ 20 percent rule—my 80 percent ally isn't my 20 percent enemy— or his eleventh commandment (Thou shall not speak ill of another

Republican). "RINO hunters" think that if you agree with the conservative movement only on selected issues, or only to a certain degree, you might *think* you're a conservative, but you are not. Instead, they say you are a "squish."

A contemporary example of someone RINO hunters deride as a squish is Senator Scott Brown, the sole Republican elected statewide in liberal Massachusetts—because he voted for the financial regulatory reform bill and is pro-choice. Conservatives' sudden disapproval of Brown marks an amazing reversal. It was not so long ago that conservative activists who now call him a RINO flooded Massachusetts to pound the pavement in support of his election to what used to be Ted Kennedy's Senate seat. Brown ran on the simple message of promising to vote against "Obamacare" (a vow he kept, although Democrats used special rules in the Senate to bypass the Republican threat of filibuster) and to fight terrorism without compunction. After winning, Senator Brown reached such heights of stardom that the conservative website *Drudge Report* even heralded him as a possible presidential candidate. But even though the senator did what he was elected to do—he opposed what he, his constituents, Senate Republicans, and the majority of the American electorate viewed as a bad health-care bill—he has been labeled a RINO because he is "not conservative enough."

But the RINO hunters have it backward. William F. Buckley Jr. always said that the rule was to support the most conservative candidate in the race who could get elected. And while Alabama or Oklahoma Republicans can put up a social and fiscal conservative who can easily win, in Delaware or Massachusetts they can't. Some conservatives argue that they would rather have thirty senators like Jim DeMint than sixty-five like Scott Brown. But that's a formula for perpetual minority status, even extinction. In the 1990s there were Republican mayors and governors in overwhelmingly Democratic states, including New York, Massachusetts, New Jersey,

Vermont, Connecticut, and Rhode Island. Many of them governed with conservative principles in mind, especially as fiscal conservatives. These Republicans included Rudy Giuliani of New York City, Dick Reardon of Los Angeles, and Stephen Goldsmith of Indianapolis. Others, like governors Bill Weld, Christine Todd Whitman, and George Pataki, represented a breed of northeastern Republican that is practically extinct today.

In my view, it's much better to have a diverse but bigger Republican Party than a smaller monolithic one. This is especially true in Congress when there are some issues on which Republicans need every vote in order to prevail—think about the effort to stop Obamacare, or the votes for the Bush tax cuts in 2001 and 2003. Conservatives who rush into the arms of "purists" such as Christine O'Donnell and Sharron Angle, two failed Senate candidates, are making a fool's bet. They get a candidate they like the most, but a candidate who loses nonetheless. Had Republicans nominated electable candidates instead of these two in 2010, they would be within reach of winning significant votes in the Senate. Instead, Harry Reid remains majority leader in 2011.

To be sure, conservatives are not alone in dealing with these issues. Liberals also have loose confederations and coalitions. That's how American politics works. But no party can hold on to power unless it works with coalitions and welcomes diverse thinking. RINO hunting is right-wing political correctness—if you're not with us 100 percent, you might as well be a traitor and are diminished to irrelevance.

The history of the conservative movement tells a story different from what the RINO hunters would have you believe. Hayek wasn't a social conservative; Irving Kristol and Milton Friedman weren't either. Reagan signed an amnesty bill, approved a tax increase, and at one time supported pro-choice legislation. Were these stalwart lions of the movement also traitors to the cause?

Some say yes. But Buckley thought otherwise. At one point early into *National Review*'s publication, at a time when the various factions were feuding with one another, Buckley famously exploded: "Conservatives must get their philosophical house in order!" This was the animating idea behind fusionism, in which the various factions learned to coexist by underscoring shared goals and muting their disagreements in order to maximize their political influence as a movement. This was the guiding spirit behind Reagan's notion of the "Big Tent."

In the coming chapters, I will lay out which conservative principles Republicans should emphasize in order to appeal to the millennial generation. I realize that others within the movement may disagree with me on some of these issues. But I know we can agree on certain fundamental points: the government that governs least governs best; lower taxes and simpler tax codes will strengthen the economy and create more jobs; deficits are a spending problem, not a revenue problem; entitlement reforms are essential if America is to avoid fiscal disaster; America's rich diversity of spiritual traditions strengthens our cultural fabric; the United States must remain the world's leading military power in order to secure our freedom at home and that of our allies abroad.

Of course, there will be areas where my conservative principles do not lead me to endorse the same policy positions as some other conservatives—especially on matters of personal privacy and individual freedoms. Our ability to appeal to the hearts and minds of millennials does not depend on everyone agreeing with me. But it does depend on people like me being able to make their case and others like me being able to say, "I'm a conservative, but I don't agree with some conservatives on certain issues." If we can't get at least that far, we won't go anywhere.

Clearly, we will need to establish priorities as a movement, much as fusionism unified the movement before the fall of Soviet Communism by making anticommunism the unifying theme of social conservatives, economic conservatives, and national security conservatives. At a time when fiscal disaster looms, thanks to an impending debt crisis and decades of irresponsible fiscal behavior in Washington, fiscal responsibility as a prescription for restoring American prosperity is a theme that, like anticommunism, will help unify conservatism's particular tribes around a central goal.

Social conservatives champion fiscal discipline because there is a *moral* imperative to restraining the federal government's intrusions into the private lives of citizens. Social conservatives no more want an expanded federal government telling them how to live their lives or educate their children than economic conservatives want the federal government's largesse to diminish economic opportunity and dynamism. Just as the urgent threat of communism brought social conservatives, economic conservatives, and national security conservatives together under one tent, so too can the existential threat of fiscal ruin serve to rally these factions as one. Introducing the reforms required to rein in the nation's runaway debt will lead to a stronger, more secure American economy, and that means a stronger national defense—an outcome that national security hawks and neoconservatives, who advocate American leadership in the world, will strongly support.

I believe that this brand of fusionism, with its emphasis on fiscal conservatism, should be embedded in the broader concept of American individualism—a framework that will appeal especially to the millennial generation. With American individualism as our integrating philosophy, and with fiscal responsibility as our action-oriented unifying political theme, I am convinced that, in reaching out to the next generation, we stand a good chance of making an enduring connection.

This modern restatement of my great-grandfather's philosophy identifies American individualism as a potent mix of rugged individualism and community spirit. It rests on three pillars.

First, it is the individual who stands at the center of American society. The freedom of the individual to pursue happiness, as immortalized in the Declaration of Independence and guaranteed by the protections of the Constitution, is sacrosanct. Yet encroachments on individual freedom constantly threaten, from government or even in the name of a majority of citizens. In every area of life, the protection of individual freedoms should be cherished, and we must never forget that we abridge the freedoms of one at great peril to freedom for all.

There are several components to individual freedom. There is the moral component: the ability of the individual to make moral choices on his or her own behalf. There is the economic component: the ability of the individual to make the best use of his or her creative spark, and to enjoy the benefits of hard work and special talents. And there is the responsibility component: the responsibility of the individual for the choices he or she makes. Freedom does not mean doing only what one wants without regard to the consequences. American individualism places a heavy responsibility on the individual not only to benefit from freedom but to act as a responsible free person should—to be completely subject to the results of one's decisions and actions.

There is another role for the state here, and it is this: protection of the individual. A strong defense is vital to the rights of the individual. Freedom, as they say, isn't free, and that is particularly true today. After all, the greatest enemies of America are particularly appalled by our individual freedoms, which we sometimes take for granted—the right of women to marry whomever they want or not at all, the right of religious minorities to worship fully and publicly, the right of free speech, and so on. Each of these rights is exercised, fundamentally, by individuals because of the protection of the state. And so American individualism makes clear that the state must exist and must serve the cause of freedom.

The second dimension of American individualism is participation in the community. American individualism does not mean that people are free from obligation to serve the community. In fact, American individualism rests squarely on the notion that the individual is the first line of defense for the community, that the individual, rather than government, must take the lead in addressing the problems of society and community. The existence of volunteer-based social and civic organizations is something that politicians often extol but do very little to support. That is because these organizations do not derive their power from political support—they exist, and get stronger, because individuals want to be part of them, not because they are required to by government.

America has always had a vibrant culture of community-based organizations and institutions. Liberals tend to believe that the best social improvements emanate from government, but in fact most of the great reforms have sprung from the individual minds of men and women acting alone or in concert with one another, oftentimes cooperating under the auspices of civic or economic organizations. America is not a nation "bowling alone," as one critic has claimed. It is connected in all kinds of ways, and a revamped American individualism will recognize that there is no difference between a Rotary Club and a Facebook group devoted to solidarity with the Iranian people—both serve a valuable social purpose, both bring together diverse peoples devoted to a worthy cause, and both make possible things that individuals could not accomplish on their own. One might meet physically, the other virtually, but they are both civic organizations, broadly defined. I believe strongly that millennials will find great appeal in this dimension of community participation based on the free choices of individuals rather than the dictates of government.

The third and final dimension of American individualism is the diversity of America's religious traditions, the spiritualism that is part of American life. A spiritual component is a necessary resource for individuals to draw upon for strength and stability, and spiritual cultivation both in private and in communities helps strengthen the fabric of society. American individualism embraces people's natural spiritual yearning and gives it room to grow, and it inspires the individual's search for faith and truth. Spiritual traditions help lead individuals toward life's intangible riches—and help balance the human experience. This is a force for good in our culture.

Cast in this way, American individualism can be a framework for communicating a new conservative sensibility to the next generation, while spotlighting the crucial fact that the most pressing threat facing America today is our fiscal disorder. An unwavering emphasis on fiscal responsibility offers a way to unify conservative factions while building a bridge to the next generation of civic-minded, politically engaged citizens—the millennial generation.

CHAPTER 3

MEET THE MILLENNIALS

*"Every generation discovers the world all new again
and knows it can improve it."*
—HERBERT HOOVER

ILLENNIALS ARE THE generation of tattoos, iTunes, texting, and Twitter. Born between the beginning of the Reagan presidency and the end of the Clinton presidency, they are the rising generation in America, fifty million strong. They are independent-minded and distrust hyperpartisan politics. And they made all the difference in Barack Obama's election to the White House.

In the 2008 election, Senator Obama and Senator McCain polled close to even among almost every major age group of the electorate. But millennials, who composed 18 percent of voters, went for Obama by a two-to-one margin. Sixty-six percent of youth voted for Obama, to 31 percent for McCain.

Now, it is conventional wisdom that the young tend to vote liberal, then come around to conservative thinking as they age. But that's not always so—young adults are not reliably liberal. In the presidential elections of 1980 and 1984, youth voted consistently for Ronald Reagan. In 2000, the year the first millennials voted in a presidential election, they split their votes evenly between George W.

Bush and Al Gore. It was only in 2004 that eighteen- to twenty-nine-year-olds broke decidedly toward the Democratic Party, gains that increased in the 2006 off-cycle elections.

Democrats had hoped that Barack Obama would solidify gains and deliver a new generation to the Democratic Party's voter rolls, just as Ronald Reagan's "Republican Revolution" did and as Franklin Delano Roosevelt and John F. Kennedy had decades earlier. Democrats now count on the votes of millennials in elections on the state and local level. They have courted these voters in new and effective ways, and have found millennials to be especially responsive to their attention.

But millennials are in no way irretrievably lost to the Republican Party. The Pew Research Center reports that only 37 percent call themselves Democrats, while 22 percent say they're Republicans, and 38 percent identify themselves as Independents. And as we have seen in the 2010 elections, when people call themselves Independents, they often have distinctly *conservative* leanings on certain issues. This presents both an opportunity and a challenge for Republicans. In order to bring Independent millennials into the party, Republicans will have to appeal to them on those issues where they are already conservative leaning. At the same time, the party will have to build a bigger tent on social issues to allow for differences of opinion where Independent millennials are more liberal leaning.

Millennials have conservative instincts when it comes to fiscal responsibility and economic policy. And against the backdrop of the astounding fiscal mismanagement of the first years of the Obama administration, there is an opening for Republicans to make headway with the millennials. Between the elections of 2008 and 2010, President Obama and the Democrats saw a decided drop in support from millennials.

To win over millennials, Republicans need to take some time to understand them, and to figure out just what attracted them to candidate Obama in the first place. If they do, Republicans will find that they stand a real chance of capturing the millennials' imaginations—and their votes.

A Snapshot of Millennials

First, let's focus on the characteristic features of the millennial generation as a whole.

- They are racially and ethnically the most diverse generation in America. Forty percent of them are nonwhite, and a full 10 percent are less white than the generation before them, while 20 percent have at least one immigrant parent. And 93 percent are comfortable with interracial dating, the highest rating of any generation.

- They are on track to become the most educated generation in America; more have attended four-year colleges or at least completed some college education than any previous generation. On average they scored higher on standardized tests than did Generation Xers. During their youth, the nation saw its rates of juvenile crime, teen pregnancy, and abortion decline.

- They are less conventionally religious but more spiritual: They identify less with organized religions than any generation before them (one in four is unaffiliated with any particular faith), yet they pray as often as their GenX predecessors and their baby boom parents did at the same point in their life cycles. According to a *Reader's Digest* poll, 67 percent say that religion is important to them, and 34 percent say they've become more spiritual in recent years.

- Millennials use digital technology the way their parents used telephones to stay socially connected to their peers. Eighty percent of them have created a profile on a social networking site such as Facebook, Twitter, MySpace, or LinkedIn. Twenty percent have posted a video of themselves online.

- Ninety-four percent of millennials rely on cell phones, but they don't use them to talk to one another as much as to text-message their friends. I remember the shock delivered to a friend's family when the cell phone bill arrived and his younger tween brother had managed to send seven hundred texts in one month—at a rate of 25 cents per message. The result: a $175 cell phone bill without a word having ever been spoken!

- Their parents spent a lot of time thinking about parenting. During their childhood, more than nine thousand books about children and parenting appeared in print, and their parents often told them they were "special" or they were "great," no matter what. Critics complain that the self-esteem movement went haywire with this generation, with kids receiving stickers and even trophies just for showing up. The result is a generation accustomed to praise and uncomfortable with criticism. Employers report that their young millennial workers require so much coddling that they have had to retrain their managers to perform essential oversight functions in ways that won't undermine their young employees' loyalty and energy.

- They volunteer in droves and are highly civic-minded. In 2005, 83 percent of new freshmen in college had volunteered regularly in high school. Sixty percent have volunteered in the last twelve months, the most of any generation. In the months and years after 9/11, this generation idolized firefighters, policemen, and soldiers. Many of them subsequently joined the ranks of those professions. They have not only a highly elevated sense of civic duty but also high expectations for the competence of their elected leaders. They are not as deeply cynical of authority as the baby boomers. Millennials have significant faith in the power and ability of government to do good. Seasoned pollsters say this is unlikely to change.

- Millennials vote. On account of their sheer numbers, in 2004 "as many raw votes were cast by those thirty and under as by those over sixty-five." Over half of all eligible millennials voted in 2008, which added up to two million more votes than in 2004. While it is true that younger voters tend to cast their ballots *less predictably* than their elders, this generation votes *in greater numbers* than previous generations at this point in their lives.

- Millennials cannot abide hyperpartisanship in their politics, which they view as divisive and destructive. If we are going to try to sell them on our politics, it will have to be a politics over-stuffed with proactive solutions to solving problems. Criticism in our politics will have to be constructive if we are going to have any hope of appealing to the millennial generation.

- Millennials are slow to start their own families—just one in five millennials (21 percent) is currently married, which amounts to half the share of their parents' generation at the same stage in their lives. And even those who would benefit from marriage and family have been reluctant to take the plunge. About a third (34 percent) are parents. In 2006, more than a third of women between the ages of eighteen and twenty-nine who had given birth were *unmarried*. This is a far higher share of unwed mothers than that experienced by any previous generation.

- And yet millennials are devoted to the families they were born into. The oldest of them, who often live on their own, have friendly relationships with their parents and communicate with them often (45 percent talk on the phone with one or both parents daily). What's more, 52 percent of millennials say being a good parent is one of the most important things in life, even though only 60 percent were raised with both parents.

- They don't have major hang-ups when it comes to sexual orientation. More than two-thirds of them think homosexuality should be accepted by society. Majorities of them that affiliate with an organized religion tend to have no moral objections to homosexuality. They are the only generation where a majority favors the legalization of same-sex marriage.

- Nearly 40 percent of them have tattoos, and half of those have more than one. Yet more than two-thirds of those tattoos are hidden beneath their clothing. For all their enthusiasm for self-expression, they still value privacy and discretion.

- Millennials don't settle. Because this group often used their high school and college summers to burnish their résumés and transcripts rather than earn money at menial jobs, they do not take easily to base-level employment. Books have been written, articles published, and consultancies spawned to deal with this new generation's entry into the workforce, and the challenges they present to managers. As one author writes, "They've been down to Machu Picchu to help excavate it. But they've never punched a time clock." Worldly and well-read young employees are always in demand, yet a lack of basic office skills turns out to be a significant handicap, especially when those basic office tasks are the first things that need to get done.

- Millennials have been hit harder by the Great Recession than any other group—37 percent of people aged eighteen to twenty-nine are unemployed or have dropped out of the workforce, the highest share among this age group in more than three decades. In 2009, only 20 percent of college students who had hoped to have a job upon graduation were successful, a drop from 51 percent two years earlier.

So here's the group portrait: Millennials are expressive, but they understand the importance of boundaries in the face of "too much information." They are innovative, tech-savvy, and entrepreneurial, but they apply those assets to more than just their careers. They tend to be strongly civic-minded. They resist ideology, and they focus more on fixing problems and making things work. They build large networks of friends, remain close to their families, and are nonjudgmental about people from different backgrounds and lifestyles. They are quietly spiritual and have demonstrated a pronounced moral sensibility, and they also place great value on doing good works. They think they can *change* the world, not just talk about changing it—and, if anything, they are determined to do the hard work themselves. And, I believe, millennials are open to certain core conservative messages.

Politics and Millennials

The oldest millennials were alive when Reagan was president, although they barely remember him in office. Vietnam, Nixon, Watergate, the Iran hostage crisis, Iran-Contra, and even the Cold War—these are all chapters in their history books. They know and like Bill Clinton, not so much on account of his presidency, which was tainted by scandal, but because of his postpresidential efforts on behalf of world health, development projects, and human rights around the world. Many of them liked George W. Bush at first, but after the mismanaged war in Iraq and the bungled federal response to Hurricane Katrina (not to mention Republican scandals in Congress through most of Bush's eight years in office), this generation soured on him, and on Republicans, dramatically.

Barack Obama's candidacy offered millennials not so much a competing political philosophy but, more important to them, an alternative to hyperpartisan politics as usual. He exuded great optimism about his ability to reduce political gridlock in Washington, to unify the nation, and to restore confidence in our governing institutions. That he has largely failed on these fronts, while chalking up mountains of debt in the process, may prove difficult for him to explain in 2012 to those millennials who supported him in 2008. Republicans have a chance to make up ground with millennials merely by focusing on those unmet promises instead of on the parties' ideological differences. The percentages of youth who during the 2010 cycle self-identified as Democrats and Republicans were back down to 2004 levels: 54 percent Democratic to 40 percent Republican. While the Democrats still maintain a large lead, Republicans have an opening.

And while millennials are liberal on social issues, such as gay rights, gender roles, or the traditional family, and while they tend to trust government more than any other generation, this doesn't mean they are reflexively liberal across the board. On a range of issues, such as the relationship between the individual and government, or the appropriate rates of taxation and of government spending, or how much government regulation is necessary, millennials are decidedly not liberal.

In fact, millennial attitudes on business regulation and government welfare are indistinct from the attitudes of baby boomers and Generation X. Millennials don't believe that government should provide an even broader safety net if it means sinking the country further into debt. They believe, more than other demographic groups, that businesses take fair profits and are not too powerful. And on certain issues, millennials are starting to catch up to other demographic groups. While they tend to favor, more than any previous generation, affirmative action programs to help minorities with preferential treatment, their support for such programs has dropped significantly—to below 50 percent—in the last few years.

So Democrats would be mistaken to interpret votes cast for John Kerry or Barack Obama as signs of a strong affinity for ideological liberalism. In significant ways, these votes represent a rejection of Republican *leadership,* not of all conservative principles. In the 2006 and 2008 election cycles, Republicans, who had dominated the executive and legislative branches, had to pay a price for their poor performance in office. And to millennials, that meant voting Democratic.

But that was before millennials felt the effects of the worst economic crisis in seventy years, and before a liberal Congress got to run the show. Evidently, millennials didn't like what they saw—although not enough to bring them to the polls in significant numbers in 2010. While they still favored Democrats in the 2010 congressional races, they were much more likely not to vote at all, with their turnout rate dropping to 20 percent, from 26 percent in 2006.

I would expect that as millennials age, fiscal conservatism will resonate even more deeply. Millennials are not just young biologically. They are young financially. To the extent they pay taxes, they are likely to be in the lowest tax brackets. They haven't yet become business owners making payrolls or investors preparing for retirement. Even if they have conservative leanings when it comes to such matters, they haven't yet reached the point where they view the price of going along with Democrats as prohibitive.

Even so, Republicans must remember that millennials retain a "liberal" view of government. They believe that government can be effective. While half of millennials agree that regulation of business does more harm than good, only 42 percent of millennials think that when something is run by the government it's usually managed inefficiently and wastefully. Or to look at it another way: 58 percent of millennials think government is good at running things.

You would have thought that after the failures of Katrina and the Iraq War, millennials would have become deeply cynical about the ability of government to do anything right. But the lesson they drew wasn't that government is incapable of handling big issues, or that government is ineffective and wasteful. They simply concluded that the *Bush administration* was incompetent. By comparison,

GenXers—at a similar stage in their lives—were much more skeptical of *government's* ability to operate efficiently. So while Republicans
can appeal to millennials on certain pocketbook issues, they have to
be mindful that the negative rhetoric of the past—even Reagan's
immortal line that "government is the problem"—will not resonate
with this new generation. The idea of limited but *energetic* government might.

Hope and Change . . . and Choice

For about the past four decades, there has been a gender gap in
American politics. Men have favored Republicans, while women
have favored Democrats. Today, in addition to a gender gap, there is a
generation gap. Yet, while the two major political parties tend to split
the support of every demographic group between them, the Democrats have held a two-to-one advantage among millennials.

*For Republicans, the key to closing that yawning generational gap is to
emphasize economic values, and de-emphasize social issues.* The Republican Party has to continue to be the party of economic growth and
opportunity. It has to represent the ideas that promise a better tomorrow—more wealth and prosperity for all Americans. Millennials grew up amid greater wealth than any previous generation, yet
thanks to the Great Recession they have learned not to take that
wealth for granted. If Republicans are to be successful with millennials, they have to make a credible case that they are the best guardians
of American prosperity.

The ground is fertile for such an appeal. Far fewer eighteen-
to twenty-nine-year-olds identify themselves as Democrats today
compared with 2008. Considering the economic struggles millennials have experienced these past few years—living at home with
their parents, sleeping on the couches of friends, putting off some
of the purchases (like homes and cars) that usually come with

adulthood—millennials appreciate all too well that without a strong economy, very few things are possible.

It is on social issues that Republicans will find themselves on shaky ground when it comes to millennials. On issues like gay rights, reproductive freedom, and religion in the public square, the most vocal representatives of the Religious Right have made it difficult for Republicans to be perceived as anything other than the fire-and-brimstone party. But it's not as if the Republicans can't alter this image. For one thing, they can talk about moral values as civic values. There is no reason for Republicans to shy away from saying that our civic life needs to be morally anchored.

After all, it is a terrible tragedy when a child goes without a father, or when a teenage girl seeks an abortion because she doesn't have the means or the support to raise a baby. What Republicans can do is focus less on the explicit commandments of the scriptures and more on the spirit of the scriptures. They can say that America needs responsible citizens to care for one another, for their families, and for their communities. Republicans need to argue that while government has a role to play in meeting certain social needs, it cannot always be a substitute for the actions of ordinary citizens and civic organizations. Republicans can and should make the case that while government is part of the solution, it can't be the only solution, because it can never be as smart and as forward-thinking as individuals acting together or alone.

Republicans would do well to adopt the "Big Society" concept introduced by a successful center-right coalition leader on the other side of the pond. As formulated by British prime minister David Cameron, the Big Society emphasizes the virtues of sacrifice and service. It recognizes that, while government should offer compassion to its neediest citizens, bloated government cannot serve the people. It holds that individuals are ultimately responsible for their lives, and must be trusted and encouraged to look out for themselves and to help others in need. Cameron describes the Big Society as "the spirit of activism, dynamism, people taking the initiative, working together to get things done." This is, essentially, a restatement of the core premise of American individualism.

Liberals, by comparison, offer a very different view of the roles and responsibilities of government and individuals. Liberalism believes that government is something you pay for with taxes and from which you can then extract the benefits, like some kind of bank. It's as if people are *owed* something by the government. And while in one sense government does owe much to its citizens, in modern liberalism's worldview the notions of personal sacrifice, initiative, and individual responsibility are overshadowed by the expectations of government largesse.

What's more, liberals have pursued the "government as bank" analogy to the point where the cost of government has become far greater than people are willing to pay. Some of the core elements of the financial contract between the citizens and the government—especially Social Security—are already in deep fiscal distress. Few millennials believe they will ever be able to collect the retirement benefits to which they are just beginning to contribute. And because Democrats, through massive spending and borrowing programs, have solidified their traditional reputation as the Party of Debt, they have exposed themselves to the criticism of millennials as a result of their having bankrupted the government "bank."

What should the Republican message be? That government is a *necessary* player in our civic life but not the *essential* one. There are certain things the government must do that individuals cannot do: defend our borders, protect our citizens, enforce our laws, keep the playing field level by ensuring the principle of equal opportunity. There are certain social benefits that government oversight makes possible: a way to save for retirement and a way for the poor to pay for their health care, principles that the New Deal and Great Society programs introduced and which most Americans now accept as part of the American system. The question that surrounds these programs today has to do with their size and how much individual initiative they allow. Republicans can and should argue that the dynamism of the individual needs to be allowed to flourish. In this context that means programs to maximize individual choice, such as private accounts within Social Security and health savings accounts for health-care spending, both of which maximize the individual's ability to make his or her own choices.

This would offer a sharp contrast to liberalism's assumption that the state must guide people's lives from cradle to grave. Millennials can do the math, and they know that our current entitlement spending and debt obligations will ultimately deprive them of the benefits they've been promised. They are open to a message of limited government responsibilities, limited government ambitions, and more freedom for individuals to handle their own affairs and build their own futures.

Finally, Republicans must make the case that government has to be willing to try new things, and in multiple ways. Instead of offering one-size-fits-all solutions to the problems of society, as Democrats often do, Republicans can and should be the party of government *customization*—giving citizens more individual choices. This is particularly true in the areas of health-care reform and education reform, where conservatives generally press for market-driven choices over government rules and restrictions.

Because of the importance of the Internet in their lives, millennials have been imbued with a sense that anything can be customized to their individual tastes and needs. Liberalism generally holds that the state can make better choices for people than people can make for themselves—on things like retirement savings, health insurance plans, and even what kinds of cars they drive. Republicans have always had a winning position on these issues: more competition means more choices, which means lower prices and better quality.

Where the party has traditionally stood for individual choices and responsibilities—education, economy and taxes, health care, retirement security and savings, personal conduct—it will have to get better at communicating what it believes, and pursue policy goals that will make those beliefs the law of the land.

But where the party has traditionally stood *against* permitting certain individual choices—be it reproductive freedom or whether two same-sex adults should be allowed to legally marry—we Republicans ought to be more philosophically consistent, recognizing that the rising generation prefers more choices and less governmental involvement in these formerly hot-button social issues. I say "formerly" because to this next generation these aren't the polarizing culture-war questions that they were to earlier generations. In fact, the majority of millennials are in agreement about these issues.

I realize that for some Republicans and social conservatives this will be a painful, if not impossible, adjustment. But if Republicans don't pledge themselves to the virtue of individual choice applied *broadly,* they may well have it thrust upon them. After all, millennials are known to manufacture their own choices. I would not be surprised if millennials embraced a dynamic third-party candidate in a national election if they remain dissatisfied with the offerings of the two major parties. A third-party candidate could easily present himself or herself as a better choice than the candidates of the major parties, drawing on the best of their respective political philosophies and casting aside the rest.

That's why neither party can take millennials for granted. The sensibilities of this cohort are diverse and sometimes, to outside eyes, appear contradictory. But what millennials will always want is more choice, because they have come to expect it. They have grown up in an age when they have had more consumer choices available to them than anyone before them, more ways to express themselves, and more sources of information, entertainment, and social friendships. Why should they expect less from their politics?

Freedom of choice is the underlying spirit of American individualism—the belief that individuals are not the same, do not want the same things, and do not necessarily want the same outcomes. That's what choice is all about—you get to choose the life you want to live, the career or interests you want to pursue, the friends you keep, and the places you live. American individualism recognizes the need to balance rights and responsibilities. To the extent that the Republican Party can become the party of individual choice and the party of civic involvement, it has a good chance to connect with millennials. If Republicans explore these values fully, they will see the need to adopt them in matters of social policy. The political payoff of consistency in the matter of individual freedom of choice will be enormous.

The next year is critical for Republicans to make this case. After all, under President Obama, trust in the government has gone down. Millennials have seen the economy stagnate. They have waited and watched as Washington has grown even more polarized, not less. And they have seen a significant increase in government power, a significant rise in government spending, and a significant increase in government debt—all without any comparable increase in their options and choices at home, at work, and elsewhere. Republicans today have their best opportunity to appeal to the sensibilities of millennials and bring them into the big tent.

CHAPTER 4

GENERATIONAL THEFT

"Blessed are the young, for they shall inherit the national debt."
—HERBERT HOOVER, JANUARY 1936

I MAGINE YOU ARRIVE late to an elegant restaurant to meet your entire extended family—parents, siblings, grandparents, aunts and uncles, and cousins—as they are wrapping up an epic celebratory dinner. They have ordered cocktails, bottles of Dom Pérignon, and a sumptuous seven-course meal, complete with appetizers, savory soups, delicious entrées, and a rich soufflé for dessert. As tuxedo-clad waiters clear away the used china, you join the celebration, steal a nibble of dessert, and delight in tasting the remnants of the expensive wines your elders ordered before you arrived. When the check arrives, you notice that most of your family has disappeared. Your grandparents left shortly after you arrived, your parents left during dessert, and as you and your siblings stay to polish off the wine, you notice that you are the only ones left at the table. Having no choice, you pay the enormously expensive bill. Although your parents and relatives haven't literally stolen money out of your pocket, they have left you with a huge tab to pay.

Right now, in America today, seniors and near retirees are essentially stealing from millennials. They have thrown themselves an extravagant party, but they won't be sticking around to pay the bill. The millennials will have to do that.

Since the 1960s, baby boomers have been enjoying what amounts to a huge party at the expense of their children and grandchildren. The parents (and grandparents) of millennials took the New Deal programs and the Great Society programs and expanded them. Social Security went on steroids. Medicare and Medicaid metastasized. The cost of government as a share of the economy ballooned.

No one should be more concerned about out-of-control government spending and deficits than members of the millennial generation. After all, they are the ones who will ultimately get stuck with the bill. Every time you hear someone argue that government isn't doing enough and has to spend more than it already does, what that person is not saying is that millennials and their children will need to be taxed more, live in a smaller economy, and be protected by a smaller military as a direct result. If there is one issue that pits old against young, generation against generation, it is cascading deficits and rising national debt. One generation spends more than it is able to afford, and demands more than it is able to pay; the next generation has to cover the costs.

Every dollar of debt today will have to be paid back, with interest, at some point in the future. Every dollar of debt accumulated today will have to be recovered by taxing someone at some point in the future. Millennials must know—and if they don't know, they will soon have to learn—that the future bill for today's spending will be paid by them, either in the form of higher taxes or diminished economic opportunity, or some combination of the two.

Now, I don't have a problem with people, or even nations, incurring responsible degrees of debt from time to time. America has carried debt for virtually its entire history. Debt financed America during the Revolution, the Civil War, both world wars, and the Cold War. Like a mortgage or a student loan, debt allows us to do something today that accrues value over time—as long as we manage the debt over time.

America, in fact, has been a great investment for people willing to lend to it. Historically, we have always paid our bills on time. And we have been the driving force for freedom and prosperity in the world for more than two hundred years, thanks in part to things we did that were financed by debt. And let's not forget about our assets. If America were truly a household or a business, we could show an incredible pile of assets that we have stored up and nurtured over time: the world's strongest military, massive natural resources and mineral rights, and some of the world's most beautiful natural wonders. Our nation has a wealth of assets.

The problem is that we are moving well past the point where all of these assets, which provided us with security in decades past, can sustain us in the future. In the past, our deficits—what we owe each year—have often remained relatively modest, on average about 2 percent of GDP. In the last few years, however, the deficit has risen to an alarming 10 percent of GDP. If this were just one bad year, America could manage. Even if it were two years, America's economy would produce enough to eventually work that debt off. But thanks to the policies of the first two years of the Obama administration, which included massive spending increases in the form of "stimulus" and the added long-term costs of "Obamacare," the government is destined to run deficits of this size for many years to come. On top of this, underfunded entitlement programs created eighty years ago are ballooning to the point where in order to pay for them, we are adding exponentially to the debt. The combination of all those years when we spent more than we had, combined with growing deficits and mounting underfunded entitlement programs, creates the kind of national debt that we see tallied in that scary debt clock near Times Square— $14 trillion and counting.

While debt and deficits represent a serious threat to our future, the fact is that people just aren't as agitated by the debt as they are by the more palpable threat of a terrorist attack, a disease, a famine, or a war. It is easy to become committed to solving any of those problems, because emotionally, when we see pain, suffering, or injustice, we want to stop it. Debt doesn't create the same sense of panic. It's a number on a piece of paper. It remains hidden. It just doesn't seem that menacing.

This isn't willful denial; it's a completely understandable lack of reaction to an invisible danger. And this is hardly a generational phenomenon. Based on the relative disinterest exhibited by politicians across the political spectrum, and the fact that politicians are rarely punished by voters for overspending (2010 is the recent exception), the rational thing for politicians to do is to ignore deficits and debt. Solutions seem more painful than the problems in many cases, so the solutions go ignored. The reality is that elected representatives will take action to fix the nation's problems only when their reelection depends on it.

I learned this firsthand working in the Bush White House in 2005, when President Bush admirably attempted to rally the Republican Senate and House to reform the ticking time bomb that is Social Security. But even with a unified legislature, mobilizing the will to fix Social Security proved impossible. Politicians ignore problems until they become crises, and even then the political will might not emerge to fix them. Unfortunately, in the absence of obvious evidence that our deficits and our debt have reached the crisis stage, there is no political will to tackle the problem. But make no mistake: a crisis is looming.

Ignoring debt and deficits is incredibly stupid and, for millennials in particular, shortsighted. Here is what deficits will do to America— especially to its youngest workers in the millennial generation. Imagine that every American household has to pay a "deficit tax" on its earnings, on top of all the other taxes it pays right now (including for Social Security, Medicare, state income, and state unemployment). If the government wanted to pay off the total national debt in five years, every American household would have to pay roughly $475 a week extra in taxes, or about $24,800 a year. Let's say the median household income is $50,000 per year, or $960 per week. That household already loses about $250 in various withholding taxes, leaving it with $710 a week. In order to pay off the deficit over five years, every American household would have to forfeit another 67 percent of its take-home pay, which would drop to $235 a week.

And here is the thing: even if everyone signed on to this deficit tax, we wouldn't be free of future debt. Because the government has piled up so many promises and continues to spend beyond what it takes in by more than $1 trillion a year, American households would have to keep paying the deficit tax, to the tune of an additional $8,850 a year, forever. Or at least until changes are made to eliminate our astronomical deficit spending.

The only good news here, from the perspective of millennials, is that they are beginning to understand this harsh reality. Some of them care deeply about the skyrocketing national debt and our inability to manage federal budgets responsibly.

Perhaps the best evidence for the rising concern about debt is the growing number of debt-related websites run by millennials. One of these websites is called WeCantPayThatTab.org. Its cofounders, Ryan Schoenike and Brandon Aitchison, track the national debt and its implications for the next generation. In typical millennial fashion, they don't discuss the issue in partisan terms. Remember, millennials are a civic generation that want to solve problems, not point fingers. They don't care what Republicans or Democrats say; they want to see the problem fixed.

They point out that unless we are willing to make hard choices to change our fiscal behavior, we'll be facing interest payments on our national debt in 2020 of more than $916 billion, a number that represents "more than we spent on education, energy, homeland security and the wars in Iraq and Afghanistan in 2009." The site tabulates the total debt of the United States at "over $73,000,000,000,000 including unfunded liabilities." That's $73 trillion in case you lost count of the zeroes.

Seventy-three trillion dollars—it's a big number. But if $1 trillion is big, what's $73 trillion? Why not go to $173 trillion? If debt hasn't hurt us yet, why should it hurt us in the future? Unfortunately, the thing with debt is that it takes two to tango. First, you need someone to spend their way into debt—in this case, the United States. That's the easy part. The harder part is finding someone who has money to lend. In this case, it's individuals and governments that are running surpluses, and they would rather invest what they have in a country that has never failed to pay on time. Countries like Germany, Japan, and China, along with their wealthier citizens, have invested in America for decades. They have had no problem writing checks for America to cash because we were very good at paying them back with interest.

But in recent years our debts have swollen so uncontrollably that those lenders are starting to have second thoughts about giving us any more of their money. Anyone who has ever applied for a loan knows that the lender is going to look at a person's credit report and income level to make a decision about whether a loan is worth the risk. For years our country's credit report was pretty solid. But now it's looking sketchy. We owe a lot of money. If our economy were bigger, this might not be as big an issue. But our economy just isn't big enough or growing fast enough—compared with the emerging markets in Asia or Latin America—to pay off our debt. To pay off what we owe will take a lot more effort and a lot more time than it did when our debts were smaller and our economy was growing.

Lenders will think, "Why give America more? What if there is a better investment out there?" And gradually, the money spigot will start to tighten. The flow of credit will begin to slow. Other borrowers less creditworthy than Uncle Sam, such as state governments, will have a tougher time getting loans. The economy as a whole will labor under the weight of a heavier load of debt and will have fewer incoming resources for investment and future growth. When countries carry debt loads of up to 30 percent of GDP, their GDP tends to grow in a healthy upward trajectory. But if their debt load balloons to 90 percent of GDP, their economy invariably slows to a trickle. That's a hard truth that Ireland, Italy, Greece, and Spain have come to know. How close are we to that breaking point? America's debt level is now at about 85 percent of its GDP. If we are not yet at that breaking point, we aren't far off.

There is a reason why Democrats are known as the party of big spending. The Democrats created the New Deal. The Democrats created Medicare and Medicaid. The Democrats just passed a massive new health care entitlement in "Obamacare" that will drive the federal budget toward even more spending in the next ten years and beyond. When Republicans suggest cutting government spending, Democrats typically protest. The central premise of modern liberalism is the virtue of government spending, the core philosophy of the left wing of the Democratic Party. The Blue Dogs, the coalition of centrist Democrats who championed fiscal responsibility through spending restraint, were largely voted out of office in 2010. There are fewer and fewer fiscally responsible Democrats in office. This could leave an opening for Republicans to bridge the generational gap. Millennials have thus far voted for Democrats, but it's not far-fetched to believe that their allegiance might now shift over the issue of deficits and debt.

Yet until the Obama administration blew up the deficit and debt, Republicans' reputation had been lacking when it came to fiscal responsibility. By any measure of spending, deficits, or debt, over the

last three decades Republicans have been only slightly better managers of taxpayer dollars. I worked in Congress when the Republicans, acting on the request of President George W. Bush, passed the
Medicare prescription drug bill. I remember thinking, "What are we
doing? How does it make any sense, now that we are in power, for
us to pass the largest federal entitlement program since LBJ?" Later,
I worked in the Bush Office of Management and Budget as deficits
and spending spiked to more than 4 percent of GDP. No fiscal conservative can be proud of the recent Republican fiscal record.

President Bush got a lot of criticism from fiscal conservatives for
never vetoing any of the Republican Congress's colossal spending
bills. But in President Bush's defense, if he had vetoed any of the
spending bills he would have risked congressional support for the
Iraq War. People forget that times were tough in 2005 and the war
wasn't going well. Al Qaeda had established itself in the northern
Anbar province and was executing regular deadly attacks on Americans and Iraqis. We were losing American lives, and congressional
Democrats weren't the only ones clamoring for a withdrawal of our
troops from Iraq. Against this backdrop, President Bush couldn't afford a fight with his own party over spending. Congressional Republicans granted the president more time and money to turn the
war around, and in exchange he went along with their irresponsible appropriations and out-of-control earmarks. They incorrectly
thought it would lead to their perpetual reelection, so they decided
to just go with the flow of the spending culture of Washington.

By the end of the Bush presidency, those of us who go on TV
to defend principles of fiscal responsibility—those of us who believe
that the Republican Party doesn't share the tax-and-spend impulses
of the Left and who believe it's our job to rein in spending and be
responsible fiscal stewards of the national economy—were silenced
by facts. President Bush gave the go-ahead to the Troubled Asset
Relief Program (TARP), a $700 billion bank bailout program, as it

morphed from a program to buy up toxic bank assets to one aimed at reliquidifying bank balance sheets. While TARP may end up costing taxpayers a fraction of its original pricetag, the view from Main Street was one of puzzlement: Why would a Republican president approve such a vast expansion of federal largesse?

In December 2008, after Obama had won the election but before he took office, Congress agreed to lend American automakers $15 billion in an effort to prevent their collapse. It was clear at the time that this was a Band-Aid applied by the Bush administration in order to get automakers through the end of the year and into the beginning of the Obama presidency. These Bush administration initiatives also proved to be too much for Republicans to defend. Some conservatives remained silent, although many others spoke out, making it clear that these moves violated conservative fiscal principles. But by then, opposition didn't matter anymore. The Democrats were in charge of the House, the Senate, and the White House, and they enjoyed the freedom to do as they pleased.

Within his first hundred days in office, President Obama signed spending bills whose total cost equaled that of the debt accumulated by every president from George Washington to George W. Bush combined. His spending spree totaled $1.2 trillion—that's roughly $24 billion a day, or $1 billion an hour. In his first two years in office, President Obama presided over the largest debt increase in history, created a vast new health insurance benefit, and considered plans for a massive energy tax. His biggest initiative to *reduce* government spending was a call for his cabinet agencies to identify $100 million in spending cuts. Now, $100 million is a lot to you and me, but it is not even one-half of 1 percent of the federal budget. Let's be honest, in the White House budget office, $100 million in spending cuts is geekspeak for a rounding error: it's "budget dust." But for Barack Obama and congressional Democrats, this served as a fig leaf of fiscal responsibility.

So now the Republicans have a chance to prove to voters of all stripes that they are, in fact, more responsible with taxpayer dollars. And because the federal deficit and the economy regularly rank among the most important issues to voters, Republicans can know that as they fight to restore their reputation for fiscal responsibility, they will also be fighting for the issues that voters care about most. It is a clarifying moment, because for many years Republican leaders thought that cutting government spending was risky politics. Now they know that cutting government spending can be popular. That is a significant awakening.

Because spending and the deficit is an issue of prime importance to millennials, Republicans can join this battle knowing that if they do what's right by fighting to bring down the deficit and opposing new forms of spending and new taxes, they will have a chance to win over millennials on fiscal issues. Because these issues are a source of concern for millennials, Republicans have an opening to earn their votes by practicing fiscal responsibility. Millennials will vote Republican if they believe the economy will be stronger and will create more jobs, and that the country's fiscal future will be in better hands.

But while most voters now say they want the government to spend less, it will be difficult for ordinary Americans of all ages to get used to smaller government. After all, when you try to cut services and programs that people have become accustomed to, they get angry. Look at Europe.

We've seen students rioting in the United Kingdom because of increases in school tuition in the face of government cutbacks in education subsidies.

In France, riots occurred in response to changes in the retirement age for those eligible for government pensions and because of shortages of gasoline for automobiles.

In Spain, protesters against austerity measures picketed government offices and staged a twenty-four-hour general strike.

Students and unions in Greece threw Molotov cocktails and beat back riot police as state benefits were decreased.

People wonder if such riots could ever happen here. Absolutely. Just look at the tens of thousands of public-sector union protesters who gathered in Madison, Wisconsin, and, defying official orders, occupied the state capitol to protest Governor Scott Walker's plan to limit their collective bargaining power. Proposals to address mounting state budget deficits in Ohio, Indiana, and elsewhere across the nation generated threats of further, escalating protests.

The longer it takes to address our unfunded mandates, the harder it will become to fix them. But we must. Here are the stakes: in 2030—if we continue on the current trajectory—we'd have to implement draconian cuts, up to half of all discretionary spending, or else impose suffocating tax increases in order to close the fiscal gap.

Even today, close to 50 percent of Americans don't pay any federal income tax because we have continually lowered the rate at which people pay federal taxes. Yes, you read that correctly. Almost half of the American population pays no federal taxes. None. Zero. Zilch. The big 0. By the year 2030, there will be more than seventy million Americans eligible to receive Social Security, but the system will have such a huge deficit that we won't have enough new workers paying into it to cover those benefits. Medicare and Medicaid, both of which are administered through state budgets and are already operating with significant deficits, will be bloated with patients, thanks to a combination of more retirees and additional enrollees through President Obama's health-care overhaul.

Thanks to the Tea Party, the protests against government fiscal policies have been caused by the fact that government spends not too little, but rather too much. There is a broad and influential constituency in America in favor of restoring fiscal sanity. And the protests we will face if we do nothing are not the protests of those who want more government largesse but of those who want less of it.

But as Republicans reach out to millennials on this issue, a few things must be remembered. First, it will be necessary to keep the tone civil, and focus on getting the work done. Pointing fingers at Democrats as the sole culprits of our financial and economic mess will ring hollow to this generation. The party that will appeal to millennials is the party that rolls up its sleeves and shows it's willing to get the job done. Millennials are hardwired to tune out partisan bickering.

Republicans need to start fresh, by credibly owning up to their past mistakes and committing to working to build coalitions across party lines to seriously address America's looming fiscal doom. Millennials want leaders who are willing to make tough choices now, so that they won't have to pay a debilitating price in the future. Republicans need to demonstrate to millennials that we are serious.

If millennials and conservatives can agree on anything, it should be restoring limits on the government's responsibilities, embracing individual freedoms, and constantly restraining federal spending and the size and power of the federal government so that it lives within its means. Government should not do things that individuals can and should do for themselves. Our objective should be to foster a robust economy that provides for an opportunity society with a safety net for those in need.

The relevant questions for the next generation are: How big a safety net do we need and who should qualify? Will it be a shared federal and state responsibility? What role should charitable organizations have? At what point is it immoral for the federal government to punish tomorrow's workers in order to pay for today's overpromised retirees? These are the questions millennials need to ask themselves. Somebody has to. The current generation of leaders is largely unwilling to do so, or to make sacrifices, even when those sacrifices appear unavoidable. Millennials, by their very nature, are frustrated when nobody is willing to do what plainly has to be done.

I believe that the modern liberal movement is not prepared to supply millennials with practical solutions to these questions. Modern liberalism, especially in its post–Great Society incarnation, as we saw in the last Democratic Congress governed by Nancy Pelosi, is based on the premise that when there is a problem, the solution is to be found in a government spending program. The bigger the problem, the more government needs to spend taxpayer money. If students are illiterate, liberalism says we need to spend more on school buildings and existing teachers, not give parents a choice of schools. If people are out of work, liberalism says we need to write them checks so they can replace some of their take-home pay, not cut taxes on corporations so they can create new jobs. And if the economy is in the tank, liberalism—which embraces Keynesian economics—says government must create vast public works projects to fill the order books of companies, not cut regulations and taxes, which prevent the economy from growing.

Remember: Every dollar we spend comes from collecting taxes from Americans, so each time liberalism calls on government to provide a service, the taxpayer is on the hook. And with each new commitment, taxes go higher, and people keep less of what they earn.

The problem is that government, by writing checks to support those who need help, is taking money away from people who are earning their own living, oftentimes struggling to do so. Now, it's one thing when government seeks to help those who are destitute or physically unable to help themselves. But it's quite another thing when roughly half the population is subsidized, in one way or another, by the other half. That's what we have in this country. And here's the thing. It's not just a questionable moral arrangement for a society. It also happens to be far more expensive than we can afford. That's why we have deficits. The government has agreed to support many people, for many reasons, but is unable to collect enough taxes from the rest of us.

The challenge for the millennial generation is to say: "Enough." Millennials already believe debts and deficits must be controlled, that government is trying to do too much, and that it's time for the government to focus on meeting the promises it is committed to meet, instead of loading on even more commitments.

So what has to change? Here is an agenda for millennials to embrace, an agenda of fiscal sanity. Some of it, admittedly, is a little wonky. One thing I learned in the Bush administration's Office of Management and Budget is that the devil is in the details. You can tell Washington to stop spending, but Washington has a million little ways to tell you it can't. Those million little ways are what preoccupy the budget wonks. And if you want to get anything done in Washington, you have to prove your budget policy chops. Otherwise, it's like trying to operate in a strange land without speaking the language.

Here are three big areas—spending reform, tax reform, and entitlement reform—where the Republican Party can take the most effective action in order to restore fiscal sanity and make our case to the millennial generation.

Spending Reform

The first thing we can do to rein in spending is implement real PAYGO. Despite the sound of it, this isn't some kind of highway toll. It's a rule that forces legislators to actually pay for new spending by cutting spending somewhere else. While President Obama praised the new PAYGO legislation in February 2010 as a way to force Congress to "pay for what it spends, just like everybody else," in fact it hasn't quite worked out that way, because Congress can ignore its own rule just by getting enough votes. In the 110th and 111th Congresses, federal lawmakers have either waived or ignored PAYGO twenty-five times. Even if a real PAYGO covering all spending is implemented, we still need lawmakers who have the integrity to play by their own rules.

We can also eliminate *earmarks,* mini-spending programs that would not pass muster if they had to compete with other government priorities but get inserted into legislation because they have a powerful sponsor in Congress. Each time an earmark is inserted into a spending bill, its cost could have gone to support something more deserving or gone unspent. More important, earmarks are a way to buy votes for legislation that might otherwise not pass or to buy votes toward future elections. In the Omnibus Spending Bill that was proposed by the lame-duck Congress in December 2010, Tea Partiers publicized $8 billion in Republican and Democratic earmarks before debate on the bill could even begin. The resulting uproar forced Senate majority leader Harry Reid to pull the bill. For years, politicians thought earmarks were good politics; not anymore, it turns out. Republicans, who are some of the worst offenders— Senator Cochrain, I'm talking to you—need to understand that if they want to connect with millennials, they need to end earmarks.

Tax Reform

The first time millennials filled out their taxes, they probably thought that the task seemed awfully complex. It's true. And, in fact, tax forms are so forbidding and impenetrable that even the most patient and the most intelligent among us are forced to hire someone to do them for us. This is wrong. It is one thing for government to ask citizens to pay their fair share (whatever that is); it's quite another to impose an additional burden on citizens as part of the process. Conservatives have always had the upper hand on this issue, and they can press their advantage with some combination of two of my favorite ideas: House budget chairman Paul Ryan's plan to simplify the tax code on personal and corporate taxes and the flat tax, first proposed by Alvin Rabushka and Robert Hall of the Hoover Institution in 1992.

Ryan's tax plan dramatically simplifies the federal tax code. It proposes only two levels of taxation: 10 percent on annual income up to $50,000 for single filers and $100,000 for couples, and 25 percent for filers with incomes above those levels. It also provides a generous standard deduction to replace itemized deductions. It further eliminates the now out-of-control alternative minimum tax, and it eliminates taxes on savings accounts, CDs, money market accounts, capital gains, dividends, and the estates of people who have already paid their taxes and are dead. In addition, it replaces the corporate income tax (which is among the highest in the world) with a business consumption tax of 8.5 percent.

The flat tax, on the other hand, is just that: a single tax rate that is paid by everyone who files an income tax return. What started out as a "crazy" proposal and "out of touch with reality" (to quote the idea's detractors) began to gain support when Steve Forbes endorsed it in the presidential election of 1992. Today, if you walk into Rabushka's office at the Hoover Institution at Stanford University, you'll see the map he keeps with flag pins denoting those nations that have adopted the flat tax. To date, more than twenty have done so— including Russia, Ukraine, Latvia, and Iceland. Millennials surely can see the appeal of either idea because they both promise the same thing: a simple way for Americans to pay their fair share, knowing they have complied with the law, and without gaming the system. It also ensures that everyone pays into the system and that everyone actually has a stake in the game.

Entitlement Reform

About 60 percent of the federal budget is spoken for and very difficult to cut because it pays for things that are already promised: Social Security, Medicare, Medicaid, and interest payments on the debt. The reality is that all the spending and tax reforms in the world won't solve our fiscal problems if we don't take on these behemoths. We have to address the problem of out-of-control entitlement programs. The bill for the promises made in the past through Social

Security, Medicare, and Medicaid is coming due, and we can't afford to pay it. Our projected unfunded liability for these entitlement programs alone reached $107 trillion in 2009, according to the National Center for Policy Analysis.

But it's not enough for Republicans to merely complain about the problem. Millennials will grow weary of such complaints unless viable solutions are forthcoming. Otherwise, they will simply conclude, correctly, that Republicans are merely whining and not offering realistic proposals to fix the problem. Fortunately, fresh faces in the Republican Party have proposed detailed solutions for the pending crisis. Paul Ryan's "Roadmap for America's Future" outlines three easy changes that could make Social Security solvent for decades. The first component would gradually increase the retirement age over time to reflect more accurately when workers actually need to stop working. When Social Security was created, the average lifespan for male workers was sixty years and the retirement age was fifty-five. Now life expectancy for men is approaching seventy-five years, but the retirement age is sixty-five. The program was designed to assist retirees for an average of five years after their retirement. Now that people are living ten or more years beyond their retirement, the program has to adjust. Ryan's plan wouldn't affect anyone who is fifty-five or older today, but it would start to raise the retirement age for those younger and give them enough time to plan to supplement their Social Security income. Part of that plan, if they choose, would include a government-managed personal account, similar to the program available to elected members of Congress and federal employees.

The final reform to Social Security would simply adjust the way we calculate future benefits. Right now, the government increases future benefits according to what people earn and multiplies that by the increase in average wages. This makes sense, but as it turns out, wages rise faster than the rate of inflation, which is what really counts to retirees. By using the inflation rate rather than the projected increase in wages to determine future benefits, we could chop off a huge chunk of what the Social Security system currently owes future retirees. People will still get what they paid into the system, and that amount will cover the way inflation eats away at savings. But those benefits will be less, as they must be, in order to make sure the program continues to exist for everyone.

Likewise, Chairman Ryan's 2011 budget that was passed by the U.S. House of Representatives courageously tackled the problem of saving Medicare. Ryan's bold plans prove that Republicans are serious about reforming entitlements and can do more than demogogue debt and deficits. This is *exactly* what millennials need to see.

But ultimately, addressing the structural problems in Medicare and Medicaid won't resolve the increasingly urgent underlying problem—the rising cost of health care. That will require reforms to the health-care marketplace, in order to make the purchase of health insurance and of health care itself more responsive to market forces through increased competition and a more empowered consumer. For example, people should be allowed to purchase health insurance across state lines, which would increase competition and lower the costs of health insurance plans, while health savings accounts should be made more portable and tax-deductible. Incentives should be in place to encourage more catastrophic health insurance plans to cover younger adults at lower costs, while medical malpractice reform would liberate doctors from the excessive costs that come with unnecessary tests and out-of-control insurance premiums. In contrast to Obamacare, free-market reforms that increase individual choice and lower costs can become a hallmark of Republican health-care reform, one that will appeal to the millennial generation.

A government can run a deficit for many reasons, and deficits are not necessarily evil. We run deficits to fight wars when winning those wars is essential to guaranteeing our freedom and the security of free nations around the world. But when we run *structural* deficits—deficits that exist regardless of whether the economy is performing well, regardless of whether tax revenues are up or down—we have committed a moral wrong. We have allowed our promises to exceed our ability to pay, and we have allowed government to occupy a place in our lives much bigger than it should be. Government that is bigger than our capacity to pay for it is, by definition, a violation of the compact between the government and the governed and between the citizens of today and the citizens of tomorrow. Millennials understand this. They may favor big government in certain cases, but they do not favor government bigger than we can afford. They don't want to spend their lives paying for their parents' entitlement-spending party. And they don't want America to go bankrupt on their watch.

President Obama has used soaring rhetoric in speaking of the importance of reducing deficits, but he has made those deficits significantly larger—in just two years—and he has offered no plan to curb future deficits. Here is what Andrew Sullivan, who usually supports Obama, had to say to millennials about the president's recent budgets: "To all those under 30 who worked so hard to get this man elected, know this: he just screwed you over. He thinks you're fools. Either the U.S. will go into default because of Obama's cowardice, or you will be paying far far more for far far less because this president has no courage when it counts. He let you down. On the critical issue of America's fiscal crisis, he represents no hope and no change. Just the same old Washington politics he once promised to end."

Our character as a nation is at stake: Will we be a debtor nation, forever requiring others to fund our deficits? Will we be forever unable to face the dangerous imbalances in our budget? Will we be unable to afford the things we want, or even the things we need, in future years, because we will be paying for the things previous generations enjoyed? Other nations have been in this position.

Other nations have chosen to ignore the problems. Those nations—once great and powerful—are now mere shadows of their former selves. America must not allow this to happen. We must face this issue squarely and face it now. And Republicans must take the lead. Millennials will see these ideas, and they will see who is proposing them. They will have a choice between a party that is simply adding to the debt, and a party that is putting forward a plan to bring it down. The choice will be clear, and no matter what other issues help shape millennials' political loyalties, no choice they face will be as stark, and as consequential for their economic fortunes and way of life, as this one.

CHAPTER 5

FREEDOM MEANS FREEDOM FOR EVERYONE

*"It's time America realized that there is no gay exemption
in the right to life, liberty, and the pursuit of happiness
in the Declaration of Independence."*
—BARRY GOLDWATER

EVERY IDEALISTIC YOUNG adult who goes to Washington, D.C., to work in public service sooner or later confronts the unavoidable reality that she's working for someone she doesn't agree with 100 percent of the time. For me, that moment arrived when I learned about the Bush-Cheney reelection campaign's anti-same-sex-marriage strategy.

I had come to the nation's capital in the spirit of patriotism after the attacks of September 11, 2001, was driven by a strong desire to serve my country, and was honored to be working for President George W. Bush. But when I learned the campaign would be supporting a divisive strategy to mobilize socially conservative voters, I suddenly realized that serving this president meant supporting a man who was willing to take measures that were detrimental to my gay friends and acquaintances, people I love and respect.

I was deeply troubled by the president's proposal to amend the

Constitution to define marriage as being exclusively between a man and a woman and by the campaign's strategy. But as a twenty-five-year-old junior staffer, I wasn't in a position to argue the point. I believed then, as I believe today, that we needed to support our nation's leadership in wartime. American troops were in harm's way in Iraq and Afghanistan; radicalized Islamist terrorists, although weakened, were still plotting 9/11-style attacks against America; and the world was less stable than it had ever been before in my lifetime. For me, it came down to the fact that I trusted President Bush to lead the country through the war more than I trusted his opponent, Senator John Kerry. I also supported President Bush's domestic policy priorities, including his tax cuts in 2001 and 2003, his dedication to improving America's failing education system, and his outreach to Hispanic Americans. But I still wondered whether this strategy—winning key states by advocating anti-gay policies—was the only way, or the best way, for a wartime president to get reelected.

I could have stood on principle and left the campaign for another job, but my departure wouldn't have made so much as a ripple. People who quit campaigns usually burn enough bridges to prevent their participation in politics in the future. I believed that remaining on the campaign staff would be better in the long run, presuming that I would find an opportunity to one day advocate within the party for a different approach to marriage freedoms. And so, even though I supported gay rights and found the campaign's tactics on this issue to be inconsistent with a conservatism that champions individual liberty, I worked hard to reelect George W. Bush.

We learned after the election that the anti-same-sex-marriage initiatives played no decisive role in securing President Bush's victory. While the marriage amendments passed in all eleven states, not all of those voters pulled the lever for Bush. For example, Michigan's rust-belt Catholics voted against same-sex marriage but still voted for John Kerry. Overall, the initiatives mobilized people *across* party lines rather than ensuring that only social conservatives showed up to vote as a bloc for President Bush.

As it turned out, the 2004 presidential election hinged on the state of Ohio, and analysis of the results in Ohio's eighty-eight counties finds no conclusive evidence that the 136,000 votes that won the state for Bush were directly tied to the ballot initiative.

This strategy was bogus from the beginning, in the opinion of the Bush-Cheney campaign's chief strategist, Matthew Dowd, who conducted extensive polling before and after the election. As Dowd later told me, "No social issues or themes were in the top five messages that motivated [social conservative] voters." Instead, they were most concerned with national security issues, such as terrorism, and economic issues, such as tax cuts. Comparing battleground states that featured anti-same-sex-marriage initiatives with those battleground states that did not, Dowd's postelection analysis found zero difference among Religious Right or social conservative voter turnout. Social conservatives voted for George W. Bush in equal numbers, regardless of whether there was an anti-gay measure on the ballot.

What the anti-same-sex-marriage initiative accomplished instead was to brand the Republican Party as the anti-gay party. The campaign decision to follow this strategy had the unfortunate effect of cementing a false narrative within the political establishment that social issues are the primary mobilizer of the Republican Party's base.

Empowered by this narrative, an elite group of prominent and vocal social conservatives, the "conservagenzia," as Dowd has dubbed them, have gained outsize influence within the Republican Party infrastructure and misrepresent the most urgent concerns of the party's base. This mythology now holds the Republican Party hostage and prevents us from reaching out to millennials and Independents— who, absent the emphasis on social issues, are quite likely to agree with the Republican Party's message on fiscal and national security issues.

The widespread acceptance of this mythology has been terrible, not only for the party's ability to attract younger voters, but because it represents a departure from one of the most important principles of the Republican Party and the conservative movement.

Yes, you heard that correctly. The Republican Party has violated one of its core premises—that it is the party of individual freedom—and by doing so, has jeopardized its own future.

When I tell people who are my age or younger that I'm in favor of gay rights, including the freedom to marry the person they love, or same-sex marriage, they seem stunned. Not because supporting equal rights for gays and lesbians strikes them as unusual. Rather, they assume it's impossible for someone to be a Republican and to support gay rights. They wonder why I have not been kicked out of the Republican Party.

From the point of view of the majority of millennials, when it comes to gay rights, the Republican Party is on the wrong side of history. They don't know about the many prominent Republicans who have publicly *supported* the freedom to marry, including former first lady Laura Bush, former vice president Dick Cheney, former solicitor general Ted Olson, and former chairman of the Republican National Committee Ken Mehlman.

Ken's experience is especially compelling. He recently came out and in the time since, he has dedicated himself to achieving equal rights for gay and lesbian Americans. Some of his efforts are behind the scenes, making the case to his fellow conservatives. But much of his energy is devoted to public efforts to raise money and awareness, just the kind of thing he did as a political operative for President Bush.

The Republican Party as a whole has yet to get credit for the individual efforts of an increasing number of Republicans, people like me, who advocate for gay rights within the GOP. Much better known to the broad public are the efforts of special interest groups such as Concerned Women for America, the Family Research Council, and the National Organization for Marriage, which aggressively lobby against equal rights for gays and lesbians. Until very recently, their message and their tone defined the Republican Party's approach toward gay rights and its image on this issue. But anyone who values the long-term interests of the Republican Party should understand that this approach is harmful.

Recall what we know about millennials. They are by no means uninterested in issues of morality; in fact they typically have strong and consistent ideas about what constitutes moral behavior. And the majority of them just don't see a correlation between sexual orientation and morality. They have grown up with gay friends, gay family members, gay coaches, and gay teachers. Millennials understand intrinsically that sexual orientation is not an active choice people make. As they see it, sexual orientation is a part of someone's personal makeup and should not in any way influence his or her rights as a citizen. And indeed, the gay rights movement has achieved its greatest success by insisting on the ordinary rights of citizens: matters such as the legal status of domestic partnerships and civil unions, hospital visitation rights, and freedom to serve in the nation's armed forces openly. These are elemental rights for most Americans, yet they are the kinds of rights for which gays and lesbians have had to struggle. No wonder millennials support their struggle: There is no reason to deprive any citizen of these basic rights.

Millennials are almost twice as likely as Americans who are sixty-five years and older to think that homosexuality should be accepted. People under thirty who identify with specific religious traditions are more likely than their older co-religionists to view homosexuality as acceptable. One might assume that acceptance of homosexuality would be much more common among the non-religious, yet even among religiously affiliated millennials the numbers prove that this generation is less likely to perceive homosexuality through the lens of religion. As many as 39 percent of young evangelicals, 69 percent of young mainline Protestants, 72 percent of young Catholics, and 51 percent of the youth in historic black Protestant churches believe homosexuality should be accepted by society. For the majority of youth, homosexuality is neither a religious nor a secular "sin" that justifies discrimination.

One of American society's most inspiring features is its ability to improve itself over time. On the issue of gay rights and acceptance of gays, as a society we have made remarkable progress in my own lifetime. When I was young, there was still strong prejudice against open homosexuality. I recall distinctly what happened when a dear friend's father came out in the late 1980s. Not only was being gay still considered taboo, but prejudices were newly reinforced by the outbreak of the AIDS virus, which was then considered to be a disease associated solely with the "gay lifestyle." At that time, the movie *Philadelphia,* which would so movingly dramatize the struggle of a gay man dying of AIDS, hadn't even been made. Magic Johnson still appeared invincible (and he is still with us today, but who knew that antiretroviral medicines were in our future?). I was in sixth grade, and another classmate hurled an insult at my friend, making fun of her gay dad. The pain she suffered from such insults affected me deeply. Her father loved her just as my father loved me, and I decided then and there that there was no reason our fathers should be viewed differently by society. Why should their love and their positions in society as fathers be held to different standards of respect and honor? Why should one man be mocked and another man be left unscathed? Why should my friend suffer because of who her father was? And why would anyone choose a "lifestyle" that would invite a lifetime of discrimination? Clearly sexual orientation wasn't a choice. These emotions raged within me, and as I worked them out in my heart and head, my sense of injustice mounted.

Over the past twenty years millions of Americans have had similar personal experiences having to do with their gay friends, family members, and acquaintances, and I believe that their individual experiences are largely responsible for the sweeping change in attitudes about gays and lesbians we have seen in this country. Politics is personal and the more that people have personal interactions with gays and lesbians, the more they support equal rights for them. Polling confirms that the number of people who say that they have a friend, relative, or acquaintance who is gay mirrors the number of people who are in favor of expanding civil rights to gay individuals.

This sea change is reflected in our popular culture. Every day Ellen DeGeneres is invited into living rooms all across America to talk about ordinary issues. She is one of America's most loved and lovable talk show hosts—and her sexuality happens to be irrelevant to her success as an entertainer. Shows such as *Queer Eye for the Straight Guy* and *Will & Grace* have made even more stereotypically flamboyant elements of gay culture more accepted throughout straight America. The situation comedy *Modern Family* debuted in 2009 and features a male couple learning the ropes of parenting after adopting a Vietnamese girl. Even the fact that Elton John, a lesbian, gay, bisexual, transgender (LGBT) movement icon, performed at Rush Limbaugh's wedding (images are available on Rush's Facebook page) proves that discrimination against gays and lesbians from all sides of the political spectrum has markedly diminished within American culture.

I started out as a Republican in part because of a family legacy. But my own personal journey, in politics and in life, has convinced me that the Republican Party, with the conservative movement's emphasis on individual freedom and its spirit of American individualism, is the natural home for equal rights. And why not? After all, this is the party that gave political force to the abolitionist movement and the woman suffrage movement. The Republican Party has individual freedom built into its DNA.

Conservatives believe that people, not government, make the best decisions for themselves, and Republicans act on this belief by advancing policy prescriptions on a variety of issues, from welfare reform to entitlement reform, health-care reform, education reform, and tax policy. The freedom of people to live their lives as they choose, and to enjoy the full benefits of their rights as enshrined in the Constitution, is entirely consistent with the central tenet of conservatism: individual freedom.

Still, there is a stark difference in how distinct generations within the Republican Party, and within all of American society, view homosexuality. I didn't fully appreciate what a generational issue this was until the time I had the chance to talk with Bill O'Reilly about California's Proposition 8, the discriminatory law in California that defines marriage as being exclusively between a man and a woman.

Let me say at the outset that even though Bill O'Reilly is the top-rated personality in cable news, most of the people who talk about him negatively have never watched his show for more than a few minutes at a time. They would rather believe everything that his detractors such as Rachel Maddow and Keith Olbermann have said about him. The truth is, Bill is a registered Independent, and sometimes his views fall more toward the center than the right. Yes, he is old-school, from a working-class background in Levittown, New York. He is culturally conservative and Catholic. He is hostile to modern liberalism precisely because he thinks liberals tend to undermine the values that have made America great, such as freedom of religion and the rights and responsibilities of families. Bill is also remarkably compassionate, and he raises and donates millions of dollars to charities annually. He genuinely cares about his viewers and sees his job as looking out for people whom the government or special interests are ignoring or mistreating. He looks out for the people in Levittown and the countless other places like it across America.

Once when I appeared on his show, Bill casually mentioned that I, as a Republican, must be opposed to same-sex marriage and in favor of Proposition 8 in California. Because TV segments fly by quickly, I had no idea how I was going to explain, in such a short amount of time, that I support the freedom of gays and lesbians to marry. I believe preventing them from marrying amounts to legal discrimination that reduces them to second-class citizens. Most people my age don't view homosexuality as a "lifestyle choice" or something that the liberal elite are pressuring us to accept as a form of political correctness. How could I fit all of this into a sound-bite-size response? So instead I took the easy way out and told him that there was no way that he'd get it, that he was just too old. At that instant I heard a loud noise and realized it was a producer from the control room who was whistling into Bill's earpiece. Bill's a pro, so he didn't flinch; but I had zinged him and he knew it. I had made my point. Unfortunately, I appeared to have tagged him as an old fuddy-duddy in front of his beloved fans. I was certain I'd never be invited back, but when I was—happily—I wondered whether this exchange had any influence on Bill, who now seems to understand that my views on gay rights reflect the sensibility of the next generation.

Ensuring that gays and lesbians attain the same rights as all other Americans has always seemed to me like one of the most obvious and most morally clear causes that Republicans can make their own, just as Republicans historically stood on the side of freedom against slavery and on the side of women's suffrage.

I am in good company defending this position. My support for gay rights is entirely consistent with American individualism and the conservative movement's most important principle: maximizing individual freedom and protecting equal opportunity for all Americans. Ronald Reagan was an early opponent of discrimination against gays and lesbians. In 1978, Reagan spoke out and campaigned against California's Proposition 6, which sought to ban homosexual teachers from public schools, as depicted in the Academy Award–winning film *Milk*. In the words of biographer Craig Shirley, "Ronald Reagan opposed any form of discrimination based on homosexuality. . . . The true American conservatism as articulated and embraced by the Gipper celebrated the individual, privacy and 'maximum freedom consistent with law and order.' "

As we all know, politics is rarely driven by a single social issue. In the 2010 campaign, the hot-button issues were fiscal responsibility, curbing federal spending, and President Obama's health-care overhaul. In 2008, it was the economy. In 2006, it was the Iraq War and Bush fatigue. It is doubtful that the issue of gay rights will ever rise to that level. But it's safe to say that as millennials assume positions of authority and leadership throughout society, the Republican Party cannot afford to be perceived as the party of bias and discrimination.

The GOP needs to recognize that supporting gay rights is historically consistent with the party's fight to expand freedoms to previously disenfranchised segments of society. Republican emphasis on individual freedom and individual choice should not be limited to our economic policy. Why should the conservative movement, which says it supports individual freedom, support it only for certain people? In the words of former vice president Dick Cheney when discussing his views on same-sex marriage and his lesbian daughter, "Freedom means freedom for everyone."

There are some on the right, however, who suggest that a person can't be a true conservative if he or she supports equal rights for gays and lesbians. While this may ring true among the traditionalists and religious conservatives, there are others within the conservative movement—economic conservatives, libertarian conservatives, national security conservatives—who support the full integration of gays and lesbians as equal citizens in society. There is considerably more diversity among Republicans and conservatives than you might imagine from watching MSNBC.

But to some conservatives, people like me who support gay rights are Republicans in Name Only—RINOs, the targets of RINO hunters, who claim to have a corner on what conservatism means. But RINO hunting on the issue of gay rights is bound to lead to a smaller conservative movement. Drumming out dissent instead of supporting what Ronald Reagan called a "big tent" will only turn people away from the GOP. And it sends a signal to all Americans—and especially millennials—that the Republican Party is close-minded and complacent, a party going nowhere.

Yet history shows us that it can be otherwise. During the past century, the Republican Party has repeatedly evolved in response to a changing world. It was at one time isolationist; it is now largely internationalist. It used to represent powerful moneyed monopolies, but now is the home of Main Street populists. The Republican Party is defined by a set of ideals and principles, including the protection of individual freedom from concentrations of power, which was essential to America's founding, has been vital to its prosperity, and remains essential to its future. If Republicans fall out of touch with those principles today, they have a diminished future as a party or a movement.

It is true that the modern conservative movement—and thus the Republican Party—has always been a bit schizophrenic on social policies. Historically the conservative movement has been most unified when it was in opposition. Mostly, though, conservatism is a cacophonous aggregation, like one of those big, happy, and somewhat offbeat families gathered for Thanksgiving dinner. Someone will always be arguing with someone about something. In the 1950s its coalition of traditionalists, economic libertarians, and anticommunists fought constantly with one another about the proper balance between progress and tradition. It was such bickering that led the godfather of the movement, William F. Buckley Jr., to say that "the conservative movement in America has got to put its theoretical house in order."

Let me suggest how today's Republicans can put their house in order and come to an understanding with gay rights advocates. For most Americans, the rights of gays and lesbians to be employed and to have access to public and private accommodations are not in dispute. What is in dispute is the question of whether gays and lesbians should be allowed to form the same bond and enter the same sacred relationship—marriage—that heterosexuals do. Those in favor of and those opposed to marriage equality engage this issue with equal intensity. Opponents of marriage freedom insist that they are concerned for the institution of marriage. They believe that marriage is an institution unique to one man and one woman, ideally for the purposes of procreation. This, they say, is the best arrangement for a healthy society.

The proponents of freedom to marry, like myself, make the same argument. I agree that marriage is humanity's most vital social institution. Marriage creates a legal and moral bond for two individuals to support each other throughout life. Indeed, many of our social institutions rely on this fundamental commitment. Next to the sanctity of the individual, the sanctity of the marriage bond is a foundational element in public life, an expression of our simultaneously self-reliant and mutually reliant society. The fabric of society is woven together and held securely by the bonds individuals form with one another and with their communities. The stronger the connective tissue between all these components, the stronger we are as a nation.

If conservatives truly cherish these values, there is no better way to support them than through policies that encourage cohesive marriages and families. Making "the big tent" a bit bigger by welcoming same-sex couples into the tradition of marriage will serve to strengthen the institution of marriage, not weaken it.

This argument should have special appeal to libertarian conservatives and others whose primary concern is to prevent the intrusion of the state into the private realm. For them, broken families are costly: delinquency, poor health, illiteracy, recidivism, and all manner of social ills stem directly from broken families. If conservatives favor a society in which individuals are less reliant on the government, then they should encourage individuals—gay or straight—to forge lifelong commitments to each other, and grant these commitments every advantage under the law. Expanding the benefits of marriage to same-sex couples strengthens the fabric of our society by cultivating an increasingly self-reliant and interdependent society, with the result that individuals become less reliant on the government.

Some conservatives believe that same-sex marriages will somehow taint heterosexual marriages, but they have failed to explain how exactly that would happen. And the truth is, as most conservatives will admit, the preponderance of no-fault divorce has done more to harm the institution of marriage than same-sex marriages.

Others argue that civil unions, which grant gay and lesbian couples all the same rights and protections under the law as marriage, should be a sufficient compromise. But by fighting for the exclusive use of the word *marriage,* they implicitly acknowledge that there is something special about the word and thus about the act itself. Indeed, the reason people oppose the use of the word *marriage* to describe same-sex commitments is because they would prefer to create a lesser category—proof that they themselves recognize that marriage is magical and distinct from every other relationship. In my view, that specialness, with all its societal implications and significance, is something that should be available to all Americans. If you agree that gays and lesbians should be able to form permanent bonds, then why not allow them to experience all the magic encapsulated in that word: marriage?

I do not believe that those who support civil unions but not legal marriage are bigots; I just don't think they have considered why nothing less than the right to marriage is what is appropriate for gays and lesbians and why something society deems special should be denied to certain citizens just because of who they are.

We've also learned in America to beware of something called separate but equal under the law. Separate is not equal. And insisting on a separate category of union other than marriage gives some of our citizens an excuse to treat other citizens differently, and that invariably leads to discrimination.

Two landmark cases, *Loving v. Virginia* in 1967, which legalized interracial marriage, and *Turner v. Safley* in 1987, which allowed prisoners the right to marry, affirmed that marriage is a right enshrined in the United States Constitution. But as conservative constitutional expert Theodore "Ted" Olson has pointed out, the Supreme Court has ruled fourteen times since 1888 that marriage is a fundamental right, the same as those enshrined in the Bill of Rights—freedom of speech, freedom of assembly, freedom to bear arms, freedom of the press. If the Supreme Court has ruled that marriage is a fundamental right, then laws forbidding marriage between homosexuals are unconstitutional. In singling out a group of citizens and denying them the freedom to marry, our laws have created a second class of citizens and institutionalized discrimination against them. When you consider that imprisoned *criminals* are allowed to marry, it seems outrageously unjust that law-abiding gays and lesbians are denied the same freedom.

The day when a majority of Americans recognize that the freedom to marry is a fundamental constitutional right is not far off. It's coming not just because millennials are rising to positions of authority, but also because the law is taking us in that direction.

I remember a gray January morning in San Francisco inside court-room number five of the U.S. District Court, Northern District of California, where I watched from a wooden gallery bench the legal dream team of David Boies and Ted Olson argue the constitutional-ity of same-sex marriage in the landmark civil rights case *Perry v. Schwarzenegger.* I was asked to join the Advisory Council of the American Foundation for Equal Rights, a bipartisan group of advocates for the nonprofit entity that brought the plaintiffs' case to court. I had come to San Francisco to witness the final days of a three-week trial.

This was not a cut-and-dried, Left-versus-Right, secular-versus-religious kind of contest. Olson is a respected constitutional conservative, a founder of the Federalist Society who successfully argued *Bush v. Gore* before the Supreme Court (among fifty-five other Supreme Court cases). He served as President George W. Bush's solicitor general. Boies was the opposing counsel in *Bush v. Gore* and is a well-known Democratic Party activist. But now these two men stood side by side in a legal quest to prove that marriage equality is a constitutional right, not a partisan issue.

The plaintiffs' legal team assembled a thorough record of evidence that Proposition 8, the California law that defined marriage as being between a man and a woman, unreasonably discriminates against gays and lesbians, relegating them to second-class citizenship.

Among the seventeen witnesses called to the stand were experts in the fields of psychology, political science, economics, sociomedical sciences, and history. Economists testified about the financial harm done to same-sex couples and their children; political scientists about their political vulnerability; sociologists and psychologists about the societal stigma attached to homosexuality; historians about the history of marriage having become available to more and more groups over time.

As the judge was about to enter the chamber, one of the lawyers in a black suit whispered to me: "You're lucky; you're right on time to see David do a cross." Indeed, Boies is known as one of the great litigators of our age. His ability to cross-examine a witness, dismantling testimony brick by brick until the entire edifice crumbles, is something his wife has described as an aphrodisiac. Boies's target that day was one of two witnesses for the defense who had earlier testified against allowing same-sex couples to marry.

The witness was David Blankenhorn, who runs the Institute for American Values. He is the author of two books on the subject, *Fatherless in America* and *The Future of Marriage*. Boies made short work of Blankenhorn. The witness found himself agreeing that marriage is better for children, regardless of the gender of the parents, and that growing up in same-sex households is better than in a single-parent home. He admitted that "adopting same-sex marriage would be likely to improve the well-being of gay and lesbian households and their children." I wondered to myself, *This man represents the people who disagree with same-sex marriage?* Finally, Boies read from Blankenhorn's book *The Future of Marriage:*

> This still-revolutionary principle—"all men [persons] are created equal"—deeply informs the American experience and character and is increasingly viewed globally as the essential universal moral law. On the issue of same-sex marriage, is this profound principle of equality and dignity the heart of the matter? After all, part of the reason why the principle is so revolutionary is that it can grow and deepen over time. Groups that had long been considered effectively outside of its moral reach—African Americans, women, people of certain colors or languages or religions—can over time, and often as a result of great struggle, enter into its

protective sphere. I believe that today the principle of equal human dignity must apply to gay and lesbian persons. In that sense, insofar as we are a nation founded on this principle we would be *more* American on the day we permitted same-sex marriage than we were the day before.

These were indeed the words of this star witness, and he could offer no argument or reason at that trial, as he spoke under oath, for why our society or its laws ought to prohibit gays and lesbians from enjoying the benefits of marriage.

Just two months earlier, I had been married in California—and it struck me on that day in the San Francisco courtroom that I had taken for granted my freedom to marry the person I loved. At the Proposition 8 trial, the arguments for marriage made by people who are not legally able to enjoy its benefits presented a clearer and more compelling justification for marriage than any that my new husband and I had considered in our prenuptial preparation. I was forcefully reminded exactly why marriage is so special and why every individual in America, gay or straight, deserves equal access to this sacred institution.

I believe the Republican Party will come around. On September 22, 2010, prominent Republicans including two former governors, one RNC finance chairman, business leaders, and several Bush-Cheney 2004 campaign staff alumni hosted a high-profile fund-raiser in support of the freedom to marry. The fund-raiser was chaired by our old boss Ken Mehlman, the campaign's manager and the former Republican National Committee chairman who had only recently come out. We raised $1.3 million for marriage freedom that day, the first public manifestation of a fundamental shift happening inside the

Republican Party. More and more Republicans are realizing that gay rights are a simple issue of freedom.

Though Republicans have been justifiably maligned for their sponsorship of anti-same-sex-marriage initiatives, the Democratic Party has fallen short as well. Once again, you heard that right. Despite liberal support for same-sex marriage, no major Democrat running for national office has openly supported freedom to marry. New York State Democrats famously failed to pass marriage equality legislation in December 2009. And don't forget that a Democratic president, Bill Clinton, signed the Defense of Marriage Act (DOMA), which prohibits states from legally recognizing same-sex marriages or civil unions conducted in other states. Even David Boies, the Democratic lawyer representing the plaintiffs in the Proposition 8 trial, chided President Obama for not supporting the court case. After all, Boies pointed out, the president's parents would not have been able to legally wed in fifteen states at the time of their marriage, and only thanks to the Supreme Court's decision in *Loving v. Virginia* was the prohibition on interracial marriage lifted in 1967.

It will take many courageous Republicans to make the case that a conservatism that champions individual freedom must also support gay rights. Democrats are very good at playing identity politics. But I believe that in the end, identity politics is a losing proposition. It may work in certain instances, but what gays and lesbians want—and what millennials expect gays and lesbians to receive—is respect and honor as citizens and individuals. That means not more privileges or pledges but the expectation of full participation in public life.

The Republican Party is changing not only thanks to leaders like Ken Mehlman but also to people like the former police chief and mayor of San Diego, Jerry Sanders. Mayor Sanders, the father of a lesbian daughter, didn't support marriage equality before his election and believed civil unions to be an acceptable compromise. The issue didn't figure in his campaign. He ran for mayor on a platform of cleaning up San Diego's legal and financial troubles after having served on the San Diego police force for twenty-six years.

In 2007, the San Diego City Council forced Mayor Sanders to take a stand after it passed a resolution supporting a court challenge to California's ban on same-sex marriage. By city law, Mayor Sanders had ten days to sign or veto the resolution supporting marriage equality. As the father of a lesbian but the mayor of a conservative city, Sanders agonized over his decision. Politically, it was a dangerous one: The mayor faced a serious reelection battle the following year and the odds against him would grow longer if he chose not to veto the resolution. He waited until the night before the deadline before making his decision. He decided to veto. While his daughter disagreed with him, she supported his decision because she believed it was more important for San Diego that her father continue to serve as the city's mayor.

The night before the ten-day deadline expired, he hosted his closest gay friends and supporters at his home, so he could explain why he intended to veto the resolution. He then listened as they expressed their disappointment. In his words, "About fifteen people spoke that night. But before the first one was finished, I shared their disappointment. It was then that I realized that all opposition to same-sex marriage, including my own opposition, was grounded in prejudice."

The next day, Mayor Sanders signed the resolution intead of vetoing it. The video of the press conference, posted online, instantly went viral and has since received more than a million views on YouTube. Mayor Sanders went on to testify for the plaintiffs in *Perry v. Schwarzenegger*, arguing that California's Proposition 8 is unconstitutional. About that testimony, and his own evolution on the issue of gay rights, he later wrote:

I hope that everyone will find someone they love deeply, someone with whom they can share life's experiences and grow old together. I cannot look anyone in the face and tell them that their relationships, their very lives, are any less meaningful than the marriage I share with my wife.

Sometimes I find it hard to believe that I came so close to making the wrong decision, and to endorsing government-sanctioned discrimination. . . . I was reelected to a second term the next year. My position on marriage equality definitely made it more difficult. . . . As someone who has spent most of his lifetime in public service, I understand that when government tolerates discrimination against any class of people, it makes it easier for citizens to do the same thing. . . . History tells us that the first step toward true equality has always been equality under the law. Denying gays and lesbians the right to marry is no different than denying black people the right to sit in a "whites only" section of the restaurant. The law and our own experience tell us that "separate but equal" is an oxymoron. Separate is never equal.

This is the testimony of someone who not only has compassion for friends and loved ones, but who has gotten closer to the heart of the American credo of personal liberty. It is also the testimony of someone who recognizes that it is a distinctly American trait to improve our system when it fails to live up to its promise, when the words *freedom, justice,* and *equality* do not apply everywhere and to everyone. This is the strength of our system, and we are stronger for identifying our own failings. I am proud to say that my great-grandfather, Herbert Hoover, wrote precisely about this process of renewal in his "American Individualism": "Many people confuse the exposure of wrongs which were below the surface with degeneration; [but in fact] their very exposure is progress. . . . A considerable experience leads me to the conviction that while we do wash our dirty linen in public, most others never wash it."

Supporting equal rights for gays and lesbians is at the core of the struggle to reinvigorate conservatism as a movement of personal freedom and responsibility. I know that the Republican Party has not led on this issue. I know, in fact, that it has been on the wrong side of this issue. But the time for such political gamesmanship is over. It didn't work before; it will never work. And it will never be right.

The Republican Party that I want to be part of proudly supports gay rights. And in doing so, it opens its ranks to a new generation that shares its enduring commitment to individual liberty.

CHAPTER 6

EDUCATION REFORM

A Civil Rights Win for the Millennial Generation

"Education spending will be most effective if it relies on parental choice and private initiative—the building blocks of success throughout our society."
—MILTON FRIEDMAN

THROUGHOUT THIS BOOK, when I refer to millennials, I have in mind that supercharged, highly educated, techno-savvy cohort whose parents and teachers have hovered over and doted on them. These millennials have shelves groaning with trophies, framed newspaper articles, and countless stickers and ribbons recognizing their achievements. They have flooded colleges and universities with résumés that have impressed admissions officers. Their community service projects have been inventive and productive. Their extracurricular activities have been awe-inspiring in their breadth. These millennials are a by-product of some of the most intensive parenting and schooling America has ever seen.

And yet there are other millennials who haven't been so fortunate. They have been raised in single-parent homes, in urban ghettos, and in rural backwaters. They struggle as all poor and forgotten people struggle—often silently, without allies, and without institutions to support them.

Ideally, America's public school system would have given these "other" millennials a way out. This is, after all, the role America's public school system was designed to play: to create an educated citizenry and to give every child a chance to learn skills and develop talents. The American education system was to be the great equalizer of opportunity—not a leveler but a common springboard from which all American youth could rise to the best of their ability, regardless of race, religion, or economic background.

The underlying ideal of equal opportunity is the basis of America's meritocracy, and it was the foundation of my great-grandfather's "American Individualism." A public school system premised on the principle that every student will have the same opportunity to receive an excellent education helps us avoid the stagnancy of societies based on class or caste or tribe. It promises to let the most talented individuals rise to the top, regardless of where, and to whom, they are born.

Tragically, this is a promise America makes but is failing to keep. We are falling dreadfully short of this ideal, and nowhere is this clearer than in the case of the millennial generation: a generation of educational haves and have-nots, a generation subject to a public school system that too often ends up cementing instead of rectifying the inequalities of birth. It would be one thing if our public school system simply had deep flaws. But the problem is far bigger: our public school system is separate and unequal. There is one educational system for children who are born into good zip codes, and another educational system for those who live in the bad zip codes.

While teens in our best public schools learn advanced math, attend language immersion classes, and rack up advanced placement credits, the rest of the education system is drifting further behind the rest of the world. Among industrialized countries, American students now rank fifteenth in reading, fourteenth in science, and nineteenth in math. What's more, seven thousand millennials drop out of high school *each day*. That's one student every nine seconds, or 1.2 million teens per year.

Since the early 1990s, approximately 70 percent of American students have graduated from high school. That means that roughly 30 percent of millennials are unlikely to have anything close to a decent career because most high-paying jobs require at least a high school diploma. We know that those leaving school before attaining a high school diploma are disproportionately African-American, Hispanic-American, or Native-American, all of whose graduation rates hover around 50 percent. This racial achievement gap flies in the face of the ideal of equal opportunity that was at the heart of the civil rights movement in America—and central to the philosophy of American individualism.

These "other" millennials who do not attain even the most basic level of education are not only disproportionately African-American, Hispanic-American, and Native-American, but they are also concentrated in a handful of schools.

Half of our nation's dropouts come from only 15 percent of America's high schools—roughly two thousand schools. These schools have earned the dubious distinction of being assigned a special name—"dropout factories"—because their rate of success is so bad. Students attending these schools have only a fifty-fifty chance of graduating. Almost 50 percent of African-Americans and nearly 40 percent of Latinos—but just 11 percent of white students—attend dropout factories.

Income is now a predictor of school achievement—how much money parents earn can determine whether a student succeeds in school, or even graduates. High school students from the lowest-income families drop out of school at six times the rate of their peers from higher-income families. Some observers have been all too willing to blame this failure on the students and their parents, and to assume that because poor neighborhoods can't support good schools, there is no sense in trying harder with poor kids. But this complacency has bred a cycle of poverty and failure. Failing neighborhoods are blamed for creating failing schools, which are blamed for creating failing kids, who go on to live in failing neighborhoods. Too many people are willing to accept this cycle, and while they may suggest we "do something" about it, they are unwilling to challenge their own assumption that a poor neighborhood means a poor school.

As a result, we have one educational system that produces whiz kids who are mostly white and from affluent or semi-affluent homes, and another educational system that cycles through poor minorities without teaching them the skills they need to survive in a global economy. Is this a system that gives its youngest citizens equal opportunity? No way.

For all the focus among the lucky millennials on the importance of diversity, and for all their ease around people of different backgrounds, they are part of a generation of Americans that has seen a resegregation of schools and a resegregation of economic opportunity—due, in part, to our school system's unequal and unfair treatment of students. If millennials truly want to promote diversity in our nation, they will resolve to reform our public school system. They should call the system what it is: separate, unequal, and unfair. They should agitate for a school system where one's zip code does not determine one's future earning power.

Many of the lucky millennials are ashamed of the educational establishment and its inequalities, not only because those inequalities are so obviously unfair, but also because those inequalities violate the core principles millennials subscribe to. Thousands stand up against those inequalities by volunteering for Teach For America, the nation's largest supplier of excellent teachers to poor urban schools. Millennials believe that government should be competent, but public schools are not competent, at least not across the board. Millennials believe that public service is supposed to be a noble calling, but they see that many of our public servants in the classroom, our teachers, do their jobs unevenly and sometimes poorly. Millennials have made Teach For America one of the most impressive and successful nongovernmental organizations in the country, and yet the reason Teach For America exists is that there is a fundamental failure of our public school establishment.

To look at it another way, imagine that someone started a new, largely volunteer nonprofit security service to supplement the work of Homeland Security. Our reaction would be, "What is so wrong with Homeland Security that someone had to come up with an alternative?" In the most basic sense, our government has failed the millennial generation in educational opportunities, and they are rising to challenge its failure.

I want to be clear. Of course there are many thousands of excellent teachers in America—and they deserve to be celebrated as American heroes. But just as with any large group, not all teachers are great, or even good. And bad teachers—and the way they are protected by union rules—are having a demonstrably negative effect on the entire educational system.

If Republicans get serious about education reform, which I believe we are in a unique position as a party to do, we will find that we have a wonderful opportunity to connect with millennials. Of all the public policy issues treated in this book—social issues, national security, the environment—the one issue that millennials understand better than anyone else is education. They are the closest to the K–12 experience and they know there are some schools that are fantastic, some teachers who are heroes, and some students who are talented beyond words. But they also know there are other schools that are beyond hopeless, other teachers who are incompetent, and other students who are trapped. If there is a single issue discussed in this book that offers an opportunity for millennials to lead, and on which they have already demonstrated leadership, it is in the crisis in American education.

Republicans can point out to millennials that our unfair educational system is a threat to their long-term economic security. Too often we think of bad schools as a social issue, as if there were no financial cost to a failing school, save the cost of teacher salaries and building maintenance. But the macroeconomic cost of dropouts is devastating. According to a recent McKinsey & Company report, if America had closed the minority achievement gap in 1998—which simply means that if we had brought all student achievement, regardless of race or ethnicity, up to the same level as that of white students—then GDP in 2009 would have been 2 to 4 percent higher. That's equal to about $310 billion to $525 billion of additional economic activity. The same report says that the achievement gap in the United States is equivalent to having "a permanent national recession." The report concludes that "cutting the dropout rate in half would yield $45 billion annually in new federal tax revenues."

The Organization for Economic Cooperation and Development (OECD) has stated that if the United States were to boost its reading, math, and science scores to the levels of those in Finland, the result would be GDP gains "on the order of $103 trillion." These are staggering figures, reflecting a troubling reality.

For millennials struggling to find their footing in a beaten-down U.S. economy, these numbers should be a wake-up call. The past failure of American policy makers to reform our school system has deprived all millennials of a more prosperous economy with more high-paying jobs. So not only have the students in failing schools suffered directly, but everyone else has as well, even those who come from the good zip codes.

The question is: What do we do about it? The first instinct is to spend more money on our schools. This is a completely understandable reaction because we believe, as Americans often believe, that we get what we pay for. But the truth is that in education, we not only don't always get what we pay for, we often get less.

Since World War II, America's spending on students has increased 40 percent per decade, nearly doubling every twenty years. But we're still not even close to leading in math or reading scores at any level. We spend between 41 and 50 percent more money on education than the average OECD country, yet we are near the bottom in the ranking of OECD student test results.

It turns out—yet again—that throwing money at a problem doesn't solve it. Liberals and Democrats have resisted this argument for years, but it has become harder to defend the status quo—let alone to invest more money in it. People are starting to wonder where all those education dollars go. And they are finding out.

If you haven't seen the movie *Waiting for "Superman,"* you are missing out on a powerful depiction of what is wrong with our public schools.

What's remarkable is that this film was made not only by a Democrat but by the same man who made Al Gore's *An Inconvenient Truth*. Davis Guggenheim was determined to present an honest, nonideological picture of what happens in bad schools. He didn't go into the project intending to point fingers but to show how things truly are. He describes how incompetent teachers are protected from dismissal by tenure. He shows how a culture of inertia has taken hold in many schools, scaring away ambitious teachers or forcing them to sell out to mediocrity.

One scene focuses on six hundred New York City teachers who have been suspended, with full pay, for violations ranging from incompetence to sexual abuse of students. These teachers report each day to a central location known as the "rubber room" and spend seven hours sitting around reading newspapers, playing cards, talking—all on the taxpayers' dime. They're impossible to fire because the procedures for terminating their employment are labyrinthine. So each year, these teachers are paid a total of $100 million of New York City and State taxpayer money to do nothing.

At the other extreme are schools that receive less money per pupil than their public counterparts—Catholic schools, charter schools, private academies for poor youth funded by wealthy donors—but have managed to buck the trend. They teach thousands of students from poor neighborhoods each year, and these kids, against incredible odds, manage to learn and manage to succeed. Even in the poorest neighborhoods, education reformers have proved that it is possible to educate disadvantaged students, and by doing so, to break the cycle of poverty.

What these examples demonstrate is not that money is irrelevant—of course schools need money. But far more important is accountability—making sure that teachers are held accountable for their students' learning, that administrators are held accountable for creating a safe and productive learning environment, that schools are held accountable to the parents and the community, and that the students are held accountable to their teachers.

What we have learned from these examples, above all, is that the spirit that drives the lucky and privileged millennials is precisely the spirit we need to see every day throughout our entire school system—a focus on creative solutions, a fundamental belief in the importance of each individual, and an unyielding sense of civic duty, because our schools are a reflection of our national strength and character. Let me share with you some examples of the millennial spirit at work in the area of education reform:

Geoffrey Canada

If the American equivalent of being knighted is being kissed on national TV by Oprah Winfrey, then Geoffrey Canada is a knight of the education reform roundtable.

Canada, who was born in Harlem, has dedicated his life to closing the education achievement gap in the neighborhoods where he grew up. His warm personality is balanced by a quiet determination. After his graduation from Harvard, Canada wanted to give something back to his community by working to turn around New York's schools. He quickly discovered that the teachers' unions would not budge, so he decided to focus on a one-hundred-square-block section of East Harlem that included the poorest neighborhoods in New York City.

In 1990 Canada launched the Harlem Children's Zone. Canada guarantees each of the eleven thousand children in the zone that if they stay with his program, he and his dedicated staff will support them and that they will get into college. The students attend public schools or charter schools, which are publicly chartered schools run without the oversight of the public school system. While it is true that charter schools spend slightly more per pupil—$16,000 versus $14,500 in a traditional public school—they also come with three assets: a 30 percent longer school year, more teacher involvement, and a guarantee against failure. The students are predominantly African-American and Latino. In Harlem, as a result of the good works of the Harlem Children's Zone, they have closed the achievement gap.

Michelle Rhee

When you meet Michelle Rhee, you know exactly what she is focused on: fixing public education in America.

In her first classroom in Baltimore, twenty years ago, she learned that despite the violence, poverty, and broken homes typical of the backgrounds of the majority of her students, excellent teachers could make a profound difference in student performance. She reached a basic conclusion: if the difference between a good school and a bad one is the quality of teachers, then the way to fix failing schools is to replace bad teachers with good ones. At first she dedicated herself to this goal through Teach For America, and then later through a nonprofit she founded called the New Teacher Project. When she met Adrian Fenty, the newly elected Democratic mayor of Washington, D.C., he offered her an opportunity to administer an entire school system. Here was her opportunity to put excellent teachers into an entire system and demonstrate improved results. When she received the power to shut down failing schools and replace bad teachers with good ones, what had previously been the worst school system in the nation was within two years leading the country in gains in math and reading at the fourth- and eighth-grade levels.

Sadly, Rhee's efforts were cut short when Mayor Fenty's rival beat him in a closed Democratic primary, thanks largely to more than $1 million in donations from teachers' unions. Sure enough, the new mayor has promised to roll back some of Rhee's reforms.

Nonetheless, Rhee's lessons endure. She demonstrated that putting excellent teachers in classrooms and incentivizing them to stay can actually improve results in the nation's worst school systems. She often poses this fact to audiences: if you took the bottom 5 percent of teachers in America's schools and replaced them with average teachers, America would go from the bottom half of educational results to being number one in education in the world. She then asks, "What CEO would not choose to fire the bottom 5 percent of underperforming employees to get that better top result in his or her bottom line?"

Rhee was willing to innovate in order to improve educational results. She questioned the teacher pay system in Washington, D.C., which rewarded teachers equally, regardless of the results they achieved. She proposed a merit pay system, especially for younger teachers who were earning $40,000 to $50,000 annually, in which they could more than double their salaries on the basis of excellent performance, with compensation reaching as high as $130,000. In return for this new pay system, teachers would have to give up tenure and thus lifelong job security. Many senior teachers favored the idea, but the teachers' union would not even let its members vote on the proposal.

Rhee's latest project is even more audacious. She has started a political organization called Students First. Inspired by the political arms of teachers' unions, it will raise money to donate to local, state, and national races for mayor and for positions on school boards. In addition, it will organize activists to demonstrate their support on behalf of students. What Rhee has learned is that the next frontier for education reform is not the classroom or the school system, but the ballot box.

Chris Christie

New Jersey's Republican governor has been sharply focused on education reform since he entered office, forming a partnership across partisan lines with Newark mayor Cory Booker to empower local education reformers and do an end run around teachers' union regulations that stifle innovation. Together, they support reforms like merit pay for teachers, charter schools, and school vouchers.

Christie has been willing to close down failing schools and reward a more entrepreneurial approach to education. Facebook founder Mark Zuckerberg donated a $100 million challenge grant in support of local reform efforts. Christie has not been shy about taking on the unions, arguing that we need to put schoolchildren first and focus on classroom results, rather than assume that simply throwing money at the problem is the key to reform, especially during a budget crisis.

Although the state spends nearly $14,000 per pupil, on average—and $24,000 per pupil in Newark—the money invested has failed to produce adequate results. In return for his political courage in taking on the teachers' unions, Christie has suffered vehement political attacks from New Jersey's formidable political Left. In a 2010 e-mail

from Bergen County teachers' union president Joe Coppola to seventeen thousand members, he wrote, "Dear Lord, this year you have
taken away my favorite actor, Patrick Swayze, my favorite actress,
Farrah Fawcett, my favorite singer, Michael Jackson, and my favorite
salesman, Billy Mays. . . . I just wanted to let you know that Chris
Christie is my favorite governor." This public declaration of what
amounts to a death wish directed at a sitting governor for bucking
the failing status quo in education illustrates how deeply entrenched
is the opposition of the teachers' unions to education reform. On
Governor Christie's watch, education reform has been given the priority it deserves, but his efforts, like Michelle Rhee's, prove that politics is the final frontier of true education reform. Christie's leadership
demonstrates that in politics Republicans have a unique opportunity
to save the American educational system because Democrats, who
rely on teachers' union funding to support their reelection bids, are
simply unable to challenge them. When courageous Democrats do
embrace education reform, they find themselves made an example of
by teachers' unions (see Fenty, Adrian).

But we can't all be pioneers like Geoffrey Canada, Michelle
Rhee, or Chris Christie. What can ordinary Republicans do to support the cause of education reform? I suggest we focus on two things.

Educational Democracy

We know that when people have a choice, whether it's between
presidential candidates or brands of soap, there is healthy competition. Choices are good, no matter what kind. One of the most
fascinating trends in the lives of millennials is the rise of educational
democracy: people voting with their feet to increase their educational
options. Most strikingly, millennials have been the first generation in
more than a century to see many of its members schooled at home.
Parents of millennials had good reason to believe that schools were
deficient in critical ways. A motley amalgam of parents—including

highly conservative Christian families, some "crunchy" liberals, and even some Crunchy Conservatives—independently came to the conclusion that our school system was no place for their children. These parents took on the job of homeschooling, providing their children with the quality of education they felt the government was incapable of delivering. From 1994 to 1999, the number of home-schooled children doubled to nearly 900,000. By 2007, the number had nearly doubled again, to 1.5 million.

That's one form of educational democracy in action, but it shouldn't be only for those parents who have the time and energy to devote to their children's educations. All parents should be able to vote with their feet. That means we need to support every effort to open up the school system to competition.

We need measures like the KIPP (Knowledge Is Power Program) academies and the charter school movement. KIPP is a national network of ninety-nine schools in twenty states and Washington, D.C., that serve more than twenty-six thousand students, from fifth grade through high school. After four years at KIPP schools, 100 percent of eighth-grade classes outperformed their district averages in both mathematics and reading, based on state tests. After four years at KIPP, these same students are performing at the eightieth percentile in math and the fifty-eighth percentile in reading. More than 85 percent of KIPP graduates are attending college. But KIPP schools are focused on lower-income students. We need competition at all levels of education.

School systems should welcome charter schools and promote magnet programs that focus on special curricula and even voucher systems that allow parents to move their tax dollars to the school of their choice.

I'll concede that vouchers are controversial. Some people oppose them because if parents use them at parochial schools, this might breach constitutional barriers against public tax money going to religious institutions. But most resistance comes from teachers' unions that don't want to see tax dollars shifted from unionized public schools to nonunionized private ones. I also suspect that some opposition is driven by people living in wealthy areas, who benefit from the geographic desirability of good school districts. When you live in a high-quality school district, it amounts to an artificial cushion inflating the value of your home. Families will always want to live in the neighborhoods that feed into the best schools.

What we have is a system in which those with high incomes and pricey homes get the best schools, which are both publicly subsidized and unlikely to admit students from low-income families. This amounts to a state-sanctioned limitation on social mobility.

Democrats have sought for years to block vouchers. President Bush and the Republican Congress created the Opportunity Scholarship Program, a small voucher program to allow Washington's underprivileged children to attend top-quality private schools, including the school that President Obama's daughters attend. But as soon as Democrats regained control of Congress, they phased out the program. One has to wonder what the Democrats were so afraid of: a few thousand poor kids attending private schools on taxpayer dollars? Indeed, what could be more in keeping with the American ideal of giving every child an opportunity to receive a high-quality education?

Such is the orthodoxy that is perpetuated by teachers' unions, which pledge themselves to one purpose: protecting public schoolteachers' jobs. And so another top priority must be to end the monopoly of the unions in order to empower education reformers.

Checking the Teachers' Unions

After Hurricane Katrina in 2005, roughly one-third of the city of New Orleans moved away. But this tragedy turned out to be an opportunity for the city's failing schools.

Before Katrina, 64 percent of New Orleans schools had been classified as "academically unacceptable" by the state of Louisiana. The school board president at the time, Ellenese Brooks-Simms, had been convicted for taking bribes; the FBI was investigating fiscal wrongdoing by the New Orleans Parish School Board, and the system had been officially declared financially bankrupt. As the city's public employees temporarily vacated New Orleans, so too did the teachers' unions, which had been the primary impediment to education reform. In that small window of time, education reformers seized their opportunity to implement meaningful reforms.

Three months after Katrina, a plan for the Louisiana Recovery School District was implemented by the state. The school district would be funded publicly, but many schools would be run privately, and they would compete with one another. The schools were given the authority to hire and fire their own teachers, without interference from the teachers' unions. The district found itself deluged with applications from teachers eager to work in a system that embraced an education reform agenda and rewarded outstanding performance.

Almost immediately, educational performance improved. The number of academically unacceptable schools is now down by more than a third, and student test scores have improved dramatically. A report by the Cowen Institute, a Tulane University think tank that monitors the school district's progress, tells a positive story: "Over half of all voters and over two-thirds of parents in the Cowen Institute's poll agreed" that "teachers are improving education in New Orleans." And the unions are not part of this story.

The opportunity New Orleans experienced in the absence of its teachers' unions in the months immediately following Hurricane Katrina illustrates an emerging consensus in America about education reform.

Public education is a highly regulated, union-dominated public monopoly that discourages the innovation necessary to solve its problems. Extraordinary individuals from all sides of the political spectrum are arriving at the same conclusions: the teachers' unions are failing our students, and the best way to fix education is to support competitive networks of private, charter, and magnet schools as an alternative. Many of today's education reformers, such as Geoffrey Canada and organizations like KIPP schools, are committed to developing programs that are insulated from the outsize influence of teachers' unions so they can focus on teaching students and avoid the political battles that have come to characterize the education agenda in America.

But others, such as Michelle Rhee, think this is not enough. They believe that the political influence of the unions has grown so strong that networks that circumvent the teachers' unions will only help a small percentage of America's disadvantaged youth. They think the time has come for the political power of the unions to be confronted head-on and for alternative political organizations to be built to compete and challenge their monopoly on the education agenda.

In this debate, Republicans have a unique opportunity to be the champions of meaningful education reform precisely because the Democrats' hands are tied. Teachers' unions are among the largest and most influential donors to the Democratic Party. In 2008, 10 percent of the delegates to the Democratic convention were representatives of two unions: the American Federation of Teachers (AFT) and the National Education Association (NEA). These two national teachers' unions donate more money to Democratic candidates and causes than any other special interest group in politics—more than the National Rifle Association, more than the pharmaceutical lobby, more even than the bigger Service Employees International Union (SEIU). Just follow the money and you'll find that in 2010, the NEA, the largest teachers' union in the country, contributed nearly $40 million to Democratic candidates in races throughout the country.

Education reform is the civil rights issue of our time, and the Republican Party can engage the millennial generation by declaring that the status quo is fundamentally unfair and dangerous for our long-term economic prosperity.

In becoming the party that champions education reform, Republicans will connect with a new generation of voters by demonstrating that we can deliver them a fairer, more effective system. Because Democrats think of themselves as the party of civil rights, the tables will turn, forcing Democrats to choose between protecting the interests of teachers' unions and the interests of African-Americans, Latinos, Native-Americans, and every other community unfairly treated by the public school system. It will give Republicans a chance to remind the entire nation that it is the Party of Lincoln, the party that abolished slavery in the nineteeth century, that is best suited to end the gross injustice of our school system in the twenty-first century.

Education reform is also an issue that can unite the Republican coalition. Christian conservatives, libertarians, and mainstream Republicans can all come together behind the education reform movement, a movement that champions individual freedom, choice, competition, and innovation. This united coalition should not be afraid to stick up for Democrats like Michelle Rhee and Adrian Fenty and thousands of other reformers in communities across America who are willing to stand up to the teachers' unions.

The issue of education has traditionally been a Democratic issue. But when it comes to improving our schools, Democrats have only two ideas: pump more money into public school budgets and defend teachers' unions under all circumstances. After decades of declining performance and rising costs, this is a stale argument. Americans of all ages, races, and economic backgrounds are desperate for new ideas and new thinking. They are ready for a fresh start. Now is the moment for Republicans to embrace a bold education reform agenda, take on the teachers' unions, and harness the enthusiasm of the millennial generation.

CHAPTER 7

A NEW REPUBLICAN FEMINISM

*"The Independent Girl prefers to fight her own battles in this life,
and sallies forth to each encounter with a martial spirit which
is quite startling."*

—LOU HENRY HOOVER, 1890

FOR AS LONG as I've been alive, the word *feminism* has been used as an expletive among conservatives and Republicans.

It probably didn't help that the background noise of my formative political years was punctuated by Rush Limbaugh's tirades about "feminazis," his crude code word for radical feminists. And my parents certainly thought the feminists of the late 1960s and 1970s went too far, by pushing an agenda that seemed to denigrate a woman's traditional role in the family as mother, wife, and household leader—all positions my mother and grandmother were proud to hold. But I was hardly alone in my aversion to the "feminist" label. The fact is, most women do not think of themselves as feminists. The last time Gallup asked the question, in 2001, only 25 percent of American women called themselves feminists.

And yet, most women sympathize broadly with some of the core successes of the modern feminist movement, specifically that women are empowered to have careers and the same social standing and legal rights enjoyed by men, in the classroom, the workplace, and all other areas of public and private life.

At the heart of contemporary feminism is something that most modern women hold dear: reproductive freedom, meaning control over when they become pregnant and whether to carry a pregnancy to term.

But "feminism" itself continues to get bad press. Lingering associations with Far Left feminists of the 1960s and 1970s are the main reason. These have stigmatized the movement, identifying it with a radical agenda that has often had little to do with the daily lives of ordinary women, and much to do with the political ideology and pet causes of its leadership.

Feminist organizations alienated more people than they attracted with bra-burning protests and negative obsessions with the "male patriarchy." They made abortion rights a core issue, perhaps with sound motives, but too often they displayed a knack for offending pro-life women. They spoke about America itself being "oppressive." And too seldom did they have positive things to say about men.

Recently, I was in a used-book store and came across a classic example of why this strain of feminism degenerated into an absurd stereotype. It was a 1972 issue of *Ms. Magazine,* the feminist bible of the Gloria Steinem era. In bold across the top of the cover was a headline article titled "Body Hair—The Final Frontier for Female Liberation." The article took the position that women should follow the example of men and stop shaving their legs, armpits, et cetera. The piece made me laugh and cringe at the same time. If we women try to assert our equality by not shaving our legs, I thought, we won't get equality, we'll just get more hair!

The next generation of feminists—the millennial generation— is more interested in individual liberty than in the hazy concept of "women's liberation." We want to *embrace* our femininity, not try to become more like men. We recognize that men and women are different—although we expect equality of opportunity in American society. We understand that we have benefited from the extraordinary effort of the pioneering women who pushed for equal rights for more than a century before us. What is interesting, and important, is that the millennial approach to feminism echoes the approach of the first wave of feminist suffragists, who framed their case for a woman's right to vote in the individual freedom enshrined in the American republic's founding documents.

I am humbled when I read about the accomplishments of women such as Elizabeth Cady Stanton and Susan B. Anthony, who agitated for the right to vote in the nineteenth and early twentieth centuries. In order to popularize their movement, they formed alliances with contemporary evangelical figures and prohibitionists such as Frances Willard. It has largely been forgotten that many of these pioneering feminists were *Republicans,* proud members of the Party of Lincoln. Christina Hoff Sommers, of the American Enterprise Institute, has written extensively about this first wave of egalitarian and conservative feminists. They were strong, independent-minded women with the courage of their convictions.

My great-grandmother Lou Henry Hoover belonged to this first wave of American feminists—although she would have preferred the label "American individualist." She was the first woman to graduate with a degree in geology from Stanford University. She was an early supporter of and lifelong leader in the Girl Scout movement, which helped to expose girls to much more than traditional household duties. She promoted the idea that there was a life for girls and women in the outdoors, in small business, and in charitable service to others. Challenging the conventional wisdom of the era, she endorsed the idea that girls should have access to the same experiences and opportunities as boys—and be treated as individuals and equals.

I certainly recognize the victories won by the second wave of feminists, in the 1960s and 1970s. While this wave had its political radicals, and generated the inevitable popular backlash, Americans have by and large internalized their core arguments as our culture has witnessed the progressive integration of women into society.

The change has been particularly evident in the workplace. In the early 1960s, when my mom joined the workforce, to the extent that women worked at all, they became secretaries, nurses, and teachers. If they happened to be especially pretty, they might become an airline stewardess, as my mother did. As glamorous as it was at the time to fly the friendly skies, it was by no means a work environment that millennial women would consider attractive.

Airline stewardesses had regular weigh-ins to ensure they stayed slim, and they donned miniskirts for work on all-male flights. My mother tells of female supervisors patting her down to make sure she wore a corset (she didn't; at 105 pounds, it was pointless). When these young women decided to marry, company policy forced them to quit their jobs. Many simply didn't tell their employers that they had gotten married—an act of dishonesty, to be sure, but one forced on them by an unfair and deeply sexist policy.

It's hard to believe these were standard practices at any American company just forty years ago. Today shows like *Mad Men* turn the memories of that era's misogyny and sexism into period entertainment, costume dramas about the distant past. Not only have women come a long way; the whole nation has.

When I decided to attend Bryn Mawr, an all-women's college, my father feared that bra-burning, male-hating, radicalized "feminazis" would have a pernicious influence on his daughter. And when my parents heard that Gloria Steinem had visited our campus, they were convinced I'd end up an acolyte of these 1970s radicals.

Much to their relief, I never embraced the radical feminism championed by faculty at my college; nor did the overwhelming majority of my friends. I recognize fully that there are challenges unique to me as a woman—not the least the challenge of someday balancing children and a career—but I never blamed an oppressive male patriarchy, as some professors no doubt hoped I would. I saw the challenges of being a woman as *personal* challenges, not social injustices, and I refused to see myself as a victim because of my gender.

What's more, I have found that my friends and most millennial women have made the same choice. When a guy treats a woman poorly, she doesn't detect a patriarchal plot to repress women but a particular jerk who needs to be put in his place.

Challenges remain: for example, even as women's freedom in the United States and the West is at an all-time high, women still haven't achieved full parity with men on the salary scale. While reveling in women's hard-won freedoms, we should not indulge in complacency. Even so, it's worth appreciating that American women today are fortunate to have been born in this country at this time in history.

So the aims of second-wave 1970s feminism have largely been internalized, while its excesses—and the label itself—have for the most part been abandoned. Nonetheless, many feminists who came of age in the 1960s and 1970s are still wedded to the identity politics of their youth, when any random issue might serve to feed the fires of group grievance.

But the millennial generation doesn't warm to identity politics. In fact, they are a "postgrievance" generation concerned with finding solutions and solving problems rather than angry finger-pointing. They are individualists first and foremost. They are uncomfortable blaming an entire group of people for any particular social ill. In addition, they're disenchanted with the hyperpartisanship they hear in the media on both the Left and the Right, especially from commentators who demonize their opponents instead of giving them the benefit of the doubt and trying to solve problems together in a constructive spirit of compromise. A feminism that appeals to the millennials isn't going to look anything like the earlier version of feminism, which they soundly reject.

Perhaps the most compelling recent example of this generational split was evident in the 2008 presidential nomination battle within the Democratic Party. Hillary Clinton's campaign was a milestone for second-wave feminists. She was, after all, a product of that wave, and firmly anchored in female identity politics. Women made up her most loyal base of support. The best-remembered line of her concession speech celebrated her supporters as "18 million cracks in the glass ceiling." And to this day, many of Clinton's longtime supporters believe that 2008 was the greatest opportunity of their lifetime to see a woman elected to the White House.

Contrast this with Barack Obama's campaign. He, not Hillary, won the hearts, minds, and votes of millennials. He accomplished this not because he was the African-American candidate or because he was the younger candidate. Neither his race nor his youth defined him. He did not campaign as the "black candidate" for president, as had other African-Americans before him. Candidate Obama was able to transcend identity politics, to the extent that some older African-American leaders initially distrusted him: they weren't sure he was "black enough," and Jesse Jackson even accused him of "acting white." Candidate Obama's postracial, postgrievance, and postpartisan rhetoric appealed to the sensibilities of millennials in a way that Hillary Clinton's female identity politics could not.

One of these days, when a woman is finally elected president (and I believe we're closer to crossing that threshold than many people think), she will have won not by pandering to a sense of grievance or by identifying herself politically as a woman but simply by demonstrating outstanding leadership. While millennial women are perfectly happy to revel in "girl power," they do not think of women as a special interest group. They understand that, in a fluid society, special interest groups end up *dis*empowering people by confining them to group definitions, and thereby undermining their individuality. Just as the sexism of the 1960s and earlier robbed women of their dreams and their voices, radical feminism's groupthink deprived individual women of the ability to think for themselves, act for themselves, and be themselves.

Millennial women have discovered that life is not an all-or-nothing, zero-sum game where women gain by men losing. For example, if women assert their sexual freedom by making sexual spectacles of themselves, we don't become freer—we just give men a cheap thrill. The increase in sexual freedom for women since the sexual revolution has done nothing to reduce the sexual objectification of women in our culture, on college campuses in particular. A sexual double standard is still in place. The negative consequences of all this are often deeply psychological, but they are also physical—the rise of sexually transmitted diseases among college-educated millennial women is one of the most underreported demographic stories today. People will say we need to practice safe sex, but the deeper lesson here is that we must use our sexual freedom more responsibly.

Millennials are the first generation raised with the concept of co-parenting, where both parents share parenting duties. The millennial experience has ushered in a reevaluation of traditional gender roles in the home, a rejection of the traditional division-of-duties family model of male breadwinner and female caretaker.

And, finally, in a comical epilogue to the *Ms. Magazine* issue that called for the free growth of women's body hair as a political final frontier, it's hard to escape the fact that women's grooming has actually gone in the opposite direction. Millennial generation women have been far more aggressive in *removing* unwanted hair than their mothers and grandmothers. But, ironically, so have men, many of whom engage in a bit of "man-scaping." So, while we didn't follow the prescriptions of the 1970s feminists when it came to body hair, we did end up achieving more egalitarian grooming practices! Who knew?

What's the bottom line? The zero-sum formulas—when women

gain, men give in—that may have been effective in helping women win basic legal rights, employment rights, and social rights become counterproductive when the issues get more complicated and come down to individual tastes and preferences.

The direction of feminism in America has huge implications for the major political parties and their platforms. That the Democratic Party has had a lock on the hearts of women is a truism. But beneath the surface a change is under way. Millennial women have made it clear that they aren't sold on the Democratic Party's adherence to female identity politics. If Republicans recognize this fact, and then act on it, we have an opportunity to capture the votes of millennial women.

I believe that millennial women are looking for a new approach to issues, one that recognizes the differences between men and women, and between women and other women—a philosophy that is deeply individualized. We need, in other words, a modern feminism rooted in the principles of American individualism.

And here the Republican Party has an opening. The GOP has an opportunity to build a new *Republican* feminism that can speak to the next generation of women. This new Republican feminism should reject the limits and arguments of identity politics and recognize that all issues are "women's issues." New Republican feminism should support the spectrum of life choices available to women, such as whether to stay at home as a primary parent or pursue a high-powered career. If men and women have equal opportunities to make successful careers, then either parent can opt to stay home as the primary caregiver. Each woman, and each family, will have the freedom to figure it out individually.

The new Republican feminism would see women as individuals first and would value each woman's unique and God-given combination of intelligence, character, skill, and creativity. Republican feminism would call upon each woman to stand up, apply her talents, contribute to society, and earn the full reward for her efforts in the free and open market. This is what millennial women want and expect—no special favors, no preferences, no barriers.

Millennial women also need new role models as diverse as the many paths they can follow—women who have both careers and families, or only families, or only careers. These include women who are scientists, nurses and physicians, astronauts, artists, journalists, and stay-at-home moms. All these role models—and many, many others I haven't listed—are essential to helping younger women determine which career and life paths might be most viable and rewarding for them. Republicans should encourage women to explore this entire spectrum of choices.

A new Republican feminism will be built upon a foundation of equality of opportunity, as well as a recognition that great gains have been made for women over the last quarter-century. But Republican feminism must also recognize that equal opportunity doesn't guarantee equal outcomes, as evidenced by the fact that there aren't yet nearly as many women as men running major organizations, occupying corner offices, or walking the halls of Congress. Despite this persistent inequality, Republican feminism should respect men as *partners* in achieving equality of opportunity and should avoid blaming men and the "oppressive male patriarchy" as we continue to work together in order to achieve genuinely equal opportunity for all women and men.

A new Republican feminism should also recognize that the most urgent battles in the twenty-first century for feminism are not those fought in the arena of American politics, but the ongoing struggles for fundamental freedom in the developing world.

Radical campus feminists sometimes forget that there are corners of the world where questions such as "Is Barbie encouraging bulimia?" are absurdly irrelevant to the more severe oppression women still endure; places where women's genitalia are mutilated,

where women are sold as property, trafficked as sex slaves, or murdered by their own family members in order to satisfy antiquated
notions of family honor.

That's why a new Republican feminism should be focused on
exporting the rights that American women have already achieved to
ever larger numbers of women around the world. It is time to put
feminism in a broader, more global context by championing not just
equality of opportunity at home, but the cause of human rights in
countries where women are too often still second-class citizens.

The next wave of feminism is global feminism, and it's being
fought on the front lines by the most inspiring of women who are
surviving and triumphing against the most barbaric societal and cultural inequalities.

Consider Somaly Mam, a survivor of Cambodia's sex trade, who
was sold into slavery at the age of ten and raped daily for several
years. Today she is a fully rehabilitated survivor who has devoted
herself to eliminating sexual slavery worldwide and whose individual
efforts have rescued more than six thousand girls from the horrors of
sexual trafficking and empowered them to pursue productive lives
within their societies.

A new Republican feminism that is global in scope will also support women like Ayaan Hirsi Ali, a Somali who was the victim of
the most misogynistic of cultural practices when she was forced to
undergo genital mutilation at a young age. She managed to flee an
arranged marriage as a young women by seeking political asylum
in the Netherlands, where she achieved citizenship and became a
member of parliament. After radicalized Islamists murdered Theo
Van Gogh and threatened Ali's life for a film they made criticizing
the lack of women's rights in certain Muslim communities, she has
become an international icon. Now she is an outspoken advocate for
liberating young women from the repressive practices of radicalized
Islamist men who perpetrate "honor crimes" on Muslim women

living in the West, and who refuse to assimilate into Western society and treat Muslim women with the dignity and respect that Western laws demand.

Women such as Nobel Peace Prize winner Aung San Suu Kyi, who until recently was a political prisoner in her home country of Myanmar, is another icon, a vocal opponent of her country's tyrannical government who has paid a high price for her leadership role in Burma's National League for Democracy (NLD) Party, standing in firm opposition to the ruling military junta. Her recent release from a seven-year detainment has reenergized the majority of Burmese citizens who hope that her leadership can help bring democracy to their country.

All of these women are survivors who have transcended the most difficult of human circumstances and who serve as role models for a new generation of feminists. A new Republican feminism will focus its energies on achieving freedom and equal opportunity for women everywhere—which means not just achieving full parity with men in America but also standing with women who struggle for basic human rights beyond our shores.

A new Republican feminism, in order to connect with millennial women, should understand that women can have diverse views about the traditional centerpiece of the feminist agenda: reproductive freedom. Millennial women feel that abortion, while an essential choice for women, is often not the right choice for individual women, and they value independence on this most personal of decisions. For example, a prominent millennial Republican, Meghan McCain, is pro-life, but she would never insist that her view, or the law, should prevent other millennials from being pro-choice. Republicans will have a much better chance of winning the support of millennial women if the party does not impose a pro-life (or pro-choice) litmus test.

In some ways, this new Republican feminism has already gained a foothold in Republican politics. Look at the new class of women elected in 2010: governors such as Susana Martinez, Nikki Haley, and Mary Falin—and members of Congress such as Nan Hayworth, Ann Marie Buerkle, and Senator Kelly Ayotte. These women represent the diversity of choices enjoyed by many modern women: they are mothers and grandmothers, they are wives and career women, and they don't represent a monolithic opinion on the issue of reproductive freedom.

This new Republican feminism is already making the case that *all* issues are women's issues. When Republican congresswoman Cathy McMorris Rodgers ran for reelection in 2010 while pregnant with her second child, she campaigned to overturn President Obama's health-care legislation by addressing women who were small-business owners. Since women are responsible for two-thirds of all small-business start-ups in the United States, women were disproportionately hurt by the exorbitant costs associated with the health insurance premium spikes that resulted from implementation of the unpopular health-care law.

Of course, it's impossible to talk about a new Republican feminism without bringing in Sarah Palin, who has herself refused to reject the feminist label. Forget that you might not agree with everything Palin says. She is the first Republican woman to appear on a national ticket, yet as a candidate she never once played the woman card. She embraced her femininity and her motherhood, but never made these the most important features of her candidacy.

The Feminist Left's hypocrisy rose to new heights when Palin hit the national scene. She was criticized for her participation in beauty contests and ridiculed as "Caribou Barbie." (Apparently, objectifying women is fine with left-wing feminists if those women don't share your politics.) Sandra Bernhard, the activist and feminist actress, even warned Sarah Palin that she'd be "gang-raped by my big black brothers if she enters Manhattan." Such ugly utterances about another woman by self-proclaimed feminists demonstrate exactly why so many women reject the label "feminist."

In the end, Sarah Palin's image may have been too maligned during the campaign for her to have any chance to become a hero to millennial women. To be sure, some of that damage was self-inflicted, but much of it resulted from a smear campaign orchestrated, ironically, by women. When it came down to it, Palin represented the greatest threat to old-line feminism—a woman who had benefited from its earlier activism but who did not share its political views, especially on the question of reproductive freedom.

I hope the variety of the women whom Republicans have elected in 2010 will catalyze the formation of a new Republican feminism, one that respects the instincts of individualism intrinsic to the first-wave American feminism and helps Republicans build a bridge to the millennial generation. In this way the Republican Party can return feminism to its roots, to its genesis in the Party of Lincoln, by engaging the political, professional, and personal challenges and choices faced by American women in the twenty-first century. Republicans have an opportunity to reach out to the millennial generation with a new Republican feminism, grounded in American individualism. *Feminism* doesn't *have* to be a dirty word, least of all to Republicans.

CHAPTER 8

THE CHOICE DILEMMA

"The federal government has no business deciding the wrongness or rightness of a woman having an abortion."
—BARRY GOLDWATER

I WAS NINETEEN WHEN I learned that a friend of mine had had an abortion. She was older than I was and confided that when she was sixteen, she had become pregnant, and her family had taken her to a clinic to undergo the procedure. Since then, she told me, every time she saw a little girl, she felt overcome by sadness. Something deep within her sensed that she had lost her own little girl.

Her sense of loss struck me. It had been six years since she had had the abortion, but to her it still felt like yesterday. For all the pro-choice arguments that focus on women's rights and reproductive freedom, I had never heard any "cons" that spoke of the emotional hardships of a would-be mother after undergoing an abortion. Surely a fetus was more than just tissue, and an abortion more than a simple medical procedure, if a young woman's emotions pulsed so strongly six years later. This personal connection with a friend's residual emotional pain from having an abortion was, for me, dramatic evidence that the choice to have an abortion wasn't as straightforward as the pro-choice activists would have us believe.

Five years later, I learned that a colleague of mine had become pregnant as a teen. Her religious beliefs had prevented her from considering an abortion, but her parents' disapproval forced her to hide her pregnancy until the school year was over and she was able to go away for the summer to have her baby. She arranged for help through a Catholic charity that supported her with room and board in a neighboring state, and also arranged for an adoption after her son was born. Tears streamed down her face as she recounted this story to me. She told me that she was tortured by the sight of stretch marks every morning in the shower. Where was her son now? she wondered. How had his life turned out? Giving up a baby to whom she had given birth, forfeiting the joy and fulfillment of holding the child she felt kick inside her for weeks, proved to be the most heart-wrenching experience of her life. This friend went on to finish high school, graduate from a top-tier university, and be accepted by one of America's premier law schools. But she never stopped wondering, *Did I make the right choice?*

These two women represent the two outcomes of the pro-choice/pro-life "best-case scenario" for teen pregnancy. One terminated an untimely pregnancy; the other carried the baby to term but gave it up. But both choices left painful emotional scars. From these two friends I learned that the practical reality of abortion and teenage motherhood is far more personal and complex than the polarized abortion debates in America suggest. It's easy to form hypothetical opinions about teenage parenthood, teenage sex, and abortion, but these real-life personal experiences exposed layers of the issue that I hadn't previously considered. And real-life experience *must* inform our discussion about abortion. My awareness of each friend's tragic situation caused me to reevaluate the pro-life/pro-choice absolutists who dominate this political debate in America while observing the issue's deeply personal and individual dimensions.

From my friends' practical experiences I learned that neither option, abortion or adoption, is a total win-win situation for the would-be teen mother. I could see that the black-and-white terms of the pro-choice versus pro-life debate fail to capture the simple but essential fact that there are no easy answers to teen pregnancy, or to the question of abortion in general. And so, like many women, I have views on abortion that are shaped by my personal interactions and experiences.

As I mentioned earlier, Irving Kristol once joked that a neoconservative was a liberal who'd been mugged by reality. I think that on the abortion issue, people on one or another side of the issue find themselves mugged by reality—pro-lifers with a pregnant teenage daughter, pro-choicers staring at an ultrasound three months after conception. The only option for me and, as it turns out, for most Americans, is to take a position that fully considers every side of this highly charged debate.

I'm with those people who adhere to a position that can be defined as "personally pro-life but politically pro-choice"—which is to say that I believe abortion is wrong, but nevertheless I think it should be legal, limited, and safe. This point of view pleases neither the pro-choice crowd nor the pro-life crowd, but it puts me in agreement with 78 percent of Republican voters, according to a 2008 study, who believe that "a woman, not the government, should make the decision to have an abortion."

A conservative movement that hopes to appeal to the millennial generation cannot make abortion a simple rallying cry, a litmus test, or a wedge issue, as have previous generations. Millennials take a mature view of this moral dilemma. While teen pregnancy first spiked and then recently hit new lows in their lifetimes, they've been inundated by a hypersexualized pop culture, and confronted by celebrity teen parents from Jamie Lynn Spears to Bristol Palin, pro-life movies like *Juno,* and reality TV series like *16 and Pregnant.* Millennials don't pay attention to the tired, predictable hyperpartisanship of the second-wave feminists and their detractors, who have been going at it since long before they were born. Remember that millennials abhor perfunctory partisanship; as soon as they hear someone spouting one-sided opinions, they become suspicious.

Which means the call-and-response of "Baby killer!" and "Take your laws out of my uterus!" screamed back and forth by activist extremists on each side of this debate are bound to alienate millennials, who, like most Americans, understand that the simplistic labels "pro-life" and "pro-choice" don't begin to describe the moral complexity of abortion.

The truth is that millennials' sensibilities on abortion mirror those of a majority of Americans. Recently there has been an uptick in the popularity of the term *pro-life*—though it hasn't been paired with a comparable rise in support for the effort to make abortion illegal. So while more than half of Americans of all ages view abortion as morally unacceptable, they are unwilling to see it outlawed in all circumstances.

Meghan McCain best describes the sensibilities of her generation on this issue: she is "pro-sex" and "pro-life" (and pro–gay marriage, incidentally). But she also specifies that this is her *personal* decision, and she wouldn't want to impose her views on anyone else. This position does not fit neatly into the old polarized, all-or-nothing activist position, but it reflects a generational sensibility that allows for personal stands of conscience without demonizing those who hold different viewpoints. A full range of opinion is respected, and there is an appreciation for the diversity of real-life decisions and compassion for those who must make them.

The Two Extremes

Pro-life absolutists leave no room for doubt. They believe that abortion should be illegal in every circumstance, including cases of incest and rape. Only when the mother's life is in danger do these ideologues pause to reflect on the complexity of this question. Suddenly "pro-life" is forced to confront a choice: which life is more valuable, the mother's or the unborn child's?   .

Remember, the *life* in the "pro-life" political position doesn't refer to the already living and independently functioning woman. It refers to the fetus developing in utero, which science has demonstrated to be more than what the radical pro-choicers dismiss as mere cells and tissue, but is still unable to survive outside the womb. From the most extreme pro-life perspective, the mother's well-being is considered secondary.

But what about a woman's ability to judge her own emotional, economic, and physical capacity to carry a child to term, and then to raise it or give it up for adoption instead? Does it make sense for the federal government to decide unilaterally, on behalf of all pregnant women, that under no circumstances should they ever have the right to choose to have an abortion? I say no.

Fundamentally, the pro-life position places the state's moral judgment ahead of the individual's. While it is clear that the state has the right—even the obligation—to protect life, the matter of abortion is unique. The question of when life begins and what protections should be accorded to the unborn are open to significant debate. And given that individuals will draw their own conclusions about the starting point of human life, an absolutist position is necessarily arbitrary. Should the federal government have the authority to make that decision? The conservatism that I've always subscribed to, that is consistent with maximum individual freedom and choice, would hold that it does not. While there is significant disagreement among the conservative movement's factions on this point, a conservatism that will appeal to the millennial generation will argue that within limits this is an individual decision among a woman, her family, her doctor, and her God, not the government.

How, then, did it come to pass that the Republican Party, that staunch champion of freedom, autonomy, and individual responsibility, supports the idea that the federal government should make these moral and biological decisions for all its citizens? In the case of abortion, the Republican Party assumes that the government can make a uniform choice for all women, in all circumstances, always. But conservatives generally say they believe that individuals make the best choices for themselves.

Is it any wonder that there is a gender gap in American politics? According to Gallup, 41 percent of women identify themselves as Democrats, 29 percent as Independents, and only 27 percent as Republicans. Perhaps this gap exists because the Republican Party, which pledges itself to smaller government, makes an exception in the case of women's most private and personal decisions.

But if moral certainty is the illness of the Right, moral surrender is the illness of the Left. Pro-choice absolutists believe that a woman should always be able to have an abortion, at any point in her pregnancy, even in the third trimester when a fetus is sufficiently developed to survive outside the womb. Consider the practice of "partial-birth" abortion. The procedure, which is now banned in most cases, strikes a majority of Americans as barbaric. Yet pro-choice absolutists insist that it is essential to reproductive rights, and they reject any effort to restrict it. Pro-choice absolutists also argue that taxpayers should help pay for abortions, both domestically and internationally. While most Americans oppose such subsidies, and the Hyde Amendment bans federal taxpayer funding of abortion, pro-choice absolutists say that denying such support is tantamount to restricting a woman's freedom.

The truth is that both extremes are wrong. An unwanted pregnancy is a dilemma, not a straightforward choice. It is a dilemma because all the alternatives are terrible. Rarely does a pro-choicer candidly address the *tragedy* of abortion—not just the tragedy of the act but the often long-lasting impact on the mother, manifested in profound feelings of remorse and regret. And similarly, rarely does a pro-lifer seriously address the gritty realities of teenage sex and unintended pregnancies, other than to preach the virtues of abstinence education. In a pro-lifer's ideal society there are no abortions and no birth control—and no sex before marriage.

Each side argues that Americans can't afford to equivocate on this issue. On the one hand, if life begins at conception, abortion is state-sanctioned infanticide. On the other hand, if a woman has a right to make decisions about her body and her future, what difference does it make whether she is two months pregnant or seven or even nine months pregnant? When do the rights of the life *inside* the mother outweigh the rights of the life of the mother? To pro-choice absolutists, the answer is never. To pro-life absolutists, the answer is always. For the majority of Americans, the answer is somewhere in between—in the first or second trimester, but not in the third.

For the hyperpolarized set, these all-or-nothing pro-life/pro-choice debates are good for business. They push people in the middle away from the kind of consensus that, opinion polls indicate, actually exists on the issue and toward implacably hostile poles of opinion. But what's good for the absolutists on either side is bad for those with unplanned pregnancies, and it's bad for our ability to talk openly about the financial, emotional, and practical challenges related to one of life's most painful personal dilemmas.

Most Americans, including millennials, reject the extremes on this issue, and instead have arrived organically at a consensus. Slim majorities of Americans *call* themselves pro-life, but most Americans—by a slightly larger majority—agree that abortion should remain legal. Most Americans take a pragmatic rather than an ideological approach, one that falls between the extremes: abortion should be rare, but a woman's decision should be left up to her.

While most Americans view abortion as morally wrong (Gallup 2010: 50 percent–38 percent), they nonetheless have a positive view of *Roe v. Wade,* the Supreme Court ruling that says a woman has a constitutional right to get an abortion within the first trimester. When Gallup last asked the question "Would you like to see the Supreme Court overturn its 1973 *Roe versus Wade* decision concerning abortion, or not?," only 33 percent of respondents replied in favor, while 52 percent said they were against overturning, and 15 percent had no opinion.

Polling also shows that Americans favor reasonable restrictions on the right to have an abortion. The majority are opposed to abortions in the final trimester: months seven, eight, and nine. They favor parental notification laws when minors seek abortions, and they don't think people's tax dollars should have to pay for abortions.

Even most Republicans agree with these views, according to Republican Majority for Choice, a pro-choice Republican group. Here are some surprising results from their 2008 poll of Republicans on the issue of abortion:

- "54% of self-described pro-life Republicans believe that women should have access to the full range of reproductive options including education, contraception, motherhood, adoption and abortion."
- "74% of Republican voters do not support an addition to the GOP platform that calls for a Constitutional Amendment that would ban all abortion, even without exceptions for rape and the life and health of the mother."
- "81% of Republicans support a GOP platform that states 'members of the GOP have differing views on the issue of abortion, and we should respectfully agree to disagree.' " [In fact, 78% of *pro-life* Republicans support a GOP platform that states that

members of the GOP have differing views on the issue of abortion, and we should respectfully agree to disagree.]

- "50% of Republicans believe that platform language that takes a specific position on the issue of abortion or other personal or moral choices is polarizing and contributes to the wedge within the Republican Party."

Despite this considerable common ground, there is a small but dedicated wing of social conservatives whose religious beliefs forbid them from conceding an inch. These anti-abortion activists are sincere in their beliefs and guided by the certainty that comes with believing they are doing God's will. This does not leave much room for disagreement or even civil conversation. The sole purpose of one of these groups, RNC for Life, is to ensure that the Republican Party remains the pro-life party, and moreover that it maintains its support for a human life amendment to the Constitution. Forget the fact that throughout its history the conservative movement has supported economic and domestic policies that put a premium on individual freedom and has sought to limit the intrusion of government into people's lives. When it comes to abortion politics, the Republican Party is beholden to its special interests.

Bad Politics

The irony, of course, is that every moment spent on the disagreement within the party on the subject of abortion is a moment lost for pursuing larger goals as a unified group. Compared with issues like the economy, fighting Islamist terrorism, reforming entitlements, and reining in debt and deficits, abortion is a second-tier issue. For the vast majority of American voters, it is one of many issues they consider when voting for a candidate. When the question was last asked by Gallup, only 15 percent of pro-lifers say a candidate must share their view. Eleven percent of pro-choicers say the same thing. That leaves 74 percent of the electorate willing to vote for someone who doesn't share their view on abortion.

Nevertheless, abortion remains a first-tier issue for an influential fraction of the Republican Party, a group that has considerable sway over the rest of the party apparatus. It conditions its support for the party on the presence in the party platform of a pledge to introduce a constitutional amendment on human life. Since 1976 the Republican Party platform has contained a commitment to the pro-life position.

Since 1980 no Republican candidate for president or vice president has been pro-choice. In the 2010 election, only a few northeastern congressional districts elected pro-choice Republicans. The fact remains that for most of the last decade pro-choice Republican politicians seemed to be extinct, and if they did exist, they knew to keep their pro-choice positions under wraps, lest they arouse the ire of the pro-life base of the party. This situation tends to minimize the opportunities within the Republican Party for pro-choice women to run for office. Even those elected Republican women who are personally pro-life but do not favor making abortion illegal, are hounded by the pro-life wing, labeled RINOs by the talk radio crowd, and accused of being "not conservative enough."

A Republican Party that would appeal to the millennial generation would tolerate diversity and rid itself of its abortion litmus test. Recent polls show that 60 percent of millennials favor keeping abortion legal, even though 53 percent feel abortion is morally wrong. What millennials don't like is the ideological rigidity that characterizes the Republican Party's stance on this issue.

Millennials also don't like a political party that seems out of touch with reality. Part of that reality is that 95 percent of Americans have sex before they get married. Forty-seven percent of teenagers have sex while they are still in high school, and the number jumps to

65 percent of college students. Most young people have sex for the first time at about age seventeen, but they do not marry until they're in their mid- to late twenties.

Republicans need to get comfortable with the fact that the sexual revolution came and went, and in its wake millennials are sexually active far earlier than any previous generation. If Republicans are going to connect with the next generation, we need to come to terms with the fact that Meghan McCain isn't the only young Republican who is "pro-sex." We also need to be honest about the fact that being pro-sex doesn't necessarily put a young woman at enormous risk of pregnancy. Ms. McCain, like the majority of women in the millennial generation, is also pro–birth control.

I believe that conservatism, as viewed through the lens of American individualism, provides a solid foundation for responding to this challenge. Because American individualism places the individual's wisdom at the center of all issues of political life, we must start there. Do we trust individuals to make the best possible decisions for themselves, especially in moments of crisis? If so, then no matter what our moral positions might be, we must give priority to the individual's right to make these decisions for herself and himself.

Moreover, as a conservative who would like to see less power and authority centralized in the federal government, I think that a proper role for mediating institutions in our culture—religious organizations, community centers, and other nonprofits—is to help women prevent unintended pregnancies, to advise them about alternatives open to them, and to pay for their abortions if that is their decision.

To be a constructive force in Republican politics, in a way that attracts the millennial generation, social conservatives and libertarian conservatives should form coalitions and work together through the country's vast network of nongovernmental institutions, including

churches, synagogues, mosques, and secular and nonsecular nonprofits, in order to transform our culture and diminish the number of
abortions. Pro-choice and pro-life conservatives can agree on the
urgent need to reduce abortions, and by advocating policies that increase adoptions and prevent unintended pregnancies we'll achieve
concrete results that will demonstrate to millennials that we are
committed to solving problems. Pro-life activists would do better
to advocate policies such as these rather than pursuing a human life
amendment to the Constitution.

The conservative impulse to elevate our moral environment
should be aligned with the conservative impulse to empower individual freedom. Those who feel strongly that abortion is immoral
should use persuasion, not legislation, to win the argument.

The best outcome would be preventing *all* unplanned
pregnancies—helping women avoid the dilemma of either having an
abortion or carrying an unwanted child to term. To this end, talking
with women, even girls, about the risks of sex is essential, as is talking to them about birth control methods. Teaching them exclusively
about abstinence is simply not going to be effective. It's not a realistic
solution. Anyone who assumes that teens can be restrained by self-
control has forgotten what it's like to be a teen. And if our message
stays stuck on abstinence-only, we'll remind millennials that we're
out of touch, and we'll become increasingly irrelevant.

I think we also ought to recognize that teen pregnancy carries
a cost to society. It tends to lead to significant economic hardships
for the mothers involved and for their children. Those children are
much more likely to impact society negatively. So while the state's
role must be limited, we must take the responsibility upon ourselves
and our civil institutions to play an active role in helping teens understand the consequences of their actions in a rigorous, fact-based,
and morally centered sex education effort. We expect our schools
to help our kids prepare for a twenty-first-century economy, but

teenage motherhood leads to high school dropouts and government assistance, and often to delinquency among children of teen parents. We should focus our efforts as conservatives on supporting sex education through mediating institutions, in order to help our kids understand the risks of unprotected sex, sexually transmitted diseases, and how to make choices that will keep them on track to benefit from the opportunities of the twenty-first-century American economy.

Palin, Millennials, and the Way Forward

For most Republicans, the Palin family looms large in the abortion debate. Sarah Palin is, in many respects, a pro-life icon. Beyond her political positions opposing abortion rights, she clearly practices what she preaches. She chose to carry to term a Down syndrome baby, Trig, whom America met during the 2008 presidential campaign and who has become an endearing symbol of the special needs community. Today, expectant parents can, and often do, have their fetuses genetically tested for Down syndrome; those with the genetic mutation are aborted roughly 90 percent of the time. Palin made it abundantly clear by the decision she made, in a situation where most women would have decided the other way, that she is strongly pro-life. Some people found her decision admirable.

Enter teenage daughter Bristol Palin. During the campaign, Bristol announced that she had become pregnant, and planned to marry the father. The announcement raised hackles in the pro-choice community. They judged Bristol to be the victim of her mother's politics, unable to abort and therefore the classic example of why teenagers should not be forced to consult their parents in order to go through with the procedure. The pro-life community applauded Bristol Palin's decision, calling her a hero to the movement.

But Bristol Palin is neither the hero nor the victim the politicized pro-lifers and pro-choicers, respectively, would have us believe she is.

She did not face the choices confronted by ordinary teen mothers. Her problem was not whether she could afford to raise a child on her own or whether her parents would disown her. She's a single teenage mom who has the support of her family and has been able to boost her own fortune by trading on her family's fame. She owns a condo, she dances with the stars, she's a celebrity who gets paid for public appearances, especially on the abstinence speakers' circuit, which enables her to pay her mortgage. She glamorously hosts traditional tea parties and dons $7,000 Carolina Herrera dresses to pose for *Harper's Bazaar* centerfolds with her baby perched on her hip.

In short, Bristol Palin is the exception to the rule. Most teenage mothers are from the poorest communities. They are statistically much more likely to be minorities and from the lowest socioeconomic backgrounds, and they're much more likely than not to come from families that can't afford to help raise their unplanned-for children. Sons of teen mothers are 13 percent more likely to serve time in prison, and daughters of teen mothers are 22 percent more likely to become unwed teen mothers themselves.

Fortunately, in the lifetime of millennials, conservatives have had much to cheer about. The teen birth rate hit a new low in 2009. And the culture is changing. The show *16 and Pregnant* on MTV has done a lot of good to reach girls and explore the unglamorized reality of being a teenage parent. According to the *Christian Science Monitor,* "82 percent of the teens who watch it say the show helps them better understand the challenges of teen pregnancy and parenthood—and why they should avoid it." What MTV has discovered is that *stories* about teenage parents—not adults lecturing them—are the most compelling way to explore the full impact of pregnancy.

This is the model we should follow when it comes to talking with teenagers about sex, pregnancy, and the abortion dilemma—not by trying to break down issues into oversimplified and out-of-touch categories but by focusing on the realities millennials face, and examining the full consequences of their options and their actions.

As conservatives, we hold fast to the idea that some individuals can handle adversity better than others; so why do we think differently about teens? Perhaps some can raise a child on their own. But to expect all teens to do so, or to bring a child to term and give it up for adoption as gracefully as did the title character in the movie *Juno,* is utterly unrealistic. And that expectation ends up becoming destructive when we condemn those who make mistakes, but we don't help them avoid those mistakes, as when we deny them the basic knowledge of the risks involved with being sexually active in the first place.

At the heart of this issue is the belief that conservatism trusts in the individual. We may not be ready to sell alcohol to a teenager, but we trust them with an extraordinary amount of authority over their own lives and their own bodies. We do them no favors by pretending they won't exercise that authority; we also do ourselves no favors by failing to teach them how to use that authority wisely. This is at the heart of American individualism: an expectation that the individual, acting with the support of the community, will make the right choices for himself or herself.

CHAPTER 9

CONSERVATIVE ENVIRONMENTALISM

"The spiritual uplift, the goodwill, cheerfulness and optimism that
accompanies every expedition to the outdoors is the peculiar spirit
that our people need in times of suspicion and doubt. . . . No other
organized joy has values comparable to the outdoor experience."
—HERBERT HOOVER, 1926

The Making of a Republican Environmentalist

I was raised in Colorado. Growing up in big-sky country in a family that valued outdoor life, I was blessed with a childhood that included an abundance of fishing, camping, hiking, and, yes, shooting.

My father was a devoted outdoorsman and hunter. He gave me my first 20-gauge shotgun when I turned twelve years old. I might have preferred a pony, but he taught me to shoot and to handle my gun responsibly—and, as it happens, I'm still a pretty decent shot. But my dad also taught me, through his words and his deeds, that responsible hunters are the most conscientious environmentalists you'll ever meet. By spending hours outdoors, they learn to appreciate, more than most people, the natural beauty of this country. Good hunters want to be sure that the animals they hunt are plentiful. And best of all, good hunters do not waste a thing.

I remember my father—who eventually graduated to hunting with only a bow and arrow—coming home with everything from turkey to deer tied down on his truck. I recall family dinners that featured the meat he brought home from his hunting trips. Everything was used up somehow, including my mother's patience. For days on end our kitchen became a meat-processing factory. My dad insisted on stuffing his own deer sausages, and would later serve them on Christmas Day.

I also knew that my family had a rich heritage of respect for nature. My great-grandmother Lou Henry Hoover learned to hunt, fish, and camp in the hills of Monterey, California, in the 1880s with her own father. She subsequently went on to devote her energies to the Girl Scouts of America, which has introduced millions of young girls to the outdoors. In a late-Victorian era that expected little more from young ladies than sewing, childbearing, and serving as ornaments for their husbands, she wanted women to experience, and to feel confident in, nature's marvels.

Herbert Hoover was a lifelong devotee of fly-fishing. There are photos of him, dressed in a suit and tie and waders, standing knee-deep in water at the edge of a stream fishing for trout. I've come to believe that the river was his church, the place where he communed with God. Although he was a devout Quaker, he stopped attending meetings while residing in Washington, D.C., because too many parishioners were "moved by the spirit" to voice their objections to his policies. Nature became his refuge, and so it remained for the rest of his life.

As a result of my family's traditions, I was raised to be an environmentalist, at least the kind who hunts, eats meat, and cherishes fresh air, fresh water, and the outdoors.

And yet, at a young age, I began to resist and resent some aspects of the environmentalist movement. I learned that there was a difference between reverence for nature and reverence for environmentalism. Reverence for nature involved simple things like not littering, leaving nature as we found it, preserving sources of clean water, changing individual habits to conserve energy, and balancing the protection of natural habitats with a responsible use of natural resources. Reverence for environmentalism seemed to be rule-bound and legalistic, and it completely discounted the fact that for millennia nature has served the needs of humanity, not vice versa. My family taught me to revere nature, yet the modern environmentalist movement aroused skepticism within me.

In Denver, where I grew up, an ominous brown cloud settled over the city in between storms, the result of car exhaust, fires, chimney smoke, and industrial pollution. When fronts blew in from the Rocky Mountains, the cloud would dissipate, but it always returned. To try to control pollution, the city introduced a "no wood-burning" policy. On specific days, as a way to reduce the smoke exacerbating the pollution problem, we weren't allowed to burn wood in the fireplace. These regulations were enforced by city employees scanning the sky with infrared binoculars to enable them to detect the heat rising from chimneys in order to determine if anyone was breaking the law, a violation that could earn you a $500 fine. Now think about that. Here were government employees using high-tech equipment to spy on ordinary citizens burning wood, and the wood burners— enjoying the crackle of a fire, the warm hearth, and the coziness of it all—were the lawbreakers, while the binocular-toting bureaucrats were playing the role of environmentalists. Go figure!

One year, the city had the nerve to declare a "no-wood-burning" day on Christmas Eve, the day when our family tradition was to gather by the fireplace, exchange gifts, and write letters to Santa that my father would "send up the chimney" for Santa to read (so we were told). My dad is a responsible, law-abiding citizen, but that year he decided enough was enough. The family tradition would go on, come what may. Would the city have suffered unacceptable pollution damage by waiving this prohibition on just this one special day, out of respect for holiday traditions? Probably not. While I'm all for encouraging individuals to change personal habits to help the environment, in the end it's better if those changes are voluntary, not enforced by the government. Anyway, I wondered what kind of Scrooge would decide to enforce a "no-wood-burning" day on Christmas Eve.

That episode left an impression on me. Normally, parents try to be a good example for their children, and I don't think my dad was trying to tell his outdoorsy kids that the environment doesn't matter. Rather, he was telling us that sometimes environmentalists focus on the wrong things. Instead of protecting nature, they worry about controlling the actions of others. They see a problem in nature, and they simply assume that humanity is the cause. But sometimes, even if people might be the cause of the problem, they can also be the solution. If you keep blaming people, and reining them in, telling them what they can or can't do, you breed resentment against your cause—and in this case perhaps, even worse, resentment against protecting the environment.

There really are different ways to be an environmentalist: One is the way of my dad, someone who uses nature but who protects it from overuse, who is a steward of the environment, who recognizes that humanity has a responsibility to treat it with respect. A second way is the way of those city bureaucrats with the infrared binoculars, those who view the American way of life—with our centrally cooled and heated homes, our two-car garages, our meat-based diets—as inherently problematic and requiring significant controls and reforms enforced by the government. In the first view, the responsibility to be a good environmental steward rests with the individual. In the second view, the responsibility rests with the state. It doesn't take much imagination to see where most conservatives, and where I as an American individualist, come down on this issue.

Historically, however, the Republican Party has been on the other side of the divide on this issue. Two of its most famous presidents—Theodore Roosevelt and Richard Nixon—were very active on environmental issues, and both used the tools of the state to pursue their policy goals.

An avid outdoorsman, Roosevelt believed that America's West—an untamed region of wild beauty—represented the essence of America's national character. He believed in the frontier, and understood how it shaped American values, behavior, and culture. As president, he sought to protect large swaths of the country from development and settlement. He was guided in this process by the nation's earliest leading environmentalists. Sierra Club founder John Muir, Boone and Crockett Club cofounder George Bird Grinnell, forestry advocate Gifford Pinchot, and buffalo breeder William Hornaday were part of Roosevelt's circle, and they advised him on what areas to protect and why—places such as the Grand Canyon, Muir Woods, Devils Tower, and Crater Lake. These lands were unique, they argued, and if not preserved against development, their pristine beauty would be lost forever. During his second term, Roosevelt dramatically expanded the federal government's control over land in the United States, creating 150 national forests and more than quadrupling acreage protected from development to nearly two hundred million acres. Included in this acreage were five national parks, eighteen national monuments, and fifty-one wildlife refuges.

But Roosevelt's actions did not forestall the rising levels of pollution caused by America's rapid industrialization. Our air and water were increasingly dirty and dangerous, and there was little to prevent companies and individuals from simply dumping whatever they needed to dispose of into public rivers, streams, and the atmosphere. And then the nation reached a breaking point: in the early summer of 1969, the Cuyahoga River caught fire near Cleveland, Ohio. It is believed that the fire was started by sparks from the wheels of a passing train, which ignited an oil slick on the river, causing it to burst into flames.

What was becoming all too apparent was that while the United States had become the most powerful and wealthiest industrialized nation in the world, it had allowed pollution to rise to dangerous levels, and we were beginning to pay the price in the alarming deterioration of our environment.

In response to the Cuyahoga River's catching fire, and just three months after the first Earth Day in 1970, another Republican president, Richard Nixon, created the Environmental Protection Agency.

Today the EPA is regarded by some conservatives as among the most dangerous and destructive of all agencies in the federal government. In fact, if Nixon were with us today, conservatives would probably call him a RINO for having created a massive government agency to regulate the environment. But as Nixon saw it, the problem of pollution was not going to be solved by the mechanics of the free market. Economists often talk about the "tragedy of the commons": when a public space like a park is owned collectively and used freely, and no individual has an incentive to take responsibility for its upkeep. There is no profit or gain in picking up litter today, after all, when the litter will return tomorrow. The result is not just an abundance of litter, but a public space that nobody wants to occupy. The solution to the tragedy of the commons is either private ownership or collective action—either a volunteer effort or a state-sponsored one—to assert control over the public space.

The nation as a whole was faced with such a problem, on a far bigger scale, and Nixon decided to take collective action. Our environment was without protection precisely because nobody owned it. And so the federal government, acting on behalf of all of us, stepped in. Perhaps economic conservatives still choke on this, but the situation was dire, as demonstrated by the blazing Cuyahoga River.

But in the process of turning environmental protection into a responsibility of the state, modern environmentalists have devalued the importance of actually experiencing nature. If you can be an environmentalist by writing laws but without ever getting outside, you almost inevitably lose touch with what nature really is about. I think many western conservatives in particular enjoy seeing liberal city-dwelling "environmentalists" go camping and struggle to cope with nature as it is: raw, uncomfortable, and challenging. And that's the thing. Sometimes what makes sense to an office-dwelling professional environmentalist makes no sense to people who actually work and live outdoors.

Think about the rules that restrict logging in our national forests. While we can all appreciate that clear-cutting a mountainside is a catastrophic way to manage our natural resources, some loggers and many forest experts say that selective logging—removing trees but not entire groves—is a smart thing to do. When you remove some trees, you reduce the underbrush and heavy growth that can feed forest fires. Indeed, those mountains that have been actively managed and selectively reduced have fared far better than those that have been managed by bureaucrats in Washington, D.C. Sometimes you have to live in nature in order to understand how best to protect it.

But over time the modern environmental movement has placed more emphasis on issues like driving a hybrid or recycling cans as opposed to the importance of getting out (and getting active!) in nature and appreciating the great outdoors. As a result, more and more Americans don't understand the vital significance of our environment in their daily lives. Teddy Roosevelt used to ride his horse from the White House up Rock Creek, where he would dismount and go swimming for relaxation before returning to the office. If he did that today, well, needless to say, he would be cited for multiple violations. Modern environmentalists have gone so far as to suggest that we should forbid car and bus access to our national parks. But if we do that, fewer people will get to see what we are trying so hard to protect.

In general, environmentalists have placed so much emphasis on what people do to harm the environment, that they have made the movement seem like those Malthusians who used to argue that there was no way the planet's population could continue to grow without causing catastrophic famines (of course, they were spectacularly wrong). There is actually a school of modern environmentalism that argues that in order to protect the planet, people must produce fewer children.

Now there is even a television series called *Life After People,* which depicts what would happen to cities, roads, landmarks, and other inhabited spaces if all of humanity were to disappear. Buildings would collapse. Animals would forage in supermarkets. Nearly extinct species would begin to flourish. Domesticated animals would struggle and die off. While this sounds like something out of a horror film, to a radical environmentalist it is closer to a vision of utopia.

Perhaps the restoration of the earth to its natural state before the rise of human civilization is not seriously the utopia of modern environmentalism, but that is the clear implication of so much of what modern left-wing environmentalism tells us to do. Don't eat meat. Don't travel on airplanes. Don't build big houses. Don't drive your car if you can avoid it. And no, don't have wood fires on Christmas Eve. If you do, we'll catch you. And if we don't, doom will descend on Planet Earth.

Looking back, the environmental philosophy of Roosevelt and Nixon was practical. Open and beautiful spaces should be protected so they can be enjoyed for generations. Clean air and clean water are valuable and need to be available to everyone. The environment is our public space, and every public space needs a caretaker, and everyone who uses it needs to be responsible.

Most Americans really do want to help protect nature and make sure the earth's water and air keep getting cleaner. They are concerned about the risks of climate change and are willing to change their ways to address it. But they have also seen how environmental challenges of great magnitude presented to them with urgency in the past—declining resources, rising pollution, questions over how to balance the needs of civilization and nature—have been answered by people developing solutions. They understand that innovation is an instinct of civilization—especially American civilization. It's not the American way to be confronted with problems and simply surrender. We figure them out. We adapt.

That's the opportunity for environmental conservatives. Most Americans really don't want the government to make decisions for them about how to treat the environment. Most Americans are willing to make sacrifices for the environment, but they want to pick which ones they will make, and when. Americans would rather be shown how innovation and creativity might steer us clear of climate change. They don't want to rely on the government to develop the solution. If conservatives position themselves as interested in environmental conservation and interested in solutions to challenges like climate change, pollution, and energy efficiency, they have a chance to prove themselves worthy to lead on those issues. And as it happens, the people who will be most responsive to these kinds of effort are millennials, the most environmentally minded generation in American history.

The Millennial Challenge

Millennials have been exposed to more information about environmental issues than any previous generation. They have been trained from a young age, often in the classroom, to be environmental warriors. School projects on endangered species, school trips focused on ecology, perhaps even vacations devoted not to the great capitals of Europe but to the great rain forests and animal preserves of the world—all these have given this generation an ingrained sense of the imminent danger facing our environment.

One of the formative events in the experience of many older millennials was the *Exxon Valdez* oil spill of 1989. I remember the heart-wrenching images, on television screens and in newspapers across the country, of birds, otters, and other wildlife smothered in oil. More recently, the BP Gulf of Mexico oil spill reinforced among younger millennials a sense of outrage about the loss of wildlife as a result of our seemingly unquenchable thirst for oil.

Growing up, millennials read Dr. Seuss's *The Lorax* and followed the exploits of the Once-ler, an industrialist who acquires great wealth by ravaging the environment, depleting the land of Truffula trees. My class even acted this story out in our fourth-grade musical. The story was a cartoon version of the standard view offered by the environmentalist movement: that industrial progress invariably comes at the expense of nature. Over time, many millennials have reached the conclusion that most human activity distorts and damages nature. But because few of them are willing to abandon the comforts of modern life, they have made it their mission to "green" human activity whenever and wherever possible. In fact, three-quarters of them demand that the products they buy be manufactured in an environmentally responsible way—using recycled or compostable materials, organic ingredients, and minimal packaging. Whether something is "green" or not has become a symbol of quality, even if the "green" feature actually serves to make it an inferior product (toilet paper made from recycled paper stock is a perfect example).

But while millennials are generally active in environmental causes, they do not always go the distance. They drive cars no less than Generation Xers. They are enthusiastic users of energy-hogging portable devices such as iPhones and laptops, all of which end up adding to the problem of dangerous chemicals leaking from the nation's trash heaps. Their zeal for going paperless creates massive demand for heat-emitting, power-sucking data centers to store all their documents, photos, and other digital information.

I am not pointing all this out in order to paint the millennials as hypocrites. Far from it. I only wish to show that millennials have decided, like the rest of us, that in some ways they will be environmentally conscious, and in some ways they won't. They pick and choose. They happen to be pickier than earlier generations of Americans. But the critical fact is that their environmentalism is driven by their own choices. They refuse, so far, to embrace a "one size fits all" approach to the problem.

They are, in other words, the ideal audience for a *conservative* approach to environmentalism, one that emphasizes the principles of American individualism: voluntary action inspired by a sense of responsibility and service to the community and the environment.

Let's start with the issue of climate change and what we need to do about it. First of all, let's agree that climate change is real. The earth's climate is getting warmer. In fact, it's been getting warmer for the past century and a half, since the end of the Little Ice Age. During that period, which lasted from about the middle of the thirteenth century to the middle of the nineteenth, temperatures were two to three degrees cooler than they are now. The Little Ice Age caused widespread crop failure and loss of life throughout the Northern Hemisphere.

But let's also stipulate that climate change is an inexact science. *Newsweek* once published a cover story titled "The Cooling World," which warned that global temperatures had dropped significantly over the course of the previous thirty-five years. The decrease was so troubling that the article wondered if we might not be entering a "new little ice age." That article was published in 1975. The lesson here is that while we can conclude that climate change is real, we should also build in some margin for human error.

Yet members of the modern environmental movement, especially those taking their cues from Al Gore, act as if they are 100 percent certain that climate change is not only real, but apocalyptic, and that the evidence is all around us. If we have a heat wave, that's climate change. If we get lots of snow, that's climate change. Deadly hurricanes? Climate change. Lack of hurricanes? Climate change.

This kind of heads-I-win, tails-you-lose logic shouldn't fool anyone. But it does. It misleads people who care deeply about the environment into thinking that we have no options left but to adopt wholesale the policy agenda of the modern left-wing environmental movement, whose top agenda item is restricting carbon emissions through the government implementation of a complex regulatory scheme that would result in a massive backdoor tax on America's middle class.

Defeating the modern left-wing environmentalist plan for implementing such a program is a fight that conservative environmentalists should absolutely take on. According to a Heritage Foundation analysis of the bill that the Democrats in the House approved in 2009, known to some as Cap-and-Trade but to conservatives as Cap-and-Tax, electricity prices would rise by 90 percent and gas prices by 74 percent. Even if those estimates overshoot the mark, we should beware of creating a new government regulatory bureaucracy that cannot even prove its effectiveness in addressing climate change, since climate scientists won't be able to produce evidence to show climate change has been halted until many, many years into the future. And, in any case, the law would only have the effect of reducing global temperatures by a mere one-tenth of one degree over the next one hundred years!

In addition, these new laws would only regulate the United States. But we are not the world's biggest polluter, and we have even decreased our carbon emissions voluntarily over the last two decades. The American economy is far less pollution- and energy-intensive than China's, India's, and other nations' economies. These rising nations are far less interested than America is in regulating carbon. They are playing economic catch-up, and that requires a lot of energy. Roughly 80 percent of the world's people want to live with the same level of comfort as the other 20 percent experience. And who can blame them?

The modern left-wing environmental movement has put forward ideas that are expensive, will lead to massive government spending and regulation, and are ineffective in solving climate change globally. How can environmental conservatives lose this argument?

Sadly, we are losing it every day. Everyone assumes that conservatives have no serious plan to address climate change. During their two-plus decades on earth, millennials have heard environmentalists sounding alarms about pollution, habitat loss, and global warming. Meanwhile, they have heard conservatives merely guffaw at the very notion of climate "science." If you were an environmentally oriented millennial, why would you listen to conservatives?

We can do better. And here are a few ways how. First, let's turn down the heat—both literally and metaphorically. There is nothing wrong with conservation. Using less energy is a smart thing for this nation, especially if it means importing less oil from the Middle East. Conservatives should recognize that the cheapest form of energy is the energy you don't use. Meanwhile, let's also turn the heat down when we talk about the issue. Instead of focusing on insisting that climate change is a myth foisted upon us by left-wing radicals attempting to reengineer the American economy, let's confront those vocal skeptics on the Right and restore our credibility with a fact-driven platform that demonstrates a healthy respect for science. We can accept that climate change exists without embracing the Left's solutions for how to combat it, and even offer alternative solutions.

Second, let's pluck the low-hanging fruit. Climate scientist Bjorn Lomborg points out that humanity has always adapted to climate change, and suggests that this time should be no different. He proposes that we take relatively simple measures to respond to the threat *right now.* For example, because cities tend to be much warmer than less populated areas, we should focus on cooling cities by planting more trees in them and by painting roofs, roads, and other large heat-absorbing dark surfaces white and other light colors. At a cost of $1 billion we could negate any potential warming in the Los Angeles basin for the next ninety years, a reasonable price compared with the massively expensive legislation proposed by congressional Democrats.

Third, we should create and sustain as many viable renewable energy technologies as possible. This includes not only advanced solar photovoltaics but also biofuels such as algae. We should encourage clean coal plants and fourth-generation nuclear reactors. Even if all the technology bets don't pay off, we need to find out what might replace fossil fuels, and at what cost. The federal government should have a hand in this, but it should be a light one. The government's history of picking technology winners and losers is checkered at best. The free market can serve us better. But there needs to be some kind of self-funding mechanism to support energy technologies—a "green bank" to provide early-stage funding for promising ideas. If the technology reduces emissions, it gets support. As its price comes down, the support is withdrawn.

Fourth, we have to champion oil, coal, and natural gas as "bridge" energy sources. That means we need to prepare our own economy for the end of affordable fossil fuels over the next fifty to one hundred years. It's important to remember that it took roughly a century for oil to become as essential as it is today. It may take another century for its significance to diminish. But like all commodities that were once highly valued and later fell into disuse (like salt's essential role as a preservative before the arrival of refrigeration), oil will one day play a lesser role. It won't happen tomorrow, but we need to start preparing for that day.

Meanwhile, we can't ignore our own energy assets. We are the Saudi Arabia of coal. With hydraulic fracturing technology, we may also be the Saudi Arabia of natural gas. And we shouldn't ignore our own considerable oil reserves in places like Alaska. We can extract significant energy stores from our own soil, a valuable way to keep energy prices as affordable as possible for as long as possible while we make the transition to new energy technologies. The central premise here is simple—no energy should be squandered. We could power our country every day for millions of years if we could harness the power of the sun efficiently. Every night, wind blows, uncaptured as a power source. The same is true for just about any energy source you can think of. There is energy to be tapped almost everywhere if we can develop the technology we need to do the job, whether it involves driving down the cost of solar panels or wind turbines, using hydraulic fracturing technology to get at tough-to-reach fossil fuels, or introducing ultracapacitors to curb line losses in electricity transmission. More than 90 percent of the electricity produced is lost along the way before it reaches the lightbulb in our homes—what if we cut that figure to 50 percent?

I'm all in favor of a conversion to clean energy sources, including wind and solar power. But I also recognize that none of these technologies is even remotely close to supplying our country's and the world's energy needs. And they're not likely to be close for at least a couple of decades. The idea that we can somehow magically turn a switch and convert the world's infrastructure to running on these technologies is ridiculous. We need to give these technologies the time and financial resources they require to be developed into viable alternatives to our current energy sources, both technologically and economically. We do need to incentivize developers of these technologies to accelerate research and development, but we also need to stress that any lasting change in our energy economy has to be market driven. Whatever replaces oil and coal will have to be as efficient and as affordable. It will have to stand on its own in the marketplace.

Will this approach resonate with millennials? I believe it will. But only if we can demonstrate that we are serious about it. So often when it comes to the environment, Republicans discuss their ideas grudgingly, even unenthusiastically. We act as if we don't really believe what we are saying when it comes to protecting the environment. Even when we do believe it, we sometimes back away for fear of being perceived as no different from the left-wing environmental radicals. But this is easily solved if Republicans will be bold enough to stake out a conservative environmental agenda that dares to talk openly about all of America's and the world's environmental challenges, from climate change to kicking our addiction to foreign oil.

More than anything else, we ought to adopt the attitude of happy warriors and have confidence that America has the capacity to figure out this problem. The government has an important role to play when it comes to protecting the environment, but it cannot—and should not—be trusted to deliver a low-carbon, energy-independent future. That has to come from individuals, working together and driven by the realities of the market. We have to insist that effective environmentalism—*conservative* environmentalism—is about results. It's about giving our children and grandchildren an environment as healthy as the one we inherited. It's about giving our economy a future independent of foreign oil. It's about creating a new energy economy that does not rely on subsidies and tax dollars. By emphasizing innovation, free-market principles, and individual initiative, conservative environmentalism holds great promise.

CHAPTER 10

A NATION OF IMMIGRANTS, A NATION OF BORDERS

"The Republican Party, unfortunately, has been cast as the anti–illegal immigration party. It is not the anti–illegal immigration party. It is the pro–legal immigration party . . . and having a legal immigration system that works begins with border security."
—SENATOR MARCO RUBIO

D URING MY JUNIOR year of college I lived in Cochabamba, Bolivia, with an incredibly loving Bolivian family while I studied at a local university. In many ways, my host family resembled my own in the United States. Delia, my "sister," was my age and studying architecture at the local university. Her brother, Alejandro, was the same age and had the same name as my younger brother in America. My Bolivian "parents" shared the same anniversary as my mom and dad. So much about my Bolivian family's structure and closeness resembled that of my own family. I lived with my Bolivian family while I studied, and secured a summer internship after the semester ended so I could extend my time in Bolivia. Despite Bolivia's status as South America's poorest country, I fell in love with all things Bolivian: my friends, the food, and the culture and the geographical richness.

While in Cochabamba, I became acquainted with several of

Delia's friends, including Emilia, whose mother operated a modest restaurant on the side of a highway staffed by Emilia's siblings and featuring her mother's recipes and cooking. In this way Emilia's mother managed to eke out a living, despite an abusive husband who drank and spent his family into oppressive debt.

Later, after returning home, I learned that Emilia's mother had arrived in the United States to try to earn enough money to pay off her husband's debts. I was eager to see her again, and to greet her with the same hospitality she had extended to me in Bolivia. By the time we reconnected, she was employed cleaning houses, was learning English, and had begun to earn far more income than her delicious *silpancho* servings in Cochabamba could ever have brought in. At an age when most women would prefer to downshift to a more comfortable pace and enjoy the company of grandchildren, this woman was a stranger in a foreign land, working a hard job, learning a new language, and tidying up a financial mess back home by cleaning houses in America.

I had no illusions about how Emilia's mother had entered the country—like nearly 40 percent of unauthorized workers, she had arrived legally and overstayed her visa. But I found it difficult to begrudge this sixty-year-old grandmother her desire to do the best she could to support her family with her limited resources. I couldn't guarantee that I wouldn't do the same thing if I were in her position. I also knew that Emilia's mother had no intention of staying in America or becoming a longtime drain on the economy through her use of public services. She would earn what she could, pay down her debts, and return home to Bolivia.

The story of Emilia's mother, one of millions of such stories, illustrates America's epidemic of illegal immigration and undocumented labor. It is a story that is part economic—the search for better-paying work. It is a story that is part national security—the inability of our nation to protect its borders against those who would enter, or remain here, without legal permission. It is a story that is part cultural—the culture of America, which has traditionally welcomed those who wanted to do better but also expects those who come temporarily to come legally and work legally, and expects those who stay to learn English and assimilate into American culture.

The case of Emilia's mother touches on all these issues. She came here to work, not to live. She arrived effortlessly and stayed as long as she needed. She provided for her family in a way she could never have in her native Bolivia. Yet what one might find admirable about one part of her story, one might resent about another. There is a reason why illegal immigration is a highly charged emotional issue for many Americans.

I tell this story as a way to convey my understanding of the compelling human element at the heart of the debates about unauthorized workers in America and the problem of illegal immigration.

I also know, however, that we cannot continue on the trajectory we are currently on as a nation—failing to secure our borders while ignoring the fact that millions of people come here to work illegally, people like Emilia's mother. The facts are troubling and cannot be ignored. Here are some prime examples from U.S. government statistics:

- There were 10.8 million undocumented immigrants living in the United States on January 1, 2009. An estimated 6.7 million were from Mexico.
- Arizona had 460,000 undocumented immigrants in 2009, out of a total population of 6.6 million.
- The U.S. Border Patrol made 650 arrests a day in its Tucson, Arizona, sector alone in 2010.
- The Phoenix Police Department reported 357 kidnappings in 2007, targeting individuals with ties to Mexican drug-smuggling gangs.

The reality is that illegal immigration exacts steep human and economic costs. When people come to the country illegally, they require schools for their children, more buses for public transportation, and other public facilities for which they rarely pay. Arizona state treasurer Dean Martin estimates that his state's government loses between $1.3 billion and $2.5 billion each year providing services for undocumented immigrants, plus other associated costs. Nationally, the costs reach $113 billion a year, according to a 2010 study by the Federation for American Immigration Reform.

Here is the dilemma that confronts us: How do we welcome immigrants who are eager to embrace the American way of life, while at the same time implementing tough and effective border security and visa enforcement? How can we encourage immigrants to contribute their unique cultural and personal attributes to the American melting pot, while also ensuring that these new arrivals learn English and assimilate into American culture?

In facing this challenge, Republicans need to frame the debate in a way that doesn't alienate the millennial generation. Millennials are the most ethnically diverse generation in American history. More than 40 percent are nonwhite, and of that group, the largest ethnic group is Hispanic. A comprehensive 2009 Pew study on millennials found that "younger people [are] more tolerant of immigrants than are older people," and that younger Americans are less apt to say immigrants have a negative impact on American customs and values. But while the study found that millennials are "much less supportive of further restrictions on immigration than other cohorts," 59 percent of millennials still believe that the federal government should secure and police our borders and manage immigration fairly and effectively.

Republicans are capable of reaching out to millennials even on the difficult issue of immigration reform. Millennials generally may have faith in the government, but they can't help but notice its utter failure to secure our borders. Also, the status quo isn't only a failure, it's compassionless: people on the border are completely at the mercy of the smugglers—just as undocumented workers in this country are victimized by criminals and unethical employers alike.

Like millennials who value competence over ideology, Republicans can express sincere outrage about the federal government's lackluster efforts at border security. Such criticism must be followed by equally sincere and realistic proposals for actually securing the border. Remember, millennials want pragmatic solutions, not rhetorical posturing. Border security must be the starting point. If the federal government could control the border, real progress could be accomplished in other key areas of comprehensive immigration reform.

A few years ago, legislation was being considered on Capitol Hill to put our country's unauthorized immigrants on a pathway to citizenship. It was a thoughtful proposal, and it had meaningful support from key members of the Senate.

I had the honor of working for the president who worked with Congress to introduce the bill. As a young Republican staffer, I had many reasons to be proud to serve under George W. Bush, but chief among them was his determined effort to meet the needs of American Latinos. As governor of Texas, Bush captured 70 percent of the Hispanic vote in his campaign for reelection in 1998. He sought to replicate that success nationally in his 2004 presidential reelection campaign. His chief strategist, Karl Rove, developed a series of outreach initiatives to Hispanics with the intention of capturing at least 40 percent of their vote—a significant target for a national Republican campaign.

Working on the Bush-Cheney 2004 reelection campaign, I took Rove's 40 percent goal seriously. As a member of the campaign's finance staff, I developed a program to organize grassroots fund-raisers in the Hispanic communities throughout the country. "Viva Bush" was our motto, and our small effort was but one of many important campaign initiatives that reflected President Bush's seriousness on behalf of Republicans to build support within the Hispanic community.

After his reelection, President Bush tackled immigration reform through the Secure Borders, Economic Opportunity and Immigration Reform Bill of 2007. Championed by President Bush, Arizona senator John McCain, and Massachusetts senator Edward Kennedy, this bill was an effort to bring the twelve million unauthorized immigrants out of the shadows. These millions were to be put on the pathway to citizenship, assuming that they had begun to learn English and that they had not committed any crimes.

The bill also included funding for a security barrier along the U.S.-Mexican border, for the installation of increased surveillance technology, and for an additional twenty thousand border patrol agents to help ramp up security.

In short, had it become law, this bill would have provided a way for unauthorized immigrants to participate in our economy legally and to become assimilated into our culture while we made the necessary investments to secure our border. The bill failed even to be brought to a vote on the floor of the Senate chamber. As it turned out, America's border states and their Republican representatives were not prepared to support a bill giving unauthorized workers a shot at citizenship until the federal government could first demonstrate that it was capable of securing the border. The bill also failed because Democrats let partisanship get in the way of serious reform and were unprepared to support a bill that would give President Bush the credit for introducing historic immigration reform.

Americans living in border states are justifiably angry that our federal government has failed for so long to live up to its constitutional obligation to secure the border. What has become obvious since 2007 is that no legislation to reform immigration will ever be politically acceptable until the federal government has first secured the border.

Even a bill as innocuous as the DREAM Act (the Development, Relief and Education for Alien Minors Act) failed to pass in December 2010. This bill would have created a pathway to citizenship for the children of unauthorized immigrants (many in the millennial generation) who are in America illegally through no fault of their own. Despite massive Democratic majorities in both houses of Congress during a lame-duck session, even this seemingly harmless bill failed to become law. The fate of the DREAM Act is the ultimate proof that the politics of immigration reform is paralyzed beyond hope until measurable success can be achieved on border security.

Our focus, therefore, has to be on securing the border, and also on ensuring that those who come here on short-term visas leave on schedule. If we do not take steps to differentiate between authorized and unauthorized immigrants, we will end up tarnishing the proud immigrant tradition of this country by placing a cloud of suspicion over every law-abiding newcomer. Enforcement of the law and protection of our border will redound not just to our benefit but to the benefit of all immigrants in America.

What can be done? As it turns out, plenty.

There have, in fact, been isolated successes in securing the border.

Yuma County, Arizona, provides a textbook example of how border security can be accomplished. It has gone from having some 138,500 unauthorized aliens enter the country across its section of border before serious border security was implemented to only 7,000 a year after implementation, a 95 percent decrease over a five-year period.

The success in Yuma County demonstrates that border security isn't rocket science. Yuma County's solution to securing the border consisted of three straightforward components: first, building miles of fencing; second, hiring a sufficient number of border patrol agents; and third, implementing Operation Streamline, a set of guidelines for how authorities should prosecute *on the spot* anyone caught trying to cross the border. The first time individuals are found crossing the border illegally they spend fourteen days in jail; the second time, thirty days; the third time, sixty days—until eventually they realize they cannot successfully cross. Imagine the results if this system could be implemented across the entire southwestern border!

This approach isn't cheap—it takes federal and state funds to pay for portable detention spaces, judges, lawyers, and court clerks. But the investment is inexpensive compared with the cost of the elaborate cat-and-mouse games involved in catching and prosecuting unauthorized immigrants elsewhere, or the cost they exact on the system as a whole.

Some of our liberal and Democratic friends have a hard time with the notion of Americans building a fence along the southern border. They think it will send a message to the world that we are isolationist and xenophobic, that we are unwelcoming of other cultures, and even that we are racists. Some have likened such a fence to the Berlin Wall, while others have dubbed it *el muro de odio,* "the wall of hate."

Any such suggestion is part of a systematic effort to paint the Republican Party as anti-immigrant, conflating the concepts of legal immigration and illegal immigration in an attempt to distort the debate. It is intended to perpetuate negative stereotypes about the Republican Party that continue to hamper its efforts to win support among not only Hispanics but also among millennials. In the eyes of many millennials, a person's (or party's) stand on immigration is more than a reflection of a particular policy. It is seen as a broader statement about attitudes toward diversity, globalism, and even civil rights. Republicans must push back on this attack by marshaling the facts.

Let's take the example of Arizona's law to enforce federal immigration rules and procedures. Despite the fact that the law has the support of 77 percent of Arizonans and 73 percent of all Americans, immediately after the bill's passage the Obama Justice Department declared that it would challenge the legislation. Attorney General Eric Holder admitted that he hadn't even read the Arizona bill when he decided to take this action. The irony of the challenge was that the administration claimed that the law infringed on the responsibilities of the federal government, despite the fact that it was precisely *because* the feds were failing to execute their constitutional responsibilities that the law had to be passed in the first place.

But what's in this law? Is it, as President Obama says, a violation of civil rights and a form of racial profiling?

Not at all. In fact, the law specifically forbids racial profiling. It merely empowers local and state law enforcement to question someone's immigration status *if that person has already broken a law.* Only at that point, and only if there is *reasonable suspicion* that the person detained might be in the country without authorization, is a law enforcement official allowed to question that person about his or her citizenship. And there is an extended list of protections defining exactly what constitutes "reasonable suspicion."

The Arizona law actually has more civil rights protections in it than federal laws. It specifies that race *cannot* be one of the criteria for "reasonable suspicion." The federal immigration law, meanwhile, does not even stipulate that a person first has to commit a crime in order to be detained or questioned about his or her immigration status. It would seem that the only thing Arizona did that might offend the feds was to say, we will enforce a law that you won't—and by the way, we will do it more fairly and equitably than you might if you ever get around to it.

Nevertheless, even with those clarifications, there is no doubt that the Arizona law is not an attempt at a comprehensive approach to immigration reform.

It does nothing about the employment of unauthorized immigrants by unscrupulous employers. It leaves out any discussion of allowing unauthorized immigrants an opportunity to resolve their status—something only the federal government has the authority to do. Its focus on "attrition through enforcement" is only one dimension of what has to be a far broader approach to the immigration problem. It is a desperate measure, by a desperate state, in the face of the federal government's failure to secure the borders.

Neither party has the confidence of the American people when it comes to border security. Republicans tried and failed to pass immigration reforms when they had control of both the White House and Capitol Hill. Democrats in the same position were unable to pass the DREAM Act.

By now, the answer should be obvious. Those who would like to see comprehensive immigration reform must first support serious improvements in border security before they attempt to do anything else. It's that simple—we must secure the borders first. Only after we have successfully secured our borders will there be a reasonable chance for comprehensive immigration reform.

Here are some ideas that can help make comprehensive immigration reform innovative and successful:

Implement Operation Streamline Broadly

As Yuma County has proved, by immediately detaining and jailing those people who try to cross the border illegally, we make it much less likely that they will keep trying. Yes, this will cost money. But it is far easier and less costly to hire judges, court clerks, prison guards, and lawyers to deal with the illegals near the border than it is to identify them once they are already in the country. Given the success of this program, it should be implemented wherever possible across the entire southwestern border.

Prioritize Skills-Based Immigration

Nobody begrudges immigrants the right to come to this country to do work Americans are unwilling to do. Yet we do not do enough to match immigrant workers with jobs in industries where there are constant labor shortages. For example, Bill Gates and other tech executives have spoken out about the need to increase the number of H-1B visas available to skilled workers who arrive in America ready to work and contribute to our economy and our culture. Likewise, if foreign students come here to be educated in areas that are important for us to maintain our competitive edge in the global economy, it doesn't make sense to have them benefit from our educational system and then kick them out of the country. We need to increase the number of long-term work visas in order to keep the American economy competitive.

End the Visa Lottery

Each year, tens of thousands of people are given visas to the United States on the basis of luck alone. No test is administered. Those given a visa might be young, they might be old, they might have skills, they might be illiterate. If immigration is going to serve the interests of the country, we have to take luck out of the equation and award visas to the deserving, especially young adults who are seeking to make a fresh start and assimilate into an adopted country. We want the best and the brightest immigrants—they will help to make our nation stronger and more competitive.

Activate E-Verify

E stands for *electronic* and this national electronic system would make it easy for employers to independently and efficiently verify whether a prospective employee is legal or not. Right now, employers have little to go on: driver's licenses are easily obtained; Social Security cards are often faked. The result is that employers have no choice but to accept what documents they are given. There is no definitive way of verifying their authenticity. Of course, once we solve the problem, employers will have no excuse for hiring unauthorized immigrants. This will be a problem not just for large agribusiness, which hires many migrant and itinerant workers on the fly. I can think of several prominent Republicans and Democrats—Zoë Baird, Linda Chavez, and Meg Whitman—who have hired unauthorized immigrants in their own homes. They broke the law, perhaps without knowing it. So the question is, why is our federal government unable to give employers a reasonable level of confidence that someone is legal or not?

It would be great if immigration reform were simply a matter of putting together a policy paper and seeing it through to law. But that's not really how it works. Because immigration is not merely a security issue and not merely an economic issue, it takes on a special intensity. After all, it touches on the lives of millions of families. And because immigration is closely tied to the legal rights and the culture of tens of millions of Hispanics, any criticism of illegal immigration tends to be misrepresented by the Left as some form of ethnic bigotry on the part of Republicans.

This means Republicans have a special challenge when it comes to talking to millennials about immigration reform. Because the millennial generation is made up of a larger percentage of Hispanics than any previous generation, Republicans must adopt a respectful and compassionate tone.

We should affirm the broadly held American values on immigration and the good that has come from being a nation of immigrants through the constant regeneration of the American dream. And we ought to make the case for effective border security on the basis of the safety of our communities, and the inherent responsibility of the federal government to secure the borders.

This is doable. In fact, it's being done.

We have a rising generation of newly elected Hispanic Republican leaders, including Senator Marco Rubio and border-state governors Brian Sandoval and Susana Martinez, to help lead the way. They can also help us make the case for the importance of assimilation. Marco Rubio has emphasized the responsibilities of immigrants who wish to become Americans: "The most important thing that recent arrivals can do for their children is make them proficient in the English language."

Senator Rubio understands, as do many immigrants who have become active in the Republican Party, that this one thing the Right fixates on—the responsibility of the immigrant to learn English—is in fact the greatest gift an immigrant can receive. Republicans must be prepared to push school systems to quickly wean immigrants off bilingual education and force more and more of them to do their schoolwork in English, the national language of the United States. But immigrants need not give up their native languages or culture even as they assimilate into American culture. And so when those on the Right say "English only," I would say instead, "English first."

While the English language is and will continue to be a unifying thread throughout American culture, we must also avoid being culturally and linguistically alone in a globalized world. I come to this issue with a personal interest and perspective. My grandmother was born in the Arizona Territory, and I've studied Spanish and Spanish literature throughout my school years. I wrote my college thesis in Spanish. Growing up in a western state with a large Latino population, I have always been comfortable hearing Spanish spoken, singing to Spanish-language music, and watching telenovelas on Univision. This familiarity with other languages and cultures can be enormously enriching and should be encouraged.

Republicans can also do something that liberal Democrats rarely do: affirm what it is that most immigrants come here for—to achieve the American dream. Republicans are the champions of entrepreneurs and small-business owners, people who take great risks to achieve a future for themselves and their families. Republicans should articulate how so much of their agenda, based on a pro-growth and pro-innovation philosophy, is vital to the dreams of all immigrants.

Republicans ought to focus in particular on the outrageous bureaucratic delays facing those who want to come to this country legally—who want to play by the rules. Because new immigrants are often fleeing governmental and economic oppression, they are the first to remind us of the incredible opportunities our country provides. They are some of the best examples of American individualism and have been the secret to the regeneration of the American dream throughout our history.

That's why I think Republicans ought to consider that a great majority of those who are in this country illegally have otherwise been law abiding and committed to the hard work and dynamism that American individualism rewards. One day, *after* the border is successfully secured, we should support efforts for them to emerge from the shadows and be given an opportunity to live in America legally. Conservative critics may call this "amnesty." But let's be honest: it's a far cry from the functional amnesty Ronald Reagan backed in the mid-1980s as part of what we now see as a flawed attempt at immigration reform.

By securing the borders first—expanding the opportunities for legal immigration, and putting in place measures like E-Verify— we can fix our broken system without encouraging new waves of unauthorized immigration. We can restore faith in legal immigration, which has always been a key ingredient of our nation's success—reviving the American dream and the spirit of American individualism through the power of the immigrant's example. Once we establish control of our borders, we can confidently and proudly assert that America remains a nation of immigrants.

CHAPTER 11

ISLAMIST SUPREMACY

A Millennial's Worst Nightmare

"The bombers of Manhattan represent fascism with an Islamic face,
and there's no point in any euphemism about it."
—CHRISTOPHER HITCHENS

O N S E P T E M B E R 11, 2001, nineteen men hijacked four commercial airplanes and used them as missiles, slamming two of the planes into the World Trade Center towers and one into the Pentagon. The hijackers piloting the fourth plane, United Airlines Flight 93, were thwarted by the heroism of the passengers on board, whose desperate resistance caused the aircraft to crash into an open field in western Pennsylvania.

These events were a defining moment in the lives of millennials and a wake-up call for all of America. In the same way that Pearl Harbor changed the Greatest Generation, and the Kennedy assassination changed baby boomers, 9/11 changed and continues to shape the millennials.

On that fateful morning, the oldest millennials were seniors in high school, while the youngest were just infants. Their lives went from being secure and carefree to uncertain and scary. For the first time in their lives, they saw that their government and their parents were not in control. Evil existed and it needed to be confronted. In the weeks and months afterward, more fear followed, sparked by bomb threats and anthrax exposure. Osama bin Laden became a household name, and to the youngest millennials he was the incarnation of their worst fears.

Millennials, like the rest of the country, understood what would happen next: a war. A war to protect our cities and borders. A war to prevent another 9/11. When America went to war against the Taliban and Al Qaeda in Afghanistan, it went proudly, and millennials saw it in the way our troops were treated, the way the flag was honored, and the way people set aside political grudges to focus on the work ahead. I suspect that it was in this period that the high expectations millennials have for their elected leaders were formed. They came to see that government should be trusted and trustworthy, and that those who give their lives to public service—soldiers, sailors, pilots, firefighters, and police—should be revered. What was for America one of the most challenging moments was also one of its most defining. Our country came through that period stronger.

But that unity of purpose did not linger long. Millennials were inspired to act by 9/11, but they soon soured on America's war in Iraq, which spurred increasing doubts about our prolonged engagement in Afghanistan. Meanwhile, in the absence of another successful attack—despite more than a dozen thwarted incidents—Americans as a whole have grown less concerned about the threat of another 9/11. The intensity is gone. The sense of shared sacrifice has dissipated. A sense of complacency threatens to take its place.

This isn't just a challenge for Republicans trying to win over millennials. This is a problem for all Americans who care about the future security of our nation. If the 9/11 generation no longer understands why we are involved in the conflicts we fight today, we have a problem.

The problem, in my view, is that as a country we never clearly established who it is we were fighting, and what we were fighting for. We looked at those nineteen men on the airplanes as representing a single isolated enemy supported by the Taliban and deployed by Al Qaeda from a remote mountainous corner of Afghanistan. We focused immediately on the tactics they might use: hijacking airplanes and turning them into missiles, deploying "dirty bombs" stuffed with radioactive material, setting off car bombs in major cities, and releasing biological and chemical agents. But we stopped thinking about who these enemies are, what their goals are and why.

Perhaps we did not have the time or imagination to think about the motivating ideology of those nineteen men and the people who planned and financed their operations. We didn't think about how they were the latest foot soldiers in a larger and ongoing movement, a broad effort to push out, through violent force when necessary, Western values from the Middle East, Africa, Asia, and even Europe. We did not recognize that these men were merely the spearhead of the most violent ideology of the twenty-first century so far—an ideology as sweeping and murderous as fascism and communism. We seemed to believe instead that all we needed to focus on were their tactics, as if we could defeat them if we just limited ourselves to three-ounce bottles of liquids in our carry-on luggage.

Initially, we called it the Global War on Terror. But America isn't fighting terror. Terror isn't an enemy. Terror is a tool of warfare, employed to achieve specific goals that other methods cannot. Terror intimidates. It forces civilized nations to spend significant sums on protecting infrastructure, transport systems, and institutions that ordinarily aren't targets of conventional warfare. It is an ancient technique, used by militants in many different times and places, including both left-wing and right-wing radicals at different points in American history. So many groups around the globe use terror that to declare a literal "war on terror" means that America must go to war against groups on every continent, in dozens of nations, including places where we have no strategic or national interests. And ultimately, calling this conflict a "war on terror" makes it impossible to declare victory—if you suffer no terror attacks, it merely means you have matched wits, for the moment, with the terror masters. You haven't eliminated the source of their strength, which is their capacity to constantly dream up new methods of mayhem.

The Bush administration deserves credit for having prevented another 9/11, but it failed to communicate clearly to the American people who it was that we were fighting. Nor have things improved in the years since the Bush administration. Neither John McCain nor Barack Obama used the term *radical Islamism* in any of the 2008 presidential debates. As soon as President Obama took office, his administration dropped the phrase "Global War on Terror" in favor of an even fuzzier "Overseas Contingency Operations." By avoiding any reference to an enemy of any kind, this terminology made our wars and our sacrifices seem like a technical problem of logistics. It gave no hint of the violent political ideology that was at the heart of 9/11 and, before that, the attacks on the USS *Cole* in 2000 and our embassies in Tanzania and Kenya in 1998. No wonder people are losing interest in securing victory in Afghanistan. A war that began as a result of the worst attack on American soil has been classified using a phrase that nobody understands and only an Orwellian could love.

We have to go back and start over from square one. We have to think about what it is we are fighting for and whom we are fighting against. Our enemies have been very open about their intentions and motives. There are certain men—this is an enemy that does not consider women to be equals (though it has begun to use women as operatives in rare cases)—who believe that their narrow, intolerant, and violent interpretation of Islam offers the only correct way to be a faithful Muslim.

They view other Muslims who subscribe to less fanatical interpretations of traditional Islamic teachings as apostates. Those Muslims who are secular, or who no longer follow the strictest interpretation of Islamic law, are condemned, sometimes to death. Those who belong to other, non-Muslim religions are considered second-class humans at best.

This political ideology is not drastically different from that of other supremacist movements we have witnessed—the Aryan supremacist movement of Nazism, the racial supremacist movement of the Ku Klux Klan and apartheid, and the countless other ideologies that have depended on the demonization of another group. Our present enemies have latched on to a highly intolerant interpretation of Islam to justify their supremacist ideology. Of course, it's not at all unusual for people of a certain faith to believe that their religion is the one true way—it is common among Hindus, Jews, Catholics, Protestants, and just about every other major religion. What sets our enemies apart today is their belief that those who don't subscribe to their view of Islam should be conquered, subjugated, and if necessary, eliminated.

Our enemies are, in a phrase, Islamist supremacists. Terrorist acts against America and other Western interests are just one tool in their toolbox. In the nations where they live, they operate schools that teach their young to hate members of all other faiths. With rare exceptions, women are treated as the property of their fathers and husbands, and they are required to veil themselves at a young age. Those who accept alternative interpretations of Islamic law and scripture are pushed aside—or worse. Those lands that once were ruled by Islamic leaders centuries ago—Spain, Israel, North Africa, Central Asia, and beyond—are regarded as lands rightfully belonging to a broad Islamic caliphate, and all non-Muslims now residing there are regarded as future subjects. In certain nations that have welcomed hundreds of thousands of Muslims—such as the Netherlands, the United Kingdom, France, and Norway—Islamist supremacists work to undermine civil authorities and laws, and agitate for the recognition of sharia as the sole law applicable to all Muslims, regardless of their desire to live under such laws.

Islamist supremacists not only view Islamic civilization as superior to Western civilization, but they also hold an especially negative view of Western civilization. To Islamist supremacists, the West is a dangerous place filled with temptations for Muslim youth such as alcohol, drugs, sexuality, equality of the sexes, and secularism.

It is not unusual for strictly observant people of *non*-Islamic faiths to regard the cultural extremes of Western society this way. But while most of the traditional strains of various faiths can accommodate Western values, and seek to promote a voluntary moral culture, Islamist supremacists can't abide the West. In their eyes, the West is decadent and immoral, and through its films, music, and other cultural exports it threatens to erode the morals of young Muslims. To Islamist supremacists, the West's liberated culture actively encourages women to oppose the wishes of fathers and husbands. In the same spirit that white supremacists took offense when a black man spoke to a white woman, Islamist supremacists have created a wall of separation around women, in the name of protecting them against male sexual aggression.

This is obviously not a live-and-let-live ideology, but an aggressive one that seeks to impose itself on others by force. It's a violent ideology based on the notion that one way of living is superior to all others, and therefore should dominate all others. This is the very definition of a supremacist movement.

With all this in mind, it is imperative that we reframe the ongoing conflict in order to more clearly communicate to the millennial generation, and all Americans, who it is exactly we are fighting. There is simply no greater threat to the liberal cultural values nourished on our nation's college campuses than Islamist supremacy. If members of the millennial generation care about women's rights or

gay rights, they must understand the present danger and evil of Islamist supremacy.

Additionally, framing the current conflict as a struggle against
Islamist supremacy makes it clear that this is not a clash of faiths, or
a clash of regions, or a clash of civilizations. It is actually a face-off
between two worldviews. One worldview is richly grounded in values of individual freedom, pluralism, and human rights, and encourages Muslims, Christians, Jews, Hindus, Catholics, Buddhists, and
members of all other faiths to practice their religion freely and to live
together peacefully. The other worldview is a political ideology of
intolerance that is fighting for the subordination of all others, including adherents of a modern and pluralistic Islam.

Framing the argument this way will help us make it unambigu-
ously clear that while the leaders of this supremacy movement may
call themselves Muslims, they do not represent the religion of Islam
or the will of the world's one billion Muslims, most of whom wish
to live in peace and do not support this xenophobic and violent
ideology.

The Bush and Obama administrations have repeatedly said that
America is not at war with Islam. And Republicans need to be vocal
about condemning anyone, in America or abroad, who seeks to lump
all Muslims together as America's enemies, whether it's a pastor in
Florida who burns the Koran, or jailed terrorists in Guantánamo
who insist that America hates Muslims. America is not at war with
Islam, and Republicans must continue to follow President Bush's example in condemning any expressions of prejudice against Muslims.

Perhaps most galling to Islamist supremacists are those Arab and
Muslim leaders who rule countries that have so far not succumbed
to Islamist fanaticism. The leaders of Saudi Arabia, Jordan, Bahrain,
Lebanon, Kuwait, and even Iraq are regarded as puppets of the West,
subject to Western whims and Western culture. And so Islamist

supremacists are often most concentrated, and most radical, in nations that are ruled by secular or pro-Western Muslim leaders. For exactly this reason, the United States is highly motivated to see the establishment of representative democratic governments in countries such as Tunisia, Egypt, Libya, and Bahrain. Islamist supremacists are often the most organized actors on the ground, and we fear they might get a foothold in governance as former dictatorships crumble.

This is not an abstract argument. It is rooted in recent human experience. Remember Afghanistan as it was run by the Taliban. This was a country in which Islamist supremacists organized what they considered to be a perfect society. Girls were forbidden to attend school and were attacked when they tried to do so. Women were confined to the home and hidden beneath heavy clothing—and had to keep their faces from view. Flying kites, an old Afghan custom, was banned, as was the playing of music. A cluster of Buddhist statues 165 feet tall and 1,700 years old, recognized as a World Heritage Site, was destroyed by dynamite and tank fire. And thousands of Afghan citizens who dared to question this supremacist rule were murdered.

It should be no surprise that the Taliban gave shelter to Osama bin Laden and Al Qaeda when they were plotting the 9/11 attacks. The mass murder of Western "infidels" is their stock-in-trade. To Islamist supremacists, the West poses a unique threat, greater than that posed by mere nonbelievers in their midst. To them, the West must be resisted, not just with the heart but with the sword.

Millennials understand the dangers of supremacist movements. They have learned about the white supremacists who once dominated the American South. They have studied the rise of Nazism and the genocidal movements in Rwanda and the Balkans, each of which proclaimed that one type of people was better than another and deserved to rule the other. Given that millennials have a strong belief in the value of pluralism and diversity, they recognize that Islamist

supremacists represent a special threat to their values and their freedoms. Indeed, Islamist supremacists are the millennial generation's
worst nightmare.

The Pew Center for Research tells us that millennials are the
most liberal generation in America. And here liberal means *socially
liberal*—"permissive" in their attitudes about sex and sexual orientation, for example. They are, of course, completely comfortable when
women participate actively in society as leaders, and in virtually any
profession they choose. Millennials have diverse and broad tastes in
music and film. They communicate readily with one another, and
with their peers in foreign countries, using social media. And by
comparison with earlier generations of Americans, they are less likely
to be affiliated with organized religion—even if they are privately
spiritual. Millennials represent the future of American individualism,
which makes them an especially despised target of the political ideology of Islamist supremacists.

But the truth is that Islamist supremacists have done more
harm to *Muslims* through their violence than to any other group.
It is not unusual for Muslims who resist Islamist supremacists to be
jailed, raped, and forced to watch family members be tortured and
murdered.

A cold-eyed realist may say, "Look, it may be terrible what this
movement does to its own people, but we can't interfere every time
there is injustice in the world." I agree that we cannot and should
not try to stop Islamist supremacy through military means wherever
it appears in the world. But we must act to contain it and confront it
when it threatens the United States.

The reason we cannot abandon Afghanistan today is that the Islamist supremacists there have not been defeated. They have fled into
neighboring Pakistan and are hoping to return to Afghanistan. And
if we leave Afghanistan before helping to secure a stable society that
can defend itself against them, they will return to power. We know

precisely what would happen if that were to occur, because we saw the effects of Taliban rule on 9/11.

Likewise, we need to remind millennials that Islamist supremacists are not just cave-dwelling insurgents. Just look at Iran: a nation that was once cosmopolitan, pluralistic, and Western oriented is now an exporter of terrorism and a repressed country whose government (though not its people) is hostile to American values and is actively trying to build nuclear weapons.

Iran's president, Mahmoud Ahmadinejad, declared before the General Assembly of the United Nations that the attacks of 9/11 were organized by the United States "to reverse the declining American economy, and its grip on the Middle East, in order to save the Zionist regime." Ahmadinejad is also a Holocaust denier who has declared that Israel should be "wiped off the face of the earth."

When Ahmadinejad went to Columbia University and was questioned about the lack of gay rights in Iran, he responded that "in Iran we don't have homosexuals like in your country." The audience of millennials could hardly subdue its laughter.

And then there's the state-sanctioned punishment for adultery: stoning. This is the medieval practice of burying a victim partially in the ground, and then taking turns throwing rocks at the victim's head, using just enough force to maximize the pain but without knocking the victim unconscious. There are, at last count, nine women sentenced to death by stoning in Iran.

The way to overcome Islamist supremacists is by empowering young Muslims around the world to think freely. We need to support Iranian millennials like those who rose up in 2009's Green Revolution against a government that had plainly stolen an election, ruined an economy, and put Iran on a path of hostile confrontation with the West. Iran's millennials have grown tired of being oppressed by a political regime led by mullahs and autocrats.

We need to connect America's millennials with those of other nations, and encourage those connections. President Obama's over-tures to the Muslim world might just help open up the minds of Muslims who would otherwise fall under the influence of Islamist supremacist thinking. We Republicans may not always agree with what President Obama says, or with the Democratic Party's foreign policy approach. But we are all Americans first, and if we are to emerge victorious in this battle against Islamist supremacists, we have to work together. Millennials look to us to uphold the proud tradi-tion that partisan politics ends at the water's edge.

Finally, we need to champion those Muslims who practice a variation of Islam that respects Western values. I think of people like Irshad Manji, a faithful Muslim who calls on her fellow Muslims around the world to reconnect with the concept of *ijtihad,* Islam's own tradition of independent reasoning. In her work she calls out the anti-Semitism, homophobia, and sexism of Muslims who have colonized her faith by imposing a narrow, tribal mind-set that vio-lates the Koran's teaching to think critically. Because of her fierce commitment to reconciling faith and freedom, Manji's life is con-stantly threatened. But her message is welcomed by youth through-out the Muslim world. They have downloaded the Urdu, Farsi, and Arabic translations of her book *The Trouble with Islam Today* from the Internet—which publishers were too fearful to print in these languages—more than two million times.

I also think of Zainab Al-Suwaij, who was forced to flee Iraq in the 1990s, and who after 9/11 went on to found the Ameri-can Islamic Congress (AIC) to give a voice to pluralist Muslims on American college campuses. She is a strong advocate of the rights of Muslim women and has devoted her work at the AIC to champion-ing interfaith understanding.

There is Zeba Khan, a writer, social media consultant, and self-described advocate of Muslim-American civic engagement. She is a quintessential millennial who in 2008 launched an online network

called Muslim-Americans for Obama to mobilize Muslim-American
voters to support President Obama's campaign. While we were on
opposite sides of the political aisle then (and probably still are today),
I want to see Khan succeed. She is the daughter of devout Muslim
parents who emigrated from India to the United States. Her parents
insisted that she learn about other faiths, so she and her brother attended Hebrew school, where she studied Hebrew for nine years
and learned to read the Torah while also attending her local mosque.
Khan is a prime example of the unusual combinations of faith traditions and backgrounds that have found a home in America over the
centuries.

Likewise, there is Suhail Khan, a young Muslim Republican whose parents also emigrated from India. He grew up in the
western United States, where he practiced his faith with his family while learning about Christianity at the Catholic school he attended. Khan worked in the White House for George W. Bush and
is deeply involved in the American conservative movement. Khan
is one of thousands of mainstream American Muslims who work to
promote Christian-Muslim understanding, in his case at the Institute
for Global Engagement. Republicans must harness the knowledge,
energy, and dynamism of people like Khan in order to mobilize, as
Zeba Kahn did for Obama, a new generation of Muslim-American
Republicans.

Republicans should champion the work of Muslims whose religious practice complements America's history of religious pluralism.
We must stand against those who use intimidation and thuggery to
silence the voices of freethinkers here in America and Europe and
the Middle East. We Republicans can show, by our own example,
that individual freedoms and liberties need not lead to lives of immo-
rality but rather to lives of discipline, creativity, and dynamism—and
to cultures of tolerance and diversity.

We must show that the dream of Islamist supremacists—an end

to the rights of women, religious minorities, homosexuals, and others who do not abide by their radicalized interpretations of the Koran—is the nightmare of all civilized people.

Republicans can connect with this new generation by reminding millennials that what they saw on September 11, 2001, represents the Islamist supremacist plan for the future. It was not a *tactic* that declared war on us that day but a political *ideology,* one as menacing, as hateful, and as anti-American as Nazism.

Millennials, the most globally oriented, most diverse generation in American history, should understand that their worldview is in the crosshairs of Islamist supremacists. This is a war that none of us— neither Republicans nor Democrats—chose. But it is a war we must win. Otherwise, values that we cherish as Americans—freedom, democracy, and diversity—will perish.

CHAPTER 12

AMERICA THE EXCEPTIONAL

"Our willingness to speak for freedom is no bargaining chip.
It's an integral part of our foreign policy."
—RONALD REAGAN

B Y 1919, WHEN Herbert Hoover turned forty-five years old, he had spent his entire adult life outside the United States, working and traveling in the Far East, the Near East, Southeast Asia, Australia, South America, Europe, and Africa. He established residencies in Australia, China, and England. He had visited every continent but Antarctica. He had circumnavigated the globe five times—and this was before the advent of commercial aviation.

He was not a dilettante traveler, casually gliding through countries as a tourist or an art collector, someone merely picking up experiences to use as dinner party fodder back home. He was working. His international travels brought him into direct contact with those who were building industries and managing emerging national governments, or clinging to feudal ones. He met all kinds of citizens in these countries, from average laborers to ruling aristocrats.

What he saw during his travels influenced him greatly. At the beginning of the twentieth century, the world was in upheaval. The old order of monarchies and empires, while still in place, was starting to be challenged. Rapidly modernizing countries such as Japan and

Germany were building up their militaries and flexing their muscles. The threat of revolution and anarchy was palpable. The ideas of Karl Marx appeared ready to overturn the ideological tables in Europe. It was a time when the assumptions that underpinned capitalism, democracy, and Western civilization were being called into question.

Hoover experienced this revolutionary upheaval. He observed that in each of the countries where revolution took hold, workers were agitated that they did not reap the benefits of their labor to an extent nearly equal to their contributions to industry. He and my great-grandmother barely escaped China's Boxer Rebellion in 1900. During the following decade, the mines he operated in Russia were seized and nationalized by Lenin's Bolshevik regime. Hoover was asked by his own government to administer massive food relief to combat the starvation and hunger-related disease caused by the First World War and its revolutionary aftermath. He saw that the landed gentry of Europe, those lucky few who hung on to the remnants of the ancient system of feudalism and peerage, were blind to their impending demise.

Hoover had no illusions, as he went about his travels, that he was an exception to the global rules of opportunity. Here was a man, once a frontier orphan of no means, who had become one of the world's wealthiest and most respected individuals. He began to think about why this was, and to wonder whether America itself was the exception—whether the American *system* was different and, in essential ways, unlike that of any other country.

He looked at countries endowed with greater natural resources, stronger educational traditions, more powerful armies and navies, and deeper cultural heritages—and yet none of them could equal America's economic might and potential at that time. He wondered whether young America, immature America, was benefiting from more than just good fortune. He began to think that perhaps America was on a distinct path because it was unique, because its founding philosophy encouraged individual achievement and placed a premium on equality of opportunity.

After the First World War, Hoover returned to the United States and began to ponder the circumstances that had catapulted the country into its position of global dominance within such a short period of time. He wondered what it was about the American formula that had made his story possible. Like the engineer he was, he began to *reverse*-engineer America. Mentally he pushed aside all the external features of its national strength and tried to peer inside the machinery, at the hardwiring. He wanted to figure out what the mechanisms were that set America apart from Europe and the rest of the world.

That search led him to craft a commencement address, which eventually became a slender volume called "American Individualism." Instead of looking at America from the top down, as a system of interconnected parts, a vast machine of political philosophy and economic organization, Hoover proceeded from the bottom up. He zeroed in on the smallest unit of society. He focused on how America was guided both culturally and politically by its celebration of the individual. In America, Hoover observed, an individual is just that—a single person, defined only as that person chooses. An individual could come from a background of poverty, be raised by uneducated parents, belong to a church of no particular note, or be born into a race just two generations removed from slavery, yet that individual could advance well beyond the circumstances of his birth. And Herbert Hoover, the orphaned boy of the frontier, the child with no privileges or advantages other than his God-given talents who rose to the greatest heights of wealth and power, understood this as well as anyone.

But Hoover worried that America would be tempted by those proposing a radical redistribution of economic spoils and political power, as the Marxists and socialists of that time prescribed. Upon his return to the United States in 1920, he saw adherents of Marxism and fascism and other ideologies lashing out at America's system. The Socialist Party in America in the late 1910s and early 1920s was regularly garnering between 2.8 percent and 6 percent of the votes in presidential elections.

Hoover wrote "American Individualism" to explain the American system, and to defend it. He wanted to inoculate America against the dangerous temptation to experiment with Europe's radical ideologies. Hoover had witnessed the failure of socialism and communism and the hardship and death it had brought to millions in Europe. And while socialists in America ignored this early evidence of ideological failure, Hoover drew attention to it. Referring to the communist experiment in Soviet Russia, he wrote that "socialism in a nation-wide application has now proved itself with rivers of blood and inconceivable misery to be an economic and spiritual fallacy and has wrecked itself finally upon the rocks of destroyed production and moral degeneracy." He understood the appeal of socialism all too well, and he considered the attempt to implement it in Russia to be useful, in that it showed humanity that socialism's uplifting ideas, when put into practice, led to destruction and misery. And having seen socialism's failure with his own eyes, he was determined to oppose it, especially in America.

It is striking that nearly a hundred years later, "American Individualism" encapsulates much of what Americans still believe about this country today, and why they resisted the temptations of socialism even in the country's darkest economic period, during the Great Depression. Hoover understood that America existed on the strength of an idea, not of national or tribal loyalties. The essence of America could not be captured in a flag or a banner or a song. America represented the collective achievements of its individual people.

Hoover didn't think that Americans were inherently superior to citizens of other countries. He merely felt that Americans were more likely to achieve their fullest potential as individuals because of the freedoms they enjoyed. He understood that America was the first nationwide experiment in economic and social freedom and mobility in history. No nation before had suggested that it was the inalienable right of an individual to pursue happiness and prosperity without fear of disrupting the social order.

Hoover presented the American system as a revolutionary system, a system without the shackles of class or caste. He understood the ambition of the revolutionaries in Europe—to bring about new systems that would offer greater opportunity for more people to share in the nation's wealth. But Hoover believed that the American system of representative democracy had its own built-in mechanisms to make possible such mobility, and that it allowed for gradual social and political reforms, thereby avoiding the need for violent or radical revolution.

It is ironic, even tragic, that my great-grandfather, the first globally minded president of our country, the first man to hold the office who had traveled so widely, is most remembered for having presided over a nation that lost its global confidence, turned inward, shut its borders, cut off its trading partners, and retreated from engagement with the world, a descent into isolation from which it would not emerge until after 1941. The Herbert Hoover of "American Individualism" believed that America was a beacon of light in the story of human freedom. And yet during his presidency and the subsequent twelve years, that light faded, just as he feared it would.

But that light was never fully extinguished. Herbert Hoover was on to something. There really was something extraordinary about the American system. Hoover's "American Individualism" was an early-twentieth-century expression of the idea of American exceptionalism, first articulated in *Democracy in America* ninety years earlier. To Alexis de Tocqueville, America was "exceptional" because at the time of its founding, it was quite literally the world's *sole exception* to antiquated governments that concentrated wealth and power in the hands of the few. Hoover's practical experience corroborated Tocqueville's observations, and he recognized that America was the first sustainable example of equality of opportunity, liberty, and social and economic mobility in human civilization. Hoover saw that America had led the world in its commitment to individual freedom, which had created unprecedented wealth and prosperity.

American exceptionalism is not a statement of arrogance or a belief that Americans are inherently better than the citizens of other nations. American exceptionalism is not the notion that America is faultless. And it is certainly not the notion that America has achieved the perfect implementation of its ideals. Rather it asserts that the American *system* is unique in its emphasis on individual liberty, and that this emphasis has produced extraordinary individuals and extraordinary achievements for humanity.

When Barack Obama was asked in his first year in office whether he believed in American exceptionalism, he said he did but in the same way that Greeks believe in Greek exceptionalism, and that the British believe in British exceptionalism. In other words, while President Obama said he personally believed America is exceptional, he was not prepared to argue that it actually *is* more exceptional than any other nation—a dodge of the question. Republicans were outraged with his answer and saw it as an example of moral equivalency— every nation is equally exceptional, none more than any other.

Republicans couldn't understand how we had elected a president who confuses the idea of American exceptionalism—which argues that the American system is better not because it's American but because it affords individuals greater freedoms and opportunities than any other system—with the base instincts of American jingoism, which is merely a reflex of the fiercely proud. Republicans like me were incensed that President Obama didn't seem to notice that the results of the American system are unmatched by any other system when it comes to securing personal freedoms and opportunity.

His view that all other nations are our equals—no better but no worse—was blasphemy to Republicans and to many Americans.

But while this statement rightly offended the sensibilities of Republicans and conservatives, President Obama's worldview that other countries are just as exceptional as America seems consistent with the values of the millennial generation. Millennials are the most global generation and the least likely to see significant differences between themselves and their international peers. The impact of globalization among millennials has been a leveling experience. The differences between nations simply fall away, and millennials do not distinguish between them. Millennials are unimpressed with the argument that America is different or special or better, because they've been taught that *everyone* is special and *everyone* is exceptional.

According to pollster Frank Luntz, this generation really is "the first to reject 'American exceptionalism,' preferring a 'We're all in this together' philosophy." They are the Facebook generation, with "friends" all over the world. They follow people on other continents via Twitter, and they have access to products from all over the globe. Luntz points out that millennials "aren't as interested in the Olympics as their parents were because they don't really like international competition—the whole country-versus-country thing—US versus Russia, US versus China. . . . They can't relate to superpower competition on any field—of battle or otherwise." On a personal level they don't think they are better than their peers in other countries, so unless they have had an opportunity to travel, they don't think the American system is better than any other system of government.

Why should they? We haven't made the case for American exceptionalism to them. And because of this, they think American exceptionalism stands for the same arrogant beliefs that President Obama thinks it does—that America is always right, that America should go it alone, and that America doesn't need allies.

I've taken a different view of American exceptionalism than

most people my age and younger, thanks as much to my own practical experiences as to any political philosophy. Partly inspired by my great-grandfather, partly by my own itch for independence, and partly because my mother was a flight attendant and I benefited from free travel vouchers, I started my adult life the same way my great-grandfather did: I traveled. Between the ages of eighteen and twenty-five (at which point my United Airlines travel passes expired), I dedicated myself to collecting passport stamps and travel visas, and even had extra pages sewn in to extend the life of my passport. I packed my university years with study-abroad experiences, with extended stays in China, Bolivia, and Mexico. When I graduated from college, I moved to Taiwan, where I landed my first job as an editor and research assistant at a Taiwanese law firm.

I wanted to see and experience an array of cultures, political systems, landscapes, and people. I loved languages and dedicated years of study to Spanish and Mandarin Chinese.

I was conscious of the fact that, in traveling the world at the dawn of a new American century, I was, in my own modest way, following in the footsteps of my great-grandfather and great-grandmother.

My experiences afforded me the ability to compare other political and economic systems with America's and reaffirmed for me that my great-grandfather's observations about American individualism were still true.

In Bolivia, the poorest of South American countries, I saw how impostors throughout their country's history have claimed to offer democracy and more prosperity but have left the country worse off. Bolivia's natural resources have been exploited to enrich the ruling elite and foreign allies, leaving the indigenous people only slightly less impoverished than at the time of the Spanish conquest more than five hundred years ago.

Even the middle class in Bolivia, a tiny share of the population, has limited economic mobility. I lived for seven months in the city of

Cochabamba with a middle-class family whose life was quite comfortable compared to that of their fellow countrymen, yet which still presented little opportunity for an improved economic position. I spent one week visiting the countryside and lived alongside the most crushing poverty of the not-yet-developing world. I herded sheep and experienced *campesino* life with a generous Aymaran family, who, after observing that their daughter and I had formed a friendship, decided that she ought to return to America with me so that she might enjoy a life of enhanced economic possibility.

In China, I saw how even the most creative and ambitious young adults avoided saying anything critical of their government or political system, aware of the watchful and stern authority that silently loomed over them. Yet their cousins in Taiwan, the thriving Chinese democracy on the other side of the Taiwan Strait, could be politically active while enjoying the economic fruits of that island marvel. All of that was possible because of the military protection and diplomatic guarantees of the United States.

I also saw how women around the world edited themselves—not just their words, but their entire personalities—so as not to offend the timeworn sensibilities of their fathers, their brothers, or their husbands. I wondered to myself what these women would be like if they lived in America. Not just how they would dress, or even talk, but how they would think. What would their lives be like? The differences between us could be boiled down to my exceptional luck in having been born under a system of government that has afforded me more freedom and opportunity than most young women around the world will ever know. This is my experience with American exceptionalism.

Most of all, I felt lucky to have been born in a country that afforded me the luxury of this ability to experience and observe, that allowed me to follow my curiosity and inclination to adventure and to test the knowledge I'd acquired from books and in classrooms. I had seen how the American system is exceptional, why it is worth fighting to preserve, and why every generation—the millennials especially—must overcome their doubts about the greatness of the American system. It is only by good fortune that we are born into a country that values individual freedom, social and economic mobility, the rule of law, and human rights. And it is too easy to take these gifts for granted.

Another reason I suspect that millennials are skeptical about American exceptionalism is that in their short lifetimes, America's foreign policy efforts have been defined by significant failures. While the millennial generation was indelibly affected by the attacks of 9/11, their attitudes toward America's assertion of power abroad were shaped by America's blunders in Iraq. And that is clear from the way millennials have voted. The first millennials to vote in a presidential election in 2000 split their votes evenly between George W. Bush and Al Gore. But their decisive break from the Republican Party occurred in the 2004 presidential election, when the defining issue was whether America should withdraw its forces from Iraq. They voted 54 percent to 45 percent for John Kerry, the Democratic nominee who had originally voted in favor of the war but who later came out against it, calling it "the wrong war, in the wrong place, at the wrong time."

The discontent with Iraq spread further in 2006, when Democratic candidates won control of both the House and the Senate, thanks in part to strong millennial turnout. And of course in 2008, millennials voted two to one for Obama, who had opposed the surge in Iraq, over McCain, who had been the first major politician to advocate in favor of it.

Unlike baby boomers during the Vietnam War, millennials do not face the risk of the military draft. There was no self-interest involved in opposing the war, and discontent with the war did not take the form of demonstrations on college campuses. Unlike the Vietnam-era campus protesters that idealized Ho Chi Minh, millennials were in no way sympathetic to Saddam Hussein, Al Qaeda in Iraq, or the multiple Islamist supremacist groups vying to replace Saddam Hussein after his ouster and execution. And millennials were not hostile to our troops, who have enjoyed significant support among all population groups, despite the unpopularity of the Iraq War.

Yet millennials fiercely opposed the war anyway—not in the run-up to the war, but after things started to go badly. They were susceptible to the constant accusations from the Left that Americans had been lied to about weapons of mass destruction. President Bush and the leaders of several nations had argued that, because Saddam Hussein had developed WMD programs in the past and had used them against the Iraqi Kurds in the late 1980s, in a post-9/11 world America could no longer risk allowing a maniacal dictator to pass WMDs on to terrorist groups hostile to the United States.

This was a powerful argument for war, but a faulty one, it turned out, because Saddam didn't have WMDs. Even worse, in the days, weeks, and months after the American military victory, Iraq descended into chaos. From the millennials' point of view, Iraq was a war fought on a false premise—WMDs—and without a clear plan for ensuring lasting victory. A 2006 survey found that a significant majority—60 percent—of millennials surveyed believed that the Iraq War was a "mistake," while nearly a third felt the United States should withdraw from Iraq immediately. They came to view Iraq as an irresponsible and incompetent adventure. This generation is not antiwar, but they oppose war waged without a clear and definable purpose. As a result, the millennial generation soured on Republican leadership in foreign policy.

Against this backdrop, Republicans have a difficult task ahead as they try to restore their credibility with the millennial generation on foreign policy. Nonetheless, I think it can be done—more important, it *must* be done. Here are five areas Republicans should

emphasize in order to win millennials back and set a confident foreign policy agenda for the next generation:

The American System Is Exceptional

America is a force for good in the world, and the American system is
worth fighting to defend. When we speak of American exceptionalism, we must be absolutely clear that this isn't a statement of superi-
ority or a belief that Americans are better than other people. There
are exceptional *individuals* in every country, but the American system, by protecting freedom and facilitating social and economic mobility, has allowed its people to reach their fullest potential in greater
numbers than is possible in any other system. Along the way it has
introduced unprecedented levels of freedom and wealth creation and
has increased standards of living for great majorities of people—not
just in the United States, but around the world.

I think it's up to us as Republicans to demonstrate to millennials that the idea of American exceptionalism stands for more than
waving the flag. We have to make the case that America champions the freedoms and liberties and privileges millennials enjoy. It is
the benefits of American exceptionalism that their peers around the
world—including those seeking freedom today in the Middle East—
desire and deserve.

Maintain a Strong Military

America spends more than any other nation on its military for good
reason. The United States must continue to be prepared to defend
its freedoms with the strongest military in the world.

We need to remind millennials that as the world's leading power
we cannot rely on other nations to defend our freedoms. Many nations of Europe have been able to prune their militaries, in some cases
to the bare branches, because for more than fifty years they have been
able to count on America to defend their freedom. But who will

come to the aid of the United States if it's unable to beat back its enemies? We must be careful not to indulge the impulse to cut military budgets just because they are large—our military budget must always be sizable, since no other nation will fight our wars and few countries will fight for the freedom of others, as America does. The system of American exceptionalism also calls for American sacrifice—military service, a strong defense, an active effort to defend our borders and our friends.

This sacrifice and service to the world has led to enormous shared prosperity. Just look at how the American Navy's securing of the seas has brought about decades of secure trade and wealth creation for the international community. It is in the interest of world prosperity that America remain a global military power. Other nations may not be willing to acknowledge it, or even thank us for it, but there are graveyards all over Europe and Asia that attest to the sacrifices we have made fighting for the freedom and security of others. In return for our sacrifices, as Colin Powell so eloquently reminded the world, all we have ever asked is for enough land to bury our dead.

Support Our Friends

America should be committed to a global strategy that focuses on supporting those countries that share our values. Rather than reach out to hostile and rogue nations such as Iran and North Korea, or aggressive nations like Russia, we must be good to our allies so they do not think America's support is only temporary. In Eastern Europe, we must keep our promise to build missile defenses to protect our friends against the threat of aggression (and not abandon these plans, as President Obama appears willing to do).

Republicans must keep in mind not only our recent struggles but also our recent successes. If not for the Pax Americana, much of the world would be living in the shadow of one form of tyranny or another. Republicans should remind millennials that America has been Israel's strongest friend in its fight for security and peace, and that we continue to provide support to South Korea and the people of Taiwan. We must recall that our friends in Colombia were once prisoners in their own nation, as drug cartels waged a vicious war of control over large swaths of that beautiful country. Thanks to American assistance, Colombia's president at the time, Álvaro Uribe, smashed the cartels and placed the future of Colombia in the hands of the Colombian people.

We should remember that one of the things that makes America exceptional is American friendship—no nation has given so much of itself for its friends, or even for those nations that have rarely supported American interests. We should be proud of that. Not just because it will resonate with millennials. But because it's true.

A Confident Foreign Policy Is Also a
Generous Foreign Policy

At the time Herbert Hoover wrote "American Individualism," he was overseeing America's first foray into foreign aid by administering the largest humanitarian food relief effort ever undertaken, to famine-ridden Soviet Russia. The American Relief Administration delivered food and medicine to tens of millions of Soviet citizens and saved millions of lives. America became the benevolent world leader, and in the spirit of the millennial generation's impulse to service, we should remind millennials how America helps the world not only by protecting our friends, but by serving needy and deserving people (even when we don't support their governments, as in the case of Hoover's humanitarian relief to the Soviets). American aid ships to Haiti, and the relief efforts after Asian tsunamis, our efforts to distribute mosquito netting to stop malaria in Africa, and our spearheading of treatments for tuberculosis worldwide—millennials see these endeavors, and they see that America alone does them on a scale that can make the difference. This is American exceptionalism in action.

Although George W. Bush gets low marks from millennials, Republicans should remind them that he led America's effort to save millions of lives in Africa through efforts to fund the distribution of HIV/AIDS medications. "[Bush] has actually done more than any American president for Africa," said British music producer Bob Geldof, one of the most outspoken advocates for aid to Africa. U2's lead singer, Bono, said much the same thing: "250,000 Africans are on anti-viral drugs; they literally owe their lives to America."

Free Trade Leads to Free People

This applies to America's approach to global trade, as well as to the free flow of ideas. Millennials are globally minded, so Republicans should point out that as emerging markets rise to compete for economic dominance, America will welcome them into the global economic marketplace, and will welcome their dynamism, their competition, their collaboration, and their innovations. We can argue that free trade and open markets do more to alleviate poverty than any other public policy. We have to make the connection to millennials—who can be skeptical of free trade because of concerns that foreign workers end up being exploited. They need to see that when we trade with a nation, we are giving that nation a chance at prosperity, while we ourselves benefit from a more globalized marketplace.

Republicans must also argue that American exceptionalism isn't just what we do around the world, but what we do at home as well. We are still a country of extraordinary opportunity. A child born under Soviet Communism can move here with his parents as a young boy and go on to found a company like Google. There is a reason this happens in America and only rarely anywhere else. It is because America does not deny legal newcomers the chance to become productive citizens. In many European countries, you can live your entire life there and yet still be considered a foreigner, simply because your parents came from another place. In America, everyone can belong.

I believe that a generation raised to think globally and act locally will understand that so long as America is free and confident, freedom and prosperity will have a chance in the world. We are, as Madeleine Albright once said, "the world's indispensable nation." I believe that millennials lost faith in the idea of American indispensability not because they lost faith in America, but because they have lost sight of the vital importance of American leadership in the world. But they do want America to be equal to its promise to give every individual an opportunity to dream, to succeed, and to be exceptional. And I think that if they are willing to fight for that, they will find many friends in the Republican Party.

ACKNOWLEDGMENTS

If American individualism is a blend of rugged individualism and a community spirit, then the effort to create this book has epitomized the spirit of its title: to be precise, a rather stubborn individual blessed with a supportive community of friends and colleagues who helped make this book possible.

My editor, Jenna Ciongoli, has been a steady champion from beginning to end—not every author is fortunate enough to have an editor who believes in her book from the moment it begins to take shape. I'd also like to thank the marketing and publicity team at Crown, especially Jennifer Robbins and Sarah Breivogel—and my agent, Ian Kleinert, for discovering this opportunity and helping me out at every step along the way.

In the realm of polishing and editing, I am grateful to Noam Neusner, my former OMB colleague and late-stage collaborator on this project, who helped ensure that I put the right words on the page. I am grateful as well to Bob Asahina for his insightful perspective on how to structure the book. And I am especially grateful to Bert Patenaude, the pristine polisher of words, whose keen eye and industrious pen swooped in at the eleventh hour.

For each of the policy sections of the book, I checked my prescriptions with friends who are experts in their respective fields, among them Stuart Gottlieb, Jen Pollom, Irshad Manji (whose moral courage inspires), and Ayann Hirsi Ali (whose friendship I treasure).

Spencer Howard and Tim Walch at the Herbert Hoover Presidential Library and Museum were invaluable in ensuring that my Hoover facts are correct.

Among those of us dedicated to restoring the good reputation of Herbert Hoover, George H. Nash stands out as the preeminent expert on both Hoover and the history of America's modern conservative movement. He is a kindred spirit in his devotion to Herbert Hoover and his dedication is deeply appreciated by the Hoover family. Likewise, film producer Austin Hoyt and historian Bert Patenaude (again) deserve recognition for drawing deeply from the archives at the Hoover Institution for their recent documentary film for PBS, *The Great Famine,* which recounts the epic story of Hoover's rescue operation in Bolshevik Russia to vanquish the Great Famine.

Ashley Koning will one day make a fine professor, but in the meantime I'm indebted to her for sacrificing her spring break from her doctoral studies in order to fact-check my work. Her prodigious talents as a researcher and her fastidious attention to detail put her in a league of her own. I also owe a debt of gratitude to Sam Abrams of Sarah Lawrence College for finding me Katelyn Bornholdt and Emily MacDonald, whose excellent research helped me immeasurably and who added their refreshing millennial perspectives to the data they supplied. Finally, many thanks to Aileen Hogan for her late-inning notes support.

I would be remiss not to thank David Eisenhower, whom I admire and respect and who first gave me the idea for this book more than ten years ago when I took his class "American Presidency and Communications" at the University of Pennsylvania.

Family and friends make life shine. And so I owe thanks first to my husband, John Avlon—Fipp and LOML—whose devotion and support are manifest throughout these pages and to whom this book is dedicated.

My parents have given me all their love all of my life—and I'm especially happy that my father has enjoyed reading the sections on his grandfather. I'm grateful that my grandmother, for whom I'm named, knew about this book. Her spirit suffuses these pages. My beloved brother and sister-in-law tolerated my absence and stress over the past year, as did my gracious in-laws, John and Dianne Avlon. Lots of love also to my Aunt Lou, whom I will now be free to visit more frequently in her new home in Los Angeles, and to my cousins: Allan and Michelle, Debbie and Jonathan, and Jimmy. And a special hug for my uncle Allan.

I am blessed with an abundance of friends who have supported me this year and steered clear during my intensive writing spells. I can't wait to reconnect with all of you—Lisa and Eric, Jenny and Scott, Libby and Chris, Judy and Bill Casey, Erika and Cameron, Natalie and Mike, Heide and Max, Muffy Lewis, Ivette Fernandez, Melissa Danforth, Christian Zaal, Maury Donahue, Jordan Salcito, Olga Arguello, Sara Dawes, Michael Ahrens, Mike Rixon, BJ Goergan, and my newfound cousin Matthew Mesher.

Likewise, Jen Heller, Lily Appelman, and Penny Rice are lifeline friends who have never flinched, even when this book forced me to shirk baby shower duties!

On a personal and professional level, I want to thank Bill O'Reilly for making me both a Culture Warrior and, to use his word, "a star"; Gretchen Carlson for her friendship; and all my friends at Fox News Channel for their support.

I am also indebted to the wonderful team of policy warriors intimately known as the Blob—Paul Singer, Annie Dickerson, Dan Senor, Michele Packman, Marge Govan, and Terry Kassel—who demonstrate the truth of Margaret Mead's aphorism that a small group of thoughtful, committed people can change the world.

Finally, for their ongoing effort to ensure that the freedom to marry is available to every American, I want to thank Chad Griffin and Adam Umhoffer at AFER, and special thanks to Ken Mehlman for his leadership in this cause. For their courage in breaking down barriers within the conservative movement, I'm grateful to Jimmy LaSalvia and Chris Barron of GOProud.

For more information on Herbert Hoover, please visit the following websites: Herbert Hoover Presidential Library and Museum, www.hoover.nara.gov; the Herbert Hoover Presidential Library Association, www.hooverassociation.org; the Hoover Institution on War, Revolution, and Peace, www.hoover.org.

NOTES

Introduction

xi *been disappointed:* "About half of millennials say the president has failed to change the way Washington works, which had been the central promise of his candidacy." http://pewresearch .org/pubs/1501/millennials-new-survey-generational-personality-upbeat-open-new-ideas-technology-bound.

xii *idealistic expectations:* Pew Research Center for People and the Press (Washington, D.C.), "A Pro-Government, Socially Liberal Generation: Democrats' Edge Among Millennials Slips," 6.

xii *favorable attitudes:* Pew poll. Ibid., 24.

xiii *saving more lives:* George H. Nash, *Reappraising the Right: The Past and Future of American Conservatism* (Wilmington, Del.: Intercollegiate Studies Institute, 2009), 309.

xiv *"contains the New and Old":* F. J. Turner to Richard Emmet [Hoover's secretary], January 18, 1923, Commerce Papers, Herbert Hoover Presidential Library, West Branch, Iowa.

1. Growing Up Hoover

1 *"He certainly has had his hand":* Lou Henry Hoover to Allan Hoover, September 26, 1931, Hoover Family Papers.

5 *He was the second son:* George H. Nash, *The Life of Herbert Hoover: The Engineer, 1874–1914* (New York: W. W. Norton, 1983), 7.

6 *He graduated to:* Herbert Hoover, *The Memoirs of Herbert Hoover: Years of Adventure, 1874–1920* (New York: Macmillan, 1951), 26–28.

6 *set sail for China:* Ibid., 35–36.

6 *German mail boat:* Nash, *The Life of Herbert Hoover,* 117–24.

7 *By the time he was:* "The Highest Salaried Man of His Age in the World," *San Francisco Chronicle,* December 8, 1901.

7 *Later, at the height:* Nash, *The Life of Herbert Hoover,* 568.

8 *"Twenty million are starving":* David Burner, *Herbert Hoover: A Public Life* (New York: Alfred A. Knopf, 1979), 131.

9 *According to Hoover's biographer:* George H. Nash, *Reappraising the Right* (Wilmington, Del.: Intercollegiate Studies Institute, 2009), 251.

9 *"let the fortune":* Will Irwin, *Herbert Hoover: A Reminiscent Biography* (New York: Grosset & Dunlap, 1928), 135.

10 *"from its records":* Herbert Hoover's 1959 statement to the Board of Trustees of Stanford University, http://www.hoover.org/about/mission-statement.

10 *encouraged to run:* Franklin D. Roosevelt, to Hugh Gibson, January 2, 1920, Pre-Commerce Papers, Herbert Hoover Presidential Library, West Branch, Iowa.

10 *"Secretary of Commerce and":* This phrase was commonly applied to Hoover in the 1920s, attributed in particular to S. Parker Gilbert, a U.S. agent general for reparations to Germany during the Coolidge administration and previously an undersecretary of the treasury. The attribution was made, without any source cited, by Oswald Garrison Villard, editor of the *Nation* at the time, in *Prophets True and False* (New York: Alfred A. Knopf, 1928), 24.

12 *"every man for himself":* Herbert Hoover, "American Individualism and Challenge to Liberty" (West Branch, Iowa: Herbert Hoover Presidential Library Association, 1989), 35.

12 *he articulated his philosophy:* Ibid., 11–12.

11 *"few great formulations":* New York Times Book Review, December 17, 1922, 1.

12 *"it contains the New":* F. J. Turner to Richard Emmet [Hoover's secretary], January 18, 1923, Commerce Papers, Herbert Hoover Presidential Library, West Branch, Iowa.

13 *low-interest loans:* Herbert Hoover, *The Memoirs of Herbert Hoover: The Cabinet and the Presidency* (New York: MacMillan, 1952), 126.

13   *"those were the days"*: Ibid., 126.

13   *"Rugged Individualism"*: Herbert Hoover, *The New Day: Campaign Speeches of Herbert Hoover, 1928* (Stanford, Calif.: Stanford University Press), 230.

14   *He proposed to Congress a $160 million tax cut:* "Annual Message to Congress on the State of the Union, December 3, 1929," *Public Papers of the Presidents: Herbert Hoover, 1929* (Washington, D.C.: U.S. Government Printing Office, 1974), 404–36.

14   *"No one in his place": New York Times*, March 2, 1930.

14   *conditions in the Midwest:* David Burner, *Herbert Hoover: A Public Life* (New York: Alfred A. Knopf, 1970), 131.

15   *4.2 percent of the:* Milton Friedman and Anna Jacobson Schwartz, *A Monetary History of the United States, 1867–1960* (Princeton, N. J.: Princeton University Press, 1963), 342.

16   *"raw ambition for power":* Thomas Fleming, "Channeling George Washington: Presidents Criticizing Presidents," George Mason University's History News Network, March 1, 2010, http://www .hnn.us/articles/123859.html.

17   *"unguarded, discredited, unloved":* William F. Buckley Jr., *Happy Days Were Here Again: Reflections of a Libertarian Journalist* (New York: Random House, 1993), 396.

17   *an injustice so petty:* Joseph E. Stevens, *Hoover Dam: An American Adventure* (Norman, Okla.: University of Oklahoma Press, 1988), 173–75.

18   *"of modern conservative thought":* Richard Norton Smith, in preface to Herbert Hoover, "American Individualism and Challenge to Liberty" (West Branch, Iowa: Herbert Hoover Presidential Library Association, 1989), vii.

18   *"cripple or abandon":* Herbert Hoover, "American Individualism and the Challenge to Liberty," 65.

19   *Hoover cited several areas:* Ibid., 124.

20   *"Hoover depression economics":* Joseph Biden, CBS interview by Katie Couric, September 22, 2008; reprinted in *Wall Street Journal*, "Rehabilitating Maligned Hoover," November 4, 2008, http:// online.wsj.com/article/SB122512986151172687.html.

20 *"ignorance was bliss"*: Ibid.

20 *"tough economic times"*: Ibid.

20 *"Obama's Hoovervilles"*: Matt Bai, "Hooverville Attacks on Obama Offers Previews of Campaign," *New York Times,* February 12, 2011, A13.

20 *"Barack 'Hoover' Obama"*: Rush Limbaugh, "Screw this Hussein business. It's Barack 'Hoover' Obama," August 12, 2010, www.rushlimbaugh.com/home/daily/site_081210/content/01125106.member.html.

22 *"what was widely believed"*: Thomas Sowell, *Intellectuals and Society* (New York: Basic Books, 2009), 71.

22 *"It's a myth"*: Burton Folsom Jr. and Anita Folsom, "Did FDR End the Depression?" *Wall Street Journal,* April 12, 2010, A17.

2. Conservative Tribalism

25 *"The term conservatism"*: Milton Friedman, *Capitalism and Freedom: Fortieth Anniversary Edition* (Chicago: University of Chicago Press, 1962), 6.

26 *homosexuality should be accepted:* Pew Research Center, "Religion Among the Millennials: Less Religiously Active Than Older Americans, but Fairly Traditional in Other Ways," February 2010, 18.

26 *As a generation:* Cathy Lynn Grossman, "Young Adults 'Less Religious,' Not Necessarily 'More Secular,' " *USA Today,* February 17, 2010, http://www.usatoday.com/news/religion/2010-02-17-pewyouth17_ST_N.htm; Cathy Lynn Grossman, "Survey: 72% of Millennials 'More Spiritual Than Religious,' " *USA Today*, October 14, 2010, http://www.usatoday.com/news/religion/2010-04-27-1Amillfaith27_ST_N.htm; Pew Research Center Forum on Religion and Public Life, "Religion Among the Millennials: Less Religiously Active Than Older Americans, but Fairly Traditional in Other Ways," February 2010, http://pewforum.org/uploadedFiles/Topics/Demographics/Age/millennials-report.pdf; "Millennials—A Portrait of Generation Next: Confident. Connected. Open to Change," Pew Research Center, February 2010,

http://pewsocialtrends.org/files/2010/10/millennials-confident-connected-open-to-change.pdf. See also "Reader's Digest Poll: Millennials Are First Generation with Unique Political Identity; Will Match Seniors in Turnout; Obama Beats McCain by Whopping 22 Points Among 18–29 Year-Olds," *PR Newswire*, May 6, 2008, http://www.prnewswire.com/news-releases/young-voters-to-have-unprecedented-impact-on-presidential-election-57162512.html.

27 *A disclaimer first:* Lee Edwards, "The Conservative Consensus: Frank Meyer, Barry Goldwater, and the Politics of Fusionism," *The Heritage Foundation: First Principles Series,* no. 8, January 22, 2007, 1.

27 *"Perhaps the most important thing":* George H. Nash, *Reappraising the Right* (Wilmington, Del.: Intercollegiate Studies Institute, 2009), 359.

29 *Buckley's mission statement:* William F. Buckley Jr., "Our Mission Statement," *National Review,* November 19, 1955, http://article.nationalreview.com/346187/our-mission-statement/william-f-buckley-jr.

29 *economic libertarians:* Nash, *Reappraising the Right,* 321.

30 *They were not even:* Friedrich A. Hayek, "Why I Am Not a Conservative," *The Constitution of Liberty* (Chicago: University of Chicago Press, 1960), 397. Hayek even dedicated an entire essay to the subject of why he refused to accept the label "conservative" for his political and economic philosophy.

30 *"free minds and free markets":* "About Reason," *Reason,* 2011, http://reason.com/about.

31 *They advocated "a revival":* Nash, *Reappraising the Right,* 320–21.

32 *"school prayer":* Ibid., 325–26.

33 *"conservagenzia":* Matthew Dowd, interviewed by author, March 9, 2011; and subsequent e-mail exchanges with author.

35 *"defiantly nationalist":* Ibid., 330.

36 *rethink their opposition:* Norman Podhoretz, "Neo-Conservatism: A Eulogy," *Commentary Magazine,* March 1996.

36 *deserved their support:* Joyce Huyett Turner and Sam Tanenhaus, "Q & A on William F. Buckley," *NYTimes.com,* February 27, 2008. http://artsbeat.blogs.nytimes.com/2008/02/27/qa-with-sam-tanenhaus-on-william-f-buckley/.

38 *Crunchy Cons:* Rod Dreher, *Crunchy Cons: The New Conservative Counterculture and Its Return Roots* (New York: Three Rivers Press, 2006).

41 *fusionism:* Nash, *Reappraising the Right,* 322.

3. Meet the Millennials

53 *"Every generation discovers":* "Concerning Honor in Public Life," a speech by Herbert Hoover broadcast nationwide from the Iowa Centennial Celebration, Des Moines, Iowa, August 30, 1951. See Herbert Hoover, *Addresses on the American Road: 1950–1955* (Stanford, Calif.: Stanford University Press, 1955), beginning on p. 111.

53 *the rising generation:* Pew Research Center, "Millennials—A Portrait of Generation Next: Confident. Connected. Open to Change," Forum on Religion and Public Life, February 2010, 4, http://pewsocialtrends.org/files/2010/10/millennials-confident-connected-open-to-change.pdf.

53 *Sixty-six percent of:* Pew Research Center, "Young Voters in the 2008 Election," by Scott Keeter, Juliana Horowitz, and Alec Tyson, November 12, 2008, 19, http://pewresearch.org/pubs/1031/young-voters-in-the-2008-election.

53 *In the presidential elections:* Patrick Fisher, "The Age Gap: Evidence of a Realignment in U.S. Politics," paper presented at the annual meeting of the Western Political Science Association, San Diego, California, March 20, 2008, http://www.allacademic.com//meta/p_mla_apa_research_citation/2/3/8/5/1/pages238512/p238512-31.php.

54 *Between the elections of 2008 and 2010:* Kirk Johnson, "Fewer Voters See Themselves as Democrats," *New York Times,* September 2, 2010, http://www.nytimes.com/2010/09/03/us/politics/03students.html.

55	*Forty percent of them are nonwhite:* Pew Research Center, "Millennials—A Portrait of Generation Next," 9.

55	*20 percent . . . at least one immigrant parent:* Morley Winograd and Michael D. Hais, "The Boomers Had Their Day. Make Way for the Millennials," *Washington Post,* February 3, 2008, http://www .washingtonpost.com/wp-dyn/content/article/2008/02/01/ AR2008020102826.html.

55	*And 93 percent are comfortable:* Pew Research Center, "Millennials— A Portrait of Generation Next," 78.

55	*most educated generation:* Pew Research Center, "Millennials—A Portrait of Generation Next," 1.

55	*juvenile crime, teen pregnancy:* Morley Winograd and Michael D. Hais, *Millennial Makeover: MySpace, YouTube, and the Future of American Politics* (Piscataway, N.J.: Rutgers University Press, 2008), 81.

55	*They are less conventionally:* Pew Research Center Forum on Religion and Public Life, "Religion Among the Millennials: Less Religiously Active Than Older Americans, but Fairly Traditional in Other Ways," February 2010, http://pewforum.org/uploaded Files/Topics/Demographics/Age/millennials-report.pdf.

55	*According to a* Reader's Digest *poll:* Carl M. Cannon, "The Facebook Election," *Reader's Digest,* June 2008.

55	*created a profile:* Pew Research Center, "Millennials—A Portrait of Generation Next," 1.

55	*video of themselves:* Ibid., 30.

56	*Ninety-four percent of millennials:* Ibid., 32–33.

56	*more than nine thousand books:* Winograd and Hais, *Millennial Makeover,* 79.

56	*Employers report that:* Morley Safer, "The 'Millennials' Are Coming," *60 Minutes,* CBS, May 23, 2008, http://www.cbsnews.com/ stories/2007/11/08/60minutes/main3475200.shtml.

56	*83 percent . . . volunteered regularly in high school:* Lynne C. Lancaster and David Stillman, *The M-Factor: How the Millennial Generation Is Rocking the Workplace* (New York: HarperCollins, 2010), 96.

56	*Sixty percent have volunteered:* Pew Research Center, "Millennials—A Portrait of Generation Next," 83.

56 *Seasoned pollsters:* Pew Research Center, "A Pro-Government, Socially Liberal Generation: Democrats' Edge Among Millennials Slips," 6, http://pewresearch.org/assets/pdf/1497.pdf, "But, compared with older cohorts, Gen Xers have remained less opposed to active government for more than a decade, suggesting that these attitudes, once formed, tend to persist at least in comparison with other age cohorts."

57 *"as many raw votes":* Cannon, "The Facebook Election."

57 *Millennials cannot abide hyperpartisanship:* Eric Greenberg and Karl Weber, "The Millennials: America's First Post-Ideological, Post-Partisan, and Post-Political Generation," *The Huffington Post,* September 14, 2008, http://www.huffingtonpost.com/eric-greenberg-and-karl-weber/the-millennials-americas_b_126205.html.

57 *currently married:* Pew Research Center, "Millennials—A Portrait of Generation Next," 11.

57 *About a third (34 percent) are parents:* Ibid., 17.

57 *higher share of unwed mothers:* Ibid., 51.

57 *devoted to the families:* Winograd and Hais, *Millennial Makeover,* 83.

57 *The oldest of them:* Pew Research Center, "Millennials—A Portrait of Generation Next," 140.

57 *45 percent talk on the phone:* Ibid., 83.

57 *What's more, 52 percent of millennials:* Ibid., 2.

58 *accepted by society:* Pew Research Center, "Religion Among the Millennials: Less Religiously Active Than Older Americans, but Fairly Traditional in Other Ways," February 2010, 18.

58 *legalization of same-sex marriage:* Pew Research Center, "Millennials—A Portrait of Generation Next," 51.

58 *Nearly 40 percent of them have tattoos:* Pew Research Center, "Millennials—A Portrait of Generation Next," 57.

58 *"They've been down":* quote from Mary Crane, in report by Morley Safer, "The 'Millennials' Are Coming," *60 Minutes,* CBS, May 23, 2008, http://www.cbsnews.com/stories/2007/11/08/60minutes/main3475200.shtml.

58 *37 percent of people aged:* Pew Research Center, "Millennials—A Portrait of Generation Next," 44.

58 *In 2009, only 20 percent:* Lynne C. Lancaster and David Stillman, *The M-Factor: How the Millennial Generation Is Rocking the Workplace* (New York: HarperCollins, 2010), 53.

60 *during the 2010 cycle:* Carl M. Cannon, "The Facebook Election," *Reader's Digest,* June 2008.

60 *On a range of issues:* Pew Research Center, "Millennials—A Portrait of Generation Next," 63.

60 *businesses take fair profits:* Ibid., 74.

60 *While they tend to favor . . . affirmative action:* Ibid., 77.

61 *While they still favored Democrats:* Kevin Brennan, "Millennials Missing from the Midterms," *Politics Daily,* November 3, 2010, http://www.politicsdaily.com/2010/11/03/millennials-missing-from-the-midterms/.

61 *turnout rate dropping:* Ibid.

61 *regulation of business:* Pew Research Center, "Millennials—A Portrait of Generation Next," 70.

62 *Far fewer eighteen- to twenty-nine-year-olds:* Kirk Johnson, "Fewer Voters See Themselves as Democrats."

63 *Republicans would do well:* David Cameron, keynote speech, Conservative Party Conference, Birmingham, England, October 6, 2010.

64 *"the spirit of activism":* Ibid.

4. Generational Theft

69 *"Blessed are the young":* "New Deal Agricultural Policies and Some Reforms," a speech by Herbert Hoover sponsored by the Nebraska Republican State Central Committee, Lincoln, Nebraska, January 16, 1936. See Herbert Hoover, *Addresses on the American Road: 1933–1936* (New York: Scribners, 1936), beginning on p. 101.

73 *WeCantPayThatTab.org:* "National Debt: The Quick Facts," *We Can't Pay That Tab,* accessed March 15, 2011, http://www.wecantpaythattab.org/debt-posts/quick-facts/.

77 *Within his first hundred days:* John Ensign, "100 Days of Bailouts and Making a Bad Situation Worse," Washington, D.C.: U.S. Senate Republican Policy Committee, April 29, 2009, http://rpc .senate.gov/public/_files/042909100DaysofBailoutsandMakinga BadSituationWorse.pdf.

77 *His spending spree:* Mike Allen, "Congress at Work: '$1 Billion an Hour,' " *Politico,* March 11, 2009, http://www.politico.com/ news/stories/0309/19884.html.

78 *We've seen students rioting:* ABC/AFP, "Riots in London After University Fee Vote," ABC News, December 10, 2010, http:// www.abc.net.au/news/stories/2010/12/10/3089663.htm.

78 *In France:* John Lichfield, "France Braces for Riots as Protests Turn Violent," *The Independent,* October 19, 2010, http://www .independent.co.uk/news/world/europe/france-braces-for-riots- as-protests-turn-violent-2110305.html.

78 *In Spain:* Fiona Govan, "General Strike in Spain to Protest Against Austerity Measures," *Telegraph,* September 29, 2010, http://www .telegraph.co.uk/travel/destinations/europe/spain/8032647/ General-strike-in-Spain-to-protest-against-austerity-measures .html.

79 *Here are the stakes:* Paul Ryan, "Roadmap to America's Future: Version 2.0," January 2010, 23, http://www.roadmap.republicans. budget.house.gov/UploadedFiles/Roadmap2Final2.pdf.

79 *Even today:* Scott A. Hodge, "Fiscal Facts: Number of Americans Paying Zero Federal Income Tax Grows to 43.4 Million," *Tax Foundation,* March 30, 2008, http://www.taxfoundation.org/news/ show/1410.html; Stephen Ohlemacher, "Nearly Half of U.S. Households Escape Fed Income Tax," Associated Press in *Yahoo! Finance,* April 7, 2010, http://finance.yahoo.com/news/Nearly- half-of-US-households-apf-1105567323.html?x=0&.v=1.

79 *By the year 2030:* Richard Wolf, "Social Security Hits First Wave of Boomers," *USA Today,* October 9, 2007, http://www.usatoday .com/news/washington/2007-10-08-boomers_N.htm.

82 *While President Obama praised:* Associated Press, "Obama Touts New 'Paygo' Budget Rules," CBSNews.com, February 13, 2010, http://

www.cbsnews.com/stories/2010/02/13/politics/main6204926
.shtml.

82 *In the 110th and 111th:* "Pelosi's PAYGO Ploy: Budgetary Gimmick
Provides Cover for Liberals," The Foundry, *The Heritage Foundation,* October 15, 2010, http://blog.heritage.org/2010/10/15/
pelosis-paygo-ploy-budgetary-gimmick-provides-cover-for-
liberals/.

85 *Our projected unfunded liability:* Pamela Villareal, "Social Security
and Medicare Projections: 2009," *National Center for Policy Analysis,* June 11, 2009, http://www.ncpa.org/pub/ba662.

87 *"those under 30 who":* Andrew Sullivan, "Obama to the Next Generation: Screw You, Suckers," *The Atlantic,* February 14, 2011, http://
www.theatlantic.com/daily-dish/archive/2011/02/obama-to-the-
next-generation-screw-you-suckers/175804/.

5. Freedom Means Freedom for Everyone

89 *"It's time America realized":* Barry Goldwater, quoted in Rebecca
Borders and C. C. Dockery, eds., *Beyond the Hill: A Directory of
Congress from 1984 to 1993* (Lanham, MD: University Press of
America, Inc., 1995), 104.

90 *anti-same-sex-marriage initiatives played no:* Daniel A. Smith, Matthew DeSantis, and Jason Kassel, "Same-Sex Marriage Ballot
Measures and the 2004 Presidential Election," *State and Local Government Review* 38, no. 2 (2006).

90 *mobilized people* across *party lines:* Simon Jackman, "Same-Sex
Marriage Ballot Initiatives and Conservative Mobilization in the
2004 Election," presentation at Institute for Research in the Social
Sciences, Stanford University, November 9, 2004, http://jackman
.stanford.edu/papers/RISSPresentation.pdf.

91 *analysis of the results in Ohio's:* Ibid.

91 *This mythology now holds:* Matthew Dowd, "When D.C. 'Wisdom'
Is Wrong: Be advised not to buy into Washington myths either before or after Election Day," *National Journal,* September 22, 2010,
http://nationaljournal.com/njmagazine/oo_20100911_3691.php.

94 *As many as 39 percent:* Pew Research Center, "Millennials—A

Portrait of Generation Next: Confident. Connected. Open to Change," Forum on Religion and Public Life, February 2010, 102, http://pewsocialtrends.org/files/2010/10/millennials-confident-connected-open-to-change.pdf.

95 *Polling confirms:* Washington Post–ABC News Poll, February 4–8, 2010 (Horsham, Penn.: TNS), http://www.washingtonpost.com/wp-srv/politics/polls/postpoll_021010.html.

95 *This sea change:* Gallup, by Lydia Saad, "Americans' Acceptance of Gay Relations Crosses 50% Threshold: Increased acceptance by men driving the change," May 25, 2010, http://www.gallup.com/poll/135764/americans-acceptance-gay-relations-crosses-threshold.aspx.

98 *"Ronald Reagan opposed":* Matt Lewis, "Are Social Conservatives Losing Clout—or Just the Gay Debate?" *Politics Daily,* December 10, 2010, http://www.politicsdaily.com/2010/12/10/are-social-conservatives-losing-clout-or-just-the-gay-debate/.

100 *"the conservative movement":* Lee Edwards, "The Conservative Consensus: Frank Meyer, Barry Goldwater, and the Politics of Fusionism," *The Heritage Foundation: First Principles Series,* no. 8, January 22, 2007, 2.

104 *"adopting same-sex marriage":* Perry v. Schwarzenegger, testimony on page 2803, lines 13–15.

104 *"This still-revolutionary":* David Blankenhorn, *The Future of Marriage* (New York: Encounter Books, 2009), 2.

107 *The next day:* Jerry Sanders, "Proud to Testify for Marriage Equality," *The Huffington Post,* January 22, 2010, http://www.huffingtonpost.com/jerry-sanders/proud-to-testify-for-marr_b_432890.html.

108 *"I hope that everyone":* Ibid.

6. Education Reform: A Civil Rights Win for the Millennial Generation

111 *"Education spending will be":* Milton Friedman, "Our Best Chance for Better Schools," *New York Post,* February 20, 2002.

112 *American students now rank:* fifteenth in reading, nineteenth in math, fourteenth in science, http://www.nationalmathandscience .org/index.php/staying-competitive/.

112 *drop out of high school:* C. A. Lehr et al., "Essential Tools: Increasing Rates of School Completion" (Minneapolis: National Center on Secondary Education and Transition, 2004), http://www .ecs.org/html/Document.asp?chouseid=6649.

113 *every nine seconds:* "Every Nine Seconds in America a Student Becomes a Dropout," American Youth Policy Forum, www.aypf.org/ publications/EveryNineSeconds.pdf.

113 *approximately 70 percent:* Ibid.

113 *leaving school:* "High School Dropouts in America," Fact Sheet, Alliance for Excellent Education, updated February 2009, www.all4ed .org/files/GraduationRates_FactSheet.pdf.

113 *"dropout factories":* Robert Balfanz and Nettie Legters, "The Graduation Rate Crisis We Know and What Can Be Done About It," Johns Hopkins University Center for Social Organization of Schools, July 12, 2006, http://web.jhu.edu/bin/a/b/Crisis_ Commentary.pdf. "Dropout factory" was first defined by Bob Balfanz and Nettie Legters at Johns Hopkins University as a high school in which "the number of seniors is routinely 60% or fewer than the number of freshmen four years earlier."

113 *from the lowest-income:* National Center for Education Statistics, U.S. Department of Education, *The Condition of Education 2004* (Washington, D.C.: U.S. Government Printing Office, 2004), 11.

116 *"a permanent national":* "High School Dropout Crisis Threatens U.S. Economic Growth and Competitiveness, Witnesses Tell House Panel," United States House Education and Labor Committee, May 12, 2009, http://democrats.edworkforce.house.gov/ newsroom/2009/05/high-school-dropout-crisis-thr.shtml.

116 *"on the order of $103 trillion":* Karin Zeitvogel, "U.S. Falls to Average in Education Ranking," Agence France-Presse, December 7, 2010.

117 *We spend between 41 and 50 percent more:* Institute of Education

Sciences, U.S. Department of Education, "Education Expenditures by Country: Contexts of Elementary and Secondary Education," http://nces.ed.gov/programs/coe/2010/section4/indicator38.asp.

120 *the power to shut down:* June Kronholz, "D.C.'s Braveheart," *Education Next* 10, no. 1 (Winter 2010), http://educationnext.org/d-c-s-braveheart/. Two years after Rhee took over as D.C.'s education chancellor, "scores on district-administered tests are up: 49 percent of elementary school students were reading at grade level, a 21-percentage-point jump in two years, according to test results released in July 2009. Among secondary-school students, 40 percent were at grade level in math, up 13 points" (36).

120 *more than $1 million in donations:* Ben Smith, "Teachers union helped unseat Fenty," *Politico,* September 15, 2010, http://www.politico.com/blogs/bensmith/0910/Teachers_union_helped_unseat_Fenty.html.

120 *bottom 5 percent of teachers:* Eric. A. Hanushek, "The Economic Value of Higher Teacher Quality," *Economics of Education Review,* 2011, doi:10.1016/j.econedurev.2010.12.006.

121 *Although the state spends:* Jessica Calefati and Jeanette Rundquist, "N.J. School Report Card Data Shows Average Per-Pupil Spending Increased Statewide, Dropped in Urban Districts," *Newark Star-Ledger,* February 8, 2011, http://www.nj.com/news/index.ssf/2011/02/nj_per-pupil_spending_increase.html.

121 *In a 2010 e-mail:* Allysia Finley, "Teachers Embrace the Power of Prayer: A New Jersey Teacher's Union Prays for Chris Christie's Death," *Wall Street Journal,* April 12, 2010, http://online.wsj.com/article/SB10001424052702303828304575180160172878050.html.

123 *From 1994 to 1999:* Kurt J. Bauman, *Home Schooling in the United States: Trends and Characteristics* (Washington, D.C.: U.S. Census Bureau, August 2001).

123 *KIPP is a national network:* "KIPP: Schools," *KIPP,* accessed March 15, 2011, http://www.kipp.org/schools.

124 *President Bush and the Republican Congress:* Susan Ferrechio, "Democrat inserted provision endangers DC Opportunity Scholarship program," posted February 23, 2009, 1:00 a.m.,

http://washingtonexaminer.com/politics/2009/02/democrat-inserted-provision-endangers-dc-opportunity-scholarship-program#ixzz1LyOiHGfV.

125 *Three months after Katrina:* Brett Michael Dykes, "New Orleans Schools Stage Impressive Turnaround after Katrina," *Yahoo! News,* August 27, 2009, http://news.yahoo.com/s/yblog_upshot/20100827/us_yblog_upshot/new-orleans-public-schools-stage-impressive-turnaround-five-years-after-katrina.

125 *"Over half of all":* "The State of Public Education in New Orleans," Cowen Institute for Public Education Initiatives, 2010, http://www.coweninstitute.com/wp-content/uploads/2010/03/SPENO-2010-Exec-Summ-WEB-22710.pdf.

126 *Just follow the money:* Liz Goodwin, "Despite Fiery Rhetoric, Largest Teachers Union Spending Big for Dems," *Yahoo! News,* October 6, 2010, http://news.yahoo.com/s/yblog_upshot/20101006/el_yblog_upshot/despite-fiery-rhetoric-largest-teachers-union-spending-big-for-dems.

7. A New Republican Feminism

129 *"The Independent Girl":* Lou Henry Hoover Papers, Subject File, School Papers, Lou Henry, High School, Reports and Misc., 1886–1990, Herbert Hoover Presidential Library, West Branch, Iowa.

130 *"Body Hair":* "Body Hair: The Final Frontier for Female Liberation," *Ms. Magazine,* July 1972.

133 *"postgrievance":* Barbara Bylenga and Marya Stark, "Have Millennial Women Moved Beyond Feminism?" *BlogHer,* October 22, 2008, http://www.blogher.com/have-millennial-women-moved-beyond-feminism-barbara-bylenga-and-marya-stark.

134 *"acting white":* Roddie A. Burris, "Jackson Slams Obama for 'Acting White,'" *The State in Politico,* September 19, 2007, http://www.politico.com/news/stories/0907/5902.html.

135 *concept of co-parenting:* Morley Winograd and Michael D. Hais, *Millennial Makeover: My Space, YouTube, and the Future of American Politics* (Piscataway, N. J.: Rutgers University Press, 2008), 71.

140 *"Caribou Barbie":* Maureen Dowd, "Now, Sarah's Folly," *New York Times*, July 4, 2009, http://www.nytimes.com/2009/07/05/opinion/05dowd.html.

140 *"gang-raped":* Tracy Miller, "Sandra Bernhard Issues 'Gang Rape' Warning to Sarah Palin," *New York Daily News*, September 19, 2008, http://www.nydailynews.com/gossip/2008/09/19/2008–09–19_sandra_bernhard_issues_gang_rape_warning-2.html.

8. The Choice Dilemma

143 *"The federal government has no business":* Barry Goldwater, from Robert Alan Goldberg, *Barry Goldwater* (New Haven: Yale University Press, 1995), 308.

145 *78 percent of Republican voters:* "Trends: Abortion," Gallup, last modified May 2010, http://www.gallup.com/poll/1576/abortion.aspx. A Gallup poll conducted May 3–6, 2010, found that 54 percent thought abortion should be "legal only under certain circumstances," and 24 percent thought it should be "legal under any circumstances." This means that 78 percent thought that abortion should be legal at least under certain circumstances. Also see Avalanche Strategic Communications, "Poll Demonstrates That a Big-Tent GOP Ticket Is More Electable," Republican Majority for Choice, August 22, 2008, https://gopchoice.electionmall.name/E-PressRelease/displaycontent.asp?a=5C5A58&z=5D. A poll conducted August 14–16, 2008, by Republican Majority for Choice found that "78% of Republican voters agreed that women should have access to the full range of reproductive options, including education, contraception, motherhood, adoption and abortion." Seventy percent of voters also said "their support for McCain would not be affected if he chose a pro-choice running mate . . ."

148 *41 percent of women identify themselves as Democrats:* Jeffrey M. Jones, "Republicans Face Steep Uphill Climb Among Women," Gallup, May 6, 2009, http://www.gallup.com/poll/118207/Republicans-Face-Steep-Uphill-Climb-Among-Women.aspx.

148 *The procedure:* "Trends: Abortion," Gallup. In a Gallup poll conducted May 10–13, 2007, the following question was asked: "Now
I would like to ask your opinion about a specific abortion procedure known as 'late term' abortion or 'partial birth' abortion,
which is sometimes performed on women during the last few
months of pregnancy. Do you think that this procedure should be
legal or illegal?" Seventy-two percent responded that this should be
illegal, up from 68 percent when the question was last polled, in
2003.

150 *most Americans view abortion as morally wrong:* Lydia Saad, "Four Moral
Issues Sharply Divide Americans," Gallup, May 26, 2010, http://
www.gallup.com/poll/137357/Four-Moral-Issues-Sharply-
Divide-Americans.aspx.

150 *"54% of self-described pro-life":* Avalanche Strategic Communications, "August 2008 National Research Inc. Poll" (Washington,
D.C.: Republican Majority for Choice, August 2008).

151 *one of these groups:* "About Us," Republican National Coalition for
Life, accessed March 15, 2011, http://www.rnclife.org/about/.

151 *When the question:* Lydia Saad, "Abortion Issue Laying Low in
2008 Campaign," Gallup, May 22, 2008, http://www.gallup.com/
poll/107458/abortion-issue-laying-low-2008-campaign.aspx.

152 *A Republican Party that would appeal:* http://www.rasmussenreports
.com/platinum/political_tracking_crosstabs/february_2011/
crosstabs_abortion_february_14_15_2010.

152 *Part of that reality:* Rebecca Wind, "Premarital Sex Is Nearly Uni-
versal Among Americans, and Has Been for Decades," Guttmacher Institute, December 19, 2006, http://www.guttmacher
.org/media/nr/2006/12/19/index.html.

152 *Forty-seven percent of teenagers:* Associated Press, "Fewer High
School Students Are Having Sex," *MSNBC.com,* July 13, 2007,
http://www.msnbc.msn.com/id/19733766/#.

153 *Most young people:* Guttmacher Institute, "Facts on American
Teens' Sexual and Reproductive Health," http://www.guttmacher
.org/pubs/FB-ATSRH.pdf.

155 *those with the genetic mutation:* Caroline Mansfield, Suellen Hop-
fer, and Theresa M. Marteau, "Termination Rates After Prenatal
Diagnosis of Down Syndrome, Spina Bifida, Anencephaly, and
Turner and Klinefelter Syndromes: A Systematic Literature Review," *Prenatal Diagnosis* 19, no. 9 (1999). Abstract available at:
http://www.ncbi.nlm.nih.gov/pubmed/10521836.

156 *Most teenage mothers:* http://www.theodora.com/teddy/newyork/
teenage.html. Also see Rebecca A. Maynard, ed., *Kids Having
Kids: A Robin Hood Foundation Special Report on the Costs of Adoles-
cent Childbearing* (New York: Robin Hood Foundation, 1996); and
R. H. Haveman, B. Wolfe, and E. Peterson, "Children of Early
Childbearers as Young Adults," in Rebecca A. Maynard, ed., *Kids
Having Kids: Economic Costs and Social Consequences of Teen Preg-
nancy* (Washington, D.C.: Urban Institute Press, 1997), 257–84.

156 *The teen birth rate:* Bill Albert, "New Survey: Teens Say Parents
Most Influence Their Decisions About Sex," The National Campaign to Prevent Teen and Unplanned Pregnancy, December 21,
2010,   http://www.thenationalcampaign.org/press/press-release.
aspx?releaseID=202.

156 *"82 percent of":* Patrik Jonsson, "A Force Behind the Lower Teen
Birthrate: MTV's '16 and Pregnant,'" *Christian Science Monitor,*
December 21, 2010, http://www.csmonitor.com/USA/Society/
2010/1221/A-force-behind-the-lower-teen-birthrate-MTV-s-16
-and-Pregnant.

9. Conservative Environmentalism

159 *"The spiritual uplift":* Herbert Hoover, National Conference on
Outdoor Recreation, Washington, D.C., January 21, 1926, Herbert Hoover Papers—Articles, Addresses, and Public Statements—
#546B.

163 *During his second term:* Information compiled and edited from research
done by the National Geographic Society and The Theodore Roosevelt Association staff. Available at: http://www.theodoreroosevelt
.org/life/conNatlForests.htm (copyright November 2005).

166 *a school of modern environmentalism:* Daniel Engber, "Global Swarming: Is It Time for Americans to Start Cutting Our Baby Emissions?" *Slate*, September 10, 2007, http://www.slate.com/id/2173458/.

168 *three-quarters of them demand:* Janis Gaudelli, "The Greenest Generation: The Truth Behind Millennials and the Green Movement," *AdvertisingAge*, April 29, 2009, http://adage.com/goodworks/post?article_id=136331.

169 Newsweek *once published a cover story:* Peter Gwynne, "The Cooling World," *Newsweek*, April 28, 1975, http://www.denisdutton.com/newsweek_coolingworld.pdf; "The Little Ice Age," *Windows to the Universe,* accessed March 15, 2011, http://windows2universe.org/earth/climate/little_ice_age.html.

170 *electricity prices would rise:* William W. Beach, David W. Kreutzer, Karen A. Campbell, and Ben Lieberman, "Son of Waxman-Markey: More Politics Makes for a More Costly Bill," *The Heritage Foundation*, May 18, 2009, http://www.heritage.org/research/reports/2009/05/son-of-waxman-markey-more-politics-makes-for-a-more-costly-bill.

172 *Climate scientist:* Bjorn Lomborg, "Cost-Effective Ways to Address Climate Change," *Washington Post*, November 17, 2010, http://www.washingtonpost.com/wp-dyn/content/article/2010/11/16/AR2010111604973.html.

10. A Nation of Immigrants, a Nation of Borders

175 *The Republican Party, unfortunately:* Marco Rubio, from Fox News Sunday interview with Chris Wallace, March 28, 2010.

177 *10.8 million undocumented immigrants:* http://www.reuters.com/article/2010/04/29/us-usa-immigration-idUSTRE63S5TY20100429.

177 *Arizona had 460,000 undocumented immigrants:* Ibid.

177 *made 650 arrests a day:* Ibid.

178 *state's government loses between:* "Expensive Aliens: How Much Do Illegal Immigrants Really Cost?" *ABC News Online:* http://

abcnews.go.com/Business/illegal-immigrants-cost-us-100-billion-year-group/story?id=10699317&page=2.

178 *$113 billion a year:* "Illegal Immigration a $113 Billion a Year Drain on U.S. Taxpayers: FAIR Releases First-of-Its-Kind Comprehensive Study of Federal, State and Local Costs of Illegal Immigration," July 6, 2010, http://www.fairus.org/site/News2?page=NewsArticle&id=23198&security=1601&news_iv_ctrl=1741.

178 *Millennials are the most ethnically diverse:* Pew Research Center, "Millennials—A Portrait of Generation Next: Confident. Connected. Open to Change," Forum on Religion and Public Life, February 2010, 79, http://pewsocialtrends.org/files/2010/10/millenials-confident-connected-open-to-change.pdf.

178 *"younger people":* Ibid.

178 *less apt to say:* Ibid.

178 *"much less supportive":* Ibid.

180 *After his reelection:* "Comprehensive Immigration Reform Act of 2007," *SourceWatch,* last modified December 17, 2008, http://www.sourcewatch.org/index.php?title=Comprehensive_Immigration_Reform_Act_of_2007.

180 *not prepared to support:* Senator Jon Kyl, "Arizona Immigration Law, State Officials," The Independent Women's Forum and The Georgetown Law Supreme Court Institute (Washington, D.C.: Georgetown University Law Center, May 20, 2010), http://www.c-spanvideo.org/program/293622–1.

181 *Yuma County, Arizona:* Lauren Gambino, "Failed virtual border fence has politicians pointing to Yuma success," *TucsonSentinel.com,* Cronkite News Service, posted January 31, 2011, 7:33 p.m., http://www.tucsonsentinel.com/local/report/013111_border.

182 *Some of our liberal:* Guy Benson, "Democrat Loretta Sanchez Compares US Border Fence to Berlin Wall," *Townhall.com,* October 6, 2010, http://townhall.com/tipsheet/guybenson/2010/10/06/democrat_loretta_sanchez_compares_us_border_fence_to_berlin_wall; Stephanie Simon, "Border-Fence Project Hits a Snag: Opposition from Environmentalists, Property Owners Slows

Construction of Final Leg," *Wall Street Journal*, February 4, 2009, http://online.wsj.com/article/SB123370523066745559.html.

182 *"muro de odio":* Stephanie Simon, "Border-Fence Project Hits a Snag: Opposition from Environmentalists, Property Owners Slows Construction of Final Leg," *Wall Street Journal*, February 4, 2009, http://online.wsj.com/article/SB123370523066745559.html; Bill Addington, "'Muro de Odio': A Border Wall of Hate and Fear," *Rio Grande Sierran*, March/April 2009, nmsierraclub.org/sites/default/ files/rgsierran_09_03_04.pdf.

183 *Despite the fact:* Andrea Nill, "Over 77 Percent of All Arizonans Support Comprehensive Immigration Reform," *Think Progress,* May 14, 2010, http://thinkprogress.org/2010/05/14/arizona-poll-immigration/.

183 *and 73 percent of all Americans:* Pew Research Center, "Democrats Divided, but Support Key Provisions: Broad Approval for New Arizona Immigration Law," May 12, 2010, http://people-press .org/reports/pdf/613.pdf.

187 *"The most important":* Rachel Rose Hartman, "Marco Rubio Defends Spanish Ad, Support for English as Official Language," The Upshot, in *Yahoo! News,* September 29, 2010, http://news.yahoo. com/s/yblog_upshot/20100929/el_yblog_upshot/marco-rubio-defends-spanish-ad-support-for-english-as-official-language.

11. Islamist Supremacy: A Millennial's Worst Nightmare

191 *"The bombers of Manhattan":* Christopher Hitchens, "Against Rationalization," *Nation*, September 20, 2001, http://www.thenation .com/article/against-rationalization. This article appeared in the print edition of the *Nation* on October 8, 2001.

191 *Islamist Supremacy:* Eli Lake, "Study: Iran Indoctrinating Children in Islamic Supremacism," *New York Sun*, March 19, 2008, http:// www.nysun.com/foreign/study-iran-indoctrinating-children-in-islamic/73162/; Robert Farley, interview by Eli Lake, "Eli Abandons 'Islamic Fascism,' Defends 'Islamic Supremacism,' " *Bloggingheads .tv,* posted January 13, 2008, http://bloggingheads.tv/diavlogs/

7939; James Taranto, " 'Islamic Supremacy': The Solution to a Co-
nundrum of Language and Policy," *Wall Street Journal*, January 16,
2009,   http://online.wsj.com/article/SB123211637982290301.
html. This term was first used by Eli Lake on *Bloggingheads.tv* and
in his *New York Sun* article, later borrowed by Taranto in *Wall Street
Journal*. I have altered it to "Islamist Supremacy."

199   *the most liberal generation:* Pew Research Center, "Millennials—A
Portrait of Generation Next," 73.

200   *Iran's president:* "Ahmadinejad: Most Blame U.S. Government
for 9/11; American Officials Call Iran Leader 'Delusional,' Walk
Out of Speech," *MSNBC.com,* September 23, 2010, http://www
.msnbc.msn.com/id/39331594/ns/world_news/.

200   *also a Holocaust denier:* Ewen MacAskill and Chris McGreal, "Israel Should Be Wiped Off the Map, Says Iran's President," *Guard-
ian*, October 27, 2005, http://www.guardian.co.uk/world/2005/
oct/27/israel.iran.

200   *When Ahmadinejad went:* "Iran President in NY Campus Row,"
BBC News, September 25, 2007, http://news.bbc.co.uk/2/hi/
7010962.stm.

200   *at last count, nine women:* Saeed Kamali Dehghan and Ian Black,
"Iranians Still Facing Death by Stoning Despite 'Reprieve,' "
Guardian.co.uk, July 8, 2010, http://www.guardian.co.uk/world/
2010/jul/08/iran-death-stoning-adultery.

201   *partisan politics ends:* Conrad Black, "A New Isolationism?" *National Review Online*, November 2, 2009, http://www.national
review.com/articles/228505/new-isolationism/conrad-black; Tony
Karon, "Why Obama Defaulted to Bush Foreign Policy Positions," *Time*, January 4, 2010, http://www.time.com/time/world/
article/0,8599,1950827,00.html. "Politics ends at the water's
edge" is a phrase associated most often with the Eisenhower and
Truman eras. It is still used in politics today, as shown by these two
recent articles.

201   *Zainab Al-Suwaij:* "American Islamic Congress: Leadership,"

American Islamic Congress, last modified 2008, http://www
.aicongress.org/about/leadership.html.

12. America the Exceptional

205 *"Our willingness to speak":* Ronald Reagan, "Remarks and a
Question-and-Answer Session in Los Angeles at a Meeting with
Editors and Broadcasters from Western States," July 1, 1982, http://
www.presidency.ucsb.edu/ws/index.php?pid=42695&st=&st1=#
ixzz1M5ByzUxj.

208 *Socialist Party:* http://www.u-s-history.com/pages/h890.html;
http://www.historycentral.com/elections/1920Pop.html.

208 *"socialism in a nation-wide":* Herbert Hoover, "American Individualism and the Challenge to Liberty" (West Branch, Iowa: Herbert
Hoover Presidential Library Association, 1989), 46.

210 *When Barack Obama was asked:* Michael D. Shear and Scott Wilson, "On European Trip, President Tries to Set a New, Pragmatic Tone," *Washington Post,* April 5, 2009, http://www
.washingtonpost.com/wp-dyn/content/article/2009/04/04/
AR2009040400700.html; James Fallows, "Obama on Exceptionalism," *Atlantic,* April 4, 2009, http://www.theatlantic.com/
technology/archive/2009/04/obama-on-exceptionalism/9874/;
Monica Crowley, "American Exceptionalism," commentary in
Washington Times, July 1, 2009, http://www.washingtontimes
.com/news/2009/jul/1/american-exceptionalism/.

211 *According to pollster:* Frank I. Luntz, *What Americans Really
Want . . . Really: The Truth About Our Hopes, Dreams, and Fears*
(New York: Hyperion, 2009), 180.

214 *But their decisive break:* Carl M. Cannon, "The Facebook Election,"
Reader's Digest, June 2008.

214 *"the wrong war":* William Kristol, "Kerry vs. Kerry: What Does
'the Wrong War in the Wrong Place at the Wrong Time'
Mean?" *The Blog,* in *The Weekly Standard,* September 7, 2004,
http://www.weeklystandard.com/Content/Public/Articles/

000/000/004/587jxocg.asp. This statement by Democratic presidential nominee and Senator John Kerry was widely quoted in the 2004 presidential election campaign.

215   *From the millennials':* Cannon, "The Facebook Election."

215   *A 2006 survey:* Frank N. Magid Associates, Inc., "The Politics of the Millennial Generation: A New Survey Comparing Political Attitudes Between Generations," *New Politics Institute,* March 2006, 8, http://ndn-newpol.civicactions.net/sites/ndn-newpol .civicactions.net/files/MillenialGenerationPolitics.pdf.

215   *This generation is:* Hilary Doe and Zachary Kolodin, "Blueprint for the Millennial America," *The Roosevelt Campus Network,* 2010, 25, http://www.rooseveltcampusnetwork.org/chapter/1875/ blueprint-millennial-america.

215   *As a result:* Cannon, "The Facebook Election."

217   *In return for:* U.S. Department of State Office of the Spokesman, "Interview of Secretary Colin L. Powell on 'Be Heard: An MTV Global Discussion with Colin Powell' " (Washington, D.C.: U.S. Department of State, February 14, 2002), http://www .solcomhouse.com/colinpowellmtv.htm.

217   *In Eastern Europe:* "Q&A: US Missile Defence," *BBC News*, September 20, 2009, http://news.bbc.co.uk/2/hi/europe/6720153 .stm.

219   *he led America's:* Jim Fisher-Thompson, "U.S. Aid to Africa Hits Record Levels: Geldof, Bono Praise Bush Before Group of Eight Summit in Scotland," *America.gov,* June 27, 2005, http://www .america.gov/st/washfile-english/2005/June/200506271748571 EJrehsiF0.8724481.html#ixzz1E2ik0cqx.

ABOUT THE AUTHOR

MARGARET HOOVER is a veteran of national political campaigns, Capitol Hill, and the Bush Administration White House. A Fox News contributor, she is committed to modernizing the Republican Party to enable it to connect with a new generation of Americans, even as it remains true to the principles of individual freedom and fiscal conservatism and continues to champion a robust U.S. foreign policy. She serves on the advisory council of the American Foundation for Equal Rights and GOProud, as well as on the boards of the Hoover Institution, the Herbert Hoover Presidential Library Association, and the Belgian American Educational Foundation. Raised in Colorado, Ms. Hoover lives in New York City with her husband.

For more information, or to contact the author, visit http:// MargaretHoover.com.